通用口笔译

● 主　编　汪莉萍　马晓云

苏州大学出版社
Soochow University Press

图书在版编目(CIP)数据

通用口笔译 / 汪莉萍,马晓云主编. —苏州:苏州大学出版社,2016.6(2021.1重印)
ISBN 978-7-5672-1601-3

Ⅰ.①通… Ⅱ.①汪…②马… Ⅲ.①翻译理论 Ⅳ.①H059

中国版本图书馆 CIP 数据核字(2016)第 025612 号

本书录音可在苏州大学出版社官网(http://www.sudapress.com)"下载中心"下载。

书　　名:	通用口笔译
主　　编:	汪莉萍　马晓云
责任编辑:	沈　琴
装帧设计:	刘　俊
出版发行:	苏州大学出版社(Soochow University Press)
出 版 人:	张建初
社　　址:	苏州市十梓街1号　邮编:215006
印　　刷:	苏州工业园区美柯乐制版印务有限责任公司
网　　址:	www.sudapress.com
E-mail　:	yanghua@suda.edu.cn
邮购热线:	0512-67480030
销售热线:	0512-65225020
开　　本:	787 mm×1 092 mm　1/16　印张:17.75　字数:438 千
版　　次:	2016 年 6 月第 1 版
印　　次:	2021 年 1 月第 5 次修订印刷
书　　号:	ISBN 978-7-5672-1601-3
定　　价:	45.00 元

凡购本社图书发现印装错误,请与本社联系调换。服务热线:0512-67481020

前 言

本教材依据《大学英语课程教学要求》设计和编写。此课程要求学生具备一定的听、说、读、写能力,通过更高要求的口笔译学习,培养其较强的实际应用能力,以顺应大学英语教学改革发展趋势,满足新时期国家和社会对人才培养的需要。编者从大量的语言素材中精选文本,进行编排。本教材主题多样,贴近生活,内容丰富,由浅入深,可作为基础口笔译课程的教材,适用于翻译初学者。

全书包括15个单元,书中不附参考译文和练习答案,为的是培养学生的自主能动性,使其在教师的引导下发现难点,分析难点,解决难点,从而为教师组织形式多样的教学活动打开空间。每个单元围绕同一个主题分别展开笔译和口译两大部分的学习。

笔译部分的教学思路是:以真实有趣的文化知识小测验和简单实用的图片词汇认知活动切入单元主题,激发学生的学习兴趣。随之展开的笔译技巧学习是为接下来的篇章中译英和英译中做好铺垫,教师可结合课文中的语言点,强化学生对所学翻译技巧的认知和应用。每篇课文均配有翻译难点的讲解,间或介绍相关内容的背景知识。课后练习部分则可以要求学生自主完成,由教师进行课堂检查。练习分别有课文句子精练、单词翻译填空、笔译技巧专项训练、句子英汉翻译、段落英汉翻译等。这些练习紧扣主题,由易到难,所选语料具有时代性、实用性,让学生在基于内容的语言输入中感受语言输出的真实性。

口译部分的教学思路是:学生可先预习口译技巧介绍,课堂上教师讲解技巧后可以以朗读或录音播放的形式为学生提供口译专项训练题,帮助学生为接下来的主题翻译进行热身。然后进入篇章英汉口译和对话口译环节,从中有选择地进行视阅翻译,部分文本可要求学生课后进行口译训练。之后同样围绕单元主题,引导学生分别进行听写填空、句子听译、段落听译、对话文本口译、情景口译、主题演讲、扩充词汇学习等活动。就情景口译环节而言,教师可根据书中所设的口译现场,通过任务分配和角色扮演,组织生动活泼的小组口译活动,这也是学生利用单元所学进行实际应用的一种形式。

另外,每个单元都在最后设置了拓展知识的自主学习活动,文本体裁多种多样,形式新颖有趣,有网络热词翻译、名家译本比较、网页翻译,还有影视翻译欣赏等。这些素材旨在进一步提高学生对翻译课程的学习兴趣和对英汉翻译的鉴赏能力。教师和学生使用本书时,可根据实际情况对本教材的内容灵活掌握,有所侧重,变通处理。

本书由江南大学的汪莉萍、马晓云编写。参与审稿的另有江南大学的林懿、马花荣,对于她们所做的大量工作,编者在此深表感谢。也特别感谢苏州大学出版社为本教材的出版所给予的大力支持。对于本教材所选用的文献和网络资源,编者在此一并致谢。

本书的编写在内容和形式上皆有新的尝试。由于编者水平有限,书中难免出现疏漏或错误,敬请读者批评指正。

编者于江南大学
2016年5月

目录
CONTENTS

Unit 1 Reception 外事接待 / 1
- Section A Translation / 2
- Section B Interpretation / 10
- Section C Further Exploration / 16

Unit 2 Shopping 购物消费 / 18
- Section A Translation / 19
- Section B Interpretation / 26
- Section C Further Exploration / 32

Unit 3 Catering Culture 饮食文化 / 34
- Section A Translation / 35
- Section B Interpretation / 45
- Section C Further Exploration / 51

Unit 4 Travelling 观光旅游 / 54
- Section A Translation / 55
- Section B Interpretation / 63
- Section C Further Exploration / 68

Unit 5 Ceremonial Speech 礼仪致辞 / 70
- Section A Translation / 71

◎ Section B　Interpretation　/ 79
◎ Section C　Further Exploration　/ 85

Unit 6　Interview　交流访谈 / 87

◎ Section A　Translation　/ 88
◎ Section B　Interpretation　/ 97
◎ Section C　Further Exploration　/ 103

Unit 7　Sports　体育运动 / 105

◎ Section A　Translation　/ 106
◎ Section B　Interpretation　/ 115
◎ Section C　Further Exploration　/ 122

Unit 8　Education Home and Abroad　中外教育 / 123

◎ Section A　Translation　/ 124
◎ Section B　Interpretation　/ 133
◎ Section C　Further Exploration　/ 139

Unit 9　Cultural Exchange　文化交流 / 143

◎ Section A　Translation　/ 144
◎ Section B　Interpretation　/ 152
◎ Section C　Further Exploration　/ 158

Unit 10　Health and Medicine　健康医疗 / 160

◎ Section A　Translation　/ 161
◎ Section B　Interpretation　/ 169
◎ Section C　Further Exploration　/ 176

Unit 11　Entertainment　影视娱乐 / 178

◎ Section A　Translation　/ 179
◎ Section B　Interpretation　/ 187
◎ Section C　Further Exploration　/ 194

目录

Unit 12 Environmental Protection 环境保护 / 195

- Section A Translation / 196
- Section B Interpretation / 206
- Section C Further Exploration / 214

Unit 13 Science and Technology 科学技术 / 215

- Section A Translation / 216
- Section B Interpretation / 224
- Section C Further Exploration / 232

Unit 14 Economy 经济活动 / 234

- Section A Translation / 235
- Section B Interpretation / 244
- Section C Further Exploration / 251

Unit 15 Laws and Regulations 法律法规 / 253

- Section A Translation / 254
- Section B Interpretation / 269
- Section C Further Exploration / 275

UNIT 1

Reception
外事接待

Learning Objectives

1. To understand the differences between Chinese and western reception etiquettes;
2. To learn to translate and interpret job titles;
3. To have some general knowledge about how to identify information in interpretation;
4. To learn how to translate / interpret passages or dialogues in the situation of reception;
5. To learn useful words and expressions related to business reception.

Lead-in

● *Quiz* (**True or False**)

_____ 1. If people don't know one another in the meeting room, you need to make introductions. You should do this by starting with the person of the lowest rank.

_____ 2. Westerners generally exchange gifts among good friends.

_____ 3. In China, people use left hand to give or receive presents to show their mutual respect.

_____ 4. In the U.S., you are not supposed to arrive early if you're invited to someone's home.

_____ 5. For a business reception, the safest option for a woman is a skirted suit with stockings and closed-toed high-heeled shoes.

_____ 6. You don't need to provide your last name when introducing yourself in a business setting.

● **What are they? Fill in the blanks with English words.**

baggage   passenger push cart   passport   flight ticket   information desk
paging board   taxi stand   airport terminal   security check   parking lot

1. _____

2. _____

3. _____

4. _____

5. _____

6. _____

7. _____

8. _____

9. _____

10. _____

Section A   Translation

Translation Technique

称谓翻译

1. 以"总……"表示的首席长官,可选择"general""chief""head"这类词表示
   总书记 general secretary   总会计师 chief accountant
   总经理 general manager   总教练 head coach
   总代理 general agent

2. 一些行业的职称头衔,如"高级"或"资深",可用"senior"来表示
   高级记者 senior reporter   高级讲师 senior lecturer

3. "首席"英语常用"chief"来表达
   首席顾问 chief advisor   首席检察官 chief inspector

4. 一些高级职务带"长"字,可用"chief""head""general"等表达
   参谋长 chief of staff   护士长 head nurse
   秘书长 secretary-general

5. 以"副"字的表示副职的行政职务头衔，可用"vice""deputy"表达

副总统 vice president   副书记 deputy secretary
副部长 vice minister   副秘书长 deputy secretary-general
副主席 vice chairman   副市长 deputy mayor

6. 学术头衔的"副"职称，常用"associate"表示

副教授 associate professor   副研究员 research associate
副审判长 associate judge   副主任医师 associate doctor

7. 学术头衔中的初级职称如"助理"，我们可以用"assistant"来称呼

助理教授 assistant professor   助理工程师 assistant engineer

8. 一般说来，"代理"可译作"acting"

代理市长 acting mayor   代理总理 acting premier
代理主任 acting director

9. "常务"可以用"managing"表示

常务理事 managing director   常务副校长 managing vice president

10. "执行"可译作"executive"

执行秘书 executive secretary   执行主席 executive chairman

11. 很多称谓的英语表达方式难以归类，这就需要我们日积月累，逐步总结

办公室主任 office manager   车间主任 workshop manager
客座教授 visiting professor   村长 village head
税务员 tax collector   股票交易员 stock dealer

12. 我们国家特有的一些荣誉称号的口译，需要平时积累

劳动模范 model worker
优秀员工 outstanding employee
标兵 pacemaker
"三好"学生 "triple-A" outstanding student; outstanding student

13. 尊称的译法

英译中时将"you""your company""your university"译成"您""贵公司""贵校"；中译英时将"尊敬的来宾"译成"distinguished guests""honorable guests"或"respected guests"。但英文中不同身份的人有不同的尊称。

（1）"陛下"（Majesty）是对"king"和"queen"的尊称。直接称谓"Your Majesty"，间接称谓"His / Her Majesty"。

（2）"殿下"（Highness）是对"Prince""Princess""Royal Duke"（王族公爵）及"Royal Duchess"的尊称。"Highness"后还可加人名和头衔，如"Your Royal Highness Princess Diana"。

（3）"阁下"（Excellency）是对"Prime Minister""Secretary""Minister""Governor""Ambassador"等高官和教士的尊称。

（4）"先生"（Honor）是对法官和某些高官的尊称。后面还可以加上具体职务称谓，如"Your Honor the Judge""His Honor the Mayor"。

以上多为英国籍英联邦体制下的尊称系列,但美国一般用"Mr. Ambassador","Mr. Governor"等。

Passage Translation 1

Vocabulary

1. 主任
2. 名片
3. 不辞辛苦
4. 拨冗
5. 远道而来
6. 会议议程表
7. 主要发言人
8. 研讨会
9. 舒适如归
10. 为……设宴洗尘

> 欢迎 John Davis 教授来访我校。请允许我做自我介绍。我叫李琳,是国际学术交流中心的主任。这是我的名片。
>
> 我很高兴能在我的家乡接待您。感谢您不辞辛苦,拨冗从美国远道而来参加我们的学术研讨会。自收到您来访日期的邮件后,我们一直期待您的到来。希望您在中国一切愉快。
>
> 我们为您预订了学术交流中心宾馆的一套客房。宾馆位于校园的中心,在湖边,去明天的会场只要走几分钟就到。宾馆设计风格独特,设施齐全,我相信您一定会喜欢。
>
> Davis 教授,这是您的会议议程表。我们的研讨会将如期在我中心举行,我很高兴地告诉您,您将作为第一轮报告会的主要发言人。
>
> 会场准备了笔记本电脑和投影仪,如果您还需要什么,请一定告诉我。我们会尽力为您服务,使您有一种舒适如归的感觉。
>
> 长途旅行之后,您应该好好休息一下。我告辞了,今晚我们将为您设宴洗尘。我 6 点来接您,晚上见!

Notes

1. "欢迎 John Davis 教授来访我校。"翻译此句时,切勿受汉语影响,不能翻成 "Welcome Professor John Davis to our university",可译为 "Welcome to our university, Professor John Davis."

2. "我叫李琳,是国际学术交流中心的主任。"在接待翻译中,自我介绍是必需的。在翻译此类介绍时，要注意调整词序，即按照所指单位的级别从小到大的顺序，译成"Director of the Center for International Academic Exchange"。此外，称谓翻译要准确，不能望文生义，例如，此处的"主任"不能译成"dean"。"dean"在英文中一般指大学的系主任。

3. "感谢您不辞辛苦，拨冗从美国远道而来参加我们的学术研讨会。"这是接待翻译中常用的套话，用来感谢他人的到来。这句套话中，需要重点掌握三个常用短语的翻译，"不辞辛苦"（in spite of the tiring journey）、"拨冗"（take time off one's busy schedule）、"远道而来"（come all the way from ...）。

4. "今晚我们将为您设宴洗尘。"在接待场合为表示对来访者的尊重，一般把"为您设宴洗尘"译成"host a banquet in your honor"。

Passage Translation 2

Vocabulary

1. Your Excellency
2. Secretary General
3. Speaker of Parliament
4. Representative of Royal Families
5. distinguished guest
6. Expo 2010 Shanghai China
7. extend a warm welcome
8. heartfelt thanks
9. showcase
10. annal

Your Excellency Jean-Pierre Lafon, President of the International Exhibitions Bureau, Your Excellency Vicente Loscertales, Secretary General of the International Exhibitions Bureau, Distinguished Heads of State and Government, Speakers of Parliament and Representatives of Royal Families, Distinguished Representatives of International Organizations, Distinguished Guests, Ladies and Gentlemen, Dear Friends,

The grand opening of Expo 2010 Shanghai China will be held this evening. On behalf of the Chinese government and people, I wish to extend a warm welcome to all the distinguished guests who have come to Shanghai for this event. I would like to express heartfelt thanks to the governments and people of all countries for the sincere help and strong support they have given to the Shanghai Expo. My thanks also go to the International Exhibitions Bureau and other international organizations and to all the friends who have contributed to Expo 2010 Shanghai.

The World Expo is a grand event to showcase the best achievements of human civilization. It is also a great occasion for people from around the world to share joy and friendship. I believe that the Expo will add a new chapter to the annals of interactions and mutual learning between the Chinese people and people of other countries and between different civilizations.

Now, I wish to propose a toast,

To a successful, splendid, and unforgettable World Expo,

To the solidarity and friendship of people of all countries,

To the development and progress of human civilization, and

To the health of all the distinguished guests and your families.

Cheers!

Notes

1. 在第一段中，出现了许多称呼，如"President""Secretary General""Speakers of Parliament and Representatives of Royal Families"，以及许多尊称，如"Your Excellency""Distinguished Guests"等。在翻译时要特别注意，依次分别译为："主席""秘书长""议长和王室代表们""阁下""贵宾"。

2. "On behalf of the Chinese government and people, I wish to extend a warm welcome to all the distinguished guests who have come to Shanghai for this event."在正式的接待场合，"extend a warm welcome"是表达欢迎的套话。

3. "I would like to express heartfelt thanks to the governments and people of all countries for the sincere help and strong support they have given to the Shanghai Expo."此句的翻译主要在于表达感谢的套话，即"express heartfelt thanks to ... for ..."。其中，"heartfelt thanks"译成"衷心的感谢"。

4. "Now, I wish to propose a toast to a successful, splendid, and unforgettable World Expo. Cheers!"祝酒句型也是接待场合常用句型。根据不同的场合，可以使用不同的句型，如较为随意的"Let's drink to ..."，也有较为正式的"May I invite you to join me in a toast to ..."等。

Sentences in Focus

1. 请允许我做自我介绍。我叫李琳，是国际学术交流中心的主任。

2. 我很高兴能在我的家乡接待您。

3. 感谢您不辞辛苦，拨冗从美国远道而来参加我们的学术研讨会。

4. 自收到您来访日期的邮件后，我们一直期待您的到来。

5. 如果您还需要什么，请一定告诉我。我们会尽力为您服务，使您有一种舒适如归的感觉。

6. 今晚我们将为您设宴洗尘。

7. On behalf of the Chinese government and people, I wish to extend a warm welcome to all the distinguished guests who have come to Shanghai for this event.

8. I would like to express heartfelt thanks to the governments and people of all countries for the sincere help and strong support they have given to the Shanghai Expo.

9. My thanks also go to the International Exhibitions Bureau and other international organizations, and to all the friends who have contributed to Expo 2010 Shanghai.

10. Now, I wish to propose a toast to a successful, splendid, and unforgettable World Expo. Cheers!

Exercises

I. Fill in the blanks with English words according to the given Chinese.

1. My colleague will _____ (接您) at the Baiyun International Airport and send you directly to the hotel.
2. Pazhou International Conference Center, the home of Canton Fair, is _____ _____ (坐落于) Yuejiang Road, Guangzhou.
3. All meeting rooms _____ (配备) the latest audio-video facilities.
4. Asia Finance Symposium will be held _____ (如期) with at least 450 participants from home and abroad.
5. Wireless Internet access and teleconference room are _____ (可提供的) free of charge during the convention.
6. It is our honor to have the attendance of _____ (嘉宾们) on the occasion of the Mid-autumn Festival.
7. The five-star hotel lies in the downtown with walking distance to the _____ _____ (会场).

8. We have _____ (预订) a table at Beijing Roast Duck Restaurant as prepared in honor of you and your wife.

9. I'd like to inform you that you will be the _____ (主要发言人) at this international forum.

10. I'd like to _____ (祝酒) to the healthy and happy life of all guests at present.

Ⅱ. Translate the following job titles.

1. sales representative _____

2. marketing manager _____

3. vice president _____

4. deputy general manager _____

5. senior accountant _____

6. 副教授 _____

7. 总工程师 _____

8. 首席执行官 _____

9. 导演 _____

10. 代理主任 _____

Ⅲ. Translate the following sentences.

1. The hotel supplies the airport pick-up service from 5 a.m. to 11:30 p.m.

2. You are going to check in Sheraton Wuxi, a luxurious five-star hotel next to the Wanda Plaza.

3. We look forward to more cultural exchange when you visit Jiangnan University for a second time.

4. The hotel is only a short taxi ride away and there're also free shuttle buses.

5. Chengdu is one of the largest metropolises in southwest China and an ancient city dating back to over 2,000 years.

6. 我们为您预订了一间单人房,包括早餐。(reserve)

7. 如果您有任何问题或特殊要求,请一定告诉我。(hesitate)

8. 我会尽力使您的上海之行成为一段愉快且有意义的经历。(rewarding)

9. 今晚,在无锡烤鸭馆,我们为总裁和所有的贵宾们设宴洗尘。(banquet)

10. 您在无锡期间,我会做您的导游,带您游遍这座美丽而又现代的城市。(show ... around)

IV. Translate the following paragraphs.

1. Three days ago, we met as strangers. Then we have visited the major scenic spots in Wuxi and enjoyed the well-known Wuxi food. Today, we bid farewell to each other as friends. As a Chinese saying goes, "It is such a delight to have friends coming from afar." I hope you'll take back happy memories of your visit to Wuxi. And I'd like to take this opportunity to extend invitation to you again and welcome you back to Wuxi next year. Ladies and gentlemen, let's drink to our friendship and health.

2. 我谨代表所有参加2014无锡国际马拉松赛(Wuxi International Marathon 2014)的运动员,向举办此次活动的组委会表达衷心感谢。我荣幸地在此欢迎从世界各地远道而来的朋友们,并祝愿大家在无锡生活愉快。谢谢!

Section B Interpretation

Interpretation Technique

口译技能：如何听辨

顾名思义，听辨不仅要"听"，还要"辨"，即思考、分析。"听辨"是口译过程中的第一个阶段。在这个过程中我们接收听到的信息，并通过种种分析手段把接收到的信息纳入我们的理解范畴，以便储存和输出。

口译中的听辨过程和平时在英语学习中所接受的听力训练是不同的，但二者又有一定的联系。

首先，英语的听力训练中比较注重语言层面，十分强调语音、语调和语言的表达及用法等。而听辨过程所注重的是意思，或是讲话者的意图，而不是具体的词句表达。所以我们在听到一段话之后在头脑中形成的是一个有逻辑关系的语意整体，而不仅仅是词句的简单集合。

其次，听力练习中主要启动听觉系统，理解只是一个被动而附带的过程。而在听辨过程中我们不仅要启动听觉系统，还要启动大脑中的分析理解机制和记忆机制。也就是说我们要边听、边分析、边理解、边记忆。所以，与一般的外语学习相比较而言，口译学习要学会"一心多用"。

再次，在听力练习过程中，信息接收是被动和跟随性的。而听辨过程中伴有很大程度的预测和判断行为，常常需要对所听内容进行分析、整理、补充和联想等。

因此，听辨训练过程较一般外语听力训练过程要复杂得多，它是一个通过听辨将信息接收和理解，再用译入语将理解了的信息加以表达的过程。

练习建议：

1. 可以选择一些英文有声资料，听完一段话后，用英文进行复述。注意在听的过程中要把注意力从词句表达上移开，而专注于整段话的逻辑意思。在复述时不要拘泥于原文的词句，更不要试图背原话。意思和逻辑关系要尽量复述得准确完整。

2. 在听辨训练的初级阶段，如果还不能完全掌握边听、边分析、边记忆的技能，可采取就所听内容进行提问的方式建立逻辑关系。比如可以将注意力放在 what、who、when and where、how and why 等几个要素上。通过这种方式增强逻辑分析意识，努力跟上讲话人的思路，从而对所听语篇内容有一个正确的理解。

Passage Interpretation 1

尊敬的各位来宾、女士们、先生们，大家晚上好！

在亚太经合组织第二十二次经济领导人会议召开之际，大家不远万里来到北京。首先，我代表中国政府和人民，代表我的夫人，也以我个人的名义对各位贵宾的到来表示热烈的欢迎！

我要感谢这次会议，让我们下了更大的决心，来保护生态环境，有利于我们今后把生态环境保护工作做得更好。也有人说，现在北京的蓝天是 APEC 蓝，美好而短暂，过了这一阵就没了。我希望并相信通过不懈的努力，APEC 蓝能够保持下去。

这是一个富有意义的夜晚，我们为亚太长远发展的共同使命而来，应该以此为契机，一起勾画亚太长远发展愿景，确定亚太未来合作方向。明天我们将相会在燕山脚下雁栖湖畔，正式拉开经济领导人会议的序幕。孔子说："智者乐水，仁者乐山。"那儿有山有水，大家可以智者见智，仁者见仁，共商亚太发展大计，共谋亚太合作愿景。

现在我提议，大家共同举杯，为亚太地区繁荣进步，为亚太经合组织蓬勃发展，为这次经济领导人非正式会议圆满成功，为各位嘉宾和家人的健康干杯！干杯！

Passage Interpretation 2

Westerners give gifts on many occasions, such as, on birthdays, at weddings, at Christmas and on some other holidays. Although gifts are always welcome, it is not necessary to exchange gifts all the time.

Generally speaking, westerners exchange gifts only among good friends; therefore, it's inappropriate to give gifts to casual acquaintances. Even though you are good friends, if you give them too many gifts, they will feel uncomfortable too, because they don't know how to reciprocate. Usually when you are invited to dinner, it is absolutely unnecessary to bring a gift except on special occasions, for example when you are going to be an overnight or weekend guest. If you wish to bring something, in most cases, the gifts should always be small, simple and inexpensive. You might bring some sweets or small toys for the children, a book, a bunch of flowers, or a bottle of wine for the host or the hostess. You can wrap the gifts, but wrapping is not always necessary. If you want to make your gifts special, you can bring some typical Chinese goods, such as tea, book markers, paper cuts or Chinese paintings.

Westerners prefer to open a gift at once and appreciate it. They would thank you and make some comment about the gift's beauty or practicality. Westerners value homemade things. When they ask you whether the gift is homemade, in fact they are praising you. They are trying to tell you that you are skillful and talented enough to make it.

Dialogue Interpretation

A：请问，您是美国来的威尔逊先生吗？
B：Yes, I am.
A：我是梅雯，中国纺织品进出口公司的秘书。
B：How do you do, Miss Mei.
A：您好，威尔逊先生，欢迎来到中国。
B：Thank you. It's very kind of you to come to meet me at the airport, Miss Mei.
A：乐意效劳。希望您在这儿过得愉快。
B：Thank you, I'm sure I will.
A：您旅途愉快吗？
B：Yes, quite a nice flight.
A：很高兴听您这么说。您将住在花园宾馆。它是城里最好的宾馆之一。我们已经预订了一间带有单独浴室的套房。在花园宾馆，每天确保有二十四小时的服务。酒店提供完备的会议服务。另外还有一个不错的餐厅、一个酒吧,以及洗衣房等。

B:Sounds great. But is it conveniently located?

A:很便利。它位于闹市区。我们马上就要到了。驱车只要十五分钟就到我们公司。

B:Miss Mei, what about tomorrow's arrangement?

A:明天早上八点半我到宾馆来接您,然后我们总经理九点钟在公司接见您。下午两位将出席一个记者招待会。晚上我们会观看一场地道的中国杂技表演。您喜欢我们的日程安排吗?

B:Very much. Thank you for such thoughtful arrangements for me.

A:我先带您去宾馆休息一下,六点再来接您去参加招待晚宴,您看好吗?

B:Perfect. Thank you for your consideration.

A:不用谢!

Exercises

I. Interpreting technique practice.

You will hear two English passages. Please try to summarize the main idea of each passage based on the following six elements: what, who, when, where, how and why.

1. _____
   _____
   _____

2. _____
   _____
   _____

II. Spot dictation.

Address a person using one's family name only, such as Mr. Chen or Ms. Hsu. The Chinese family name comes first and is usually one syllable. A one- or two-syllable (1)_____ name follows a family name. For example, in the case of Teng Peinian, Teng is the family name and Peinian is the given name. In some instances, westernized Chinese might (2)_____ their names when visiting and sending correspondence abroad. Therefore, it is always a good idea to ask a native speaker which name is the family name.

For business (3)_____, it is traditionally acceptable to call a Chinese person by the surname, together with a title, such as "Director Wang" or "Chairman Li". (4)_____ using someone's given name unless you have known him or her for a long period of time. Formality is a sign of respect, and it is (5)_____ to clarify how you will address someone very early in a relationship, generally during your first meeting.

Do not try to become too (6)_____ too soon, and do not insist that your Chinese counterparts address you by your given name. The western pattern of quick informality should be (7)_____.

The Chinese way of greeting is a nod or slight bow. However, when (8)_____ with westerners, Chinese usually shake hands. Bear in mind that a soft handshake and a lack of eye (9)_____ do not necessarily indicate timidity. It only implies that the person is not (10)_____ to the firm handshakes commonly used in the west.

III. Sentence listening and translation.

1. _____
2. _____
3. _____
4. _____
5. _____

IV. Paragraph listening and translation.

_____
_____
_____
_____
_____

V. Dialogue interpretation.

A: What a beautiful city! Where shall I be staying?
B: 您将住在和平饭店,城里最好的宾馆之一。
A: I remember that it is a five-star hotel, isn't it?
B: 是的。我们已经预订了一间带有阳台的单人间。您一定会喜欢的。
A: Sounds great, but is it conveniently located?
B: 很便利。它位于闹市区。我们马上就要到了。
A: Mr. Wang, what about tomorrow's arrangement?
B: 明天早上八点半我到宾馆来接您,然后我们总经理九点钟在公司会见您。
A: I've been looking forward to meeting him since I received his invitation.
B: 明天晚上七点我们在花园饭店为您设宴洗尘。
A: Thank you so much for your thoughtful arrangement.
B: 不客气。布朗先生,我们到了。

VI. Interpreting in groups.

Role-play the following situation with your partners, acting as the Chinese speaker, English speaker and the interpreter respectively. One group will be invited to perform in class.

Participants: 1. Mr. Zhang, assistant manager
　　　　　　　 2. Mr. Peter Wright, personnel manager
　　　　　　　 3. An interpreter

Location: Airport

Task: Mr. Zhang meets Mr. Wright at the airport by greeting him, making self-introduction and a small talk. On the way to the hotel, Mr. Zhang introduces the hotel and the schedule of that day.

VII. 3-minute talk on the given topic.

Talk on the following topic in three minutes based on the given reference questions.

Topic: Meeting guests at the airport

Questions for Reference:

1. What will you do before you go to the airport to pick up your guests?
2. How will you greet your guests at the airport?
3. What else will you do for the guests after greeting?

VIII. Theme-related expressions.

机场大楼	terminal building
问讯处	information/inquiry desk
安全检查	security check
登机卡	boarding pass
办理海关例行手续	go through customs formalities
海关行李申报单	customs baggage/luggage declaration form
应纳关税物品	dutiable goods/ articles
往返票	round-trip ticket; return ticket
入境/出境/过境签证	entry/exit/transit visa
旅游签证	tourist visa
外交护照	diplomatic passport
免税店	duty-free shop
随身携带行李	carry-on baggage
行李标签牌	luggage/ baggage tag

● 行李提取处	luggage/ baggage claim
● 机场班车	airport shuttle bus
● 出租车候车处	taxi stand/ rank
● 盛大招待会	grand reception
● 宾馆登记表	hotel registration form
● 宾馆休息大厅	hotel lobby
● 入住/退房	check in/ out
● 总统/豪华套房	presidential/luxury suite
● 外事办	foreign affair office
● 活动日程	itinerary/schedule
● 招待会	reception party
● 欢迎/告别词	welcome/farewell speech

1. 见面语

☞ 请允许我介绍一下自己,我叫……,口译员。
Allow me to introduce myself. I am ... , the interpreter.

☞ 很高兴能请到您。
It's a great pleasure to have you here with us.

☞ 您一定是我们期盼已久的客人——从匹兹堡大学来的格林教授吧。
You must be our long-expected guest, Professor Green from University of Pittsburgh!

☞ 谢谢您专程赶来接待我!
Thank you very much for coming all the way to meet me in person.

☞ 我们又见面了。
Small world, isn't it?

☞ 我很高兴能与您结识。
I'm delighted to make your acquaintance.

☞ 我很高兴能在我的家乡接待您。
I'm glad/happy/delighted to meet you in my hometown.

2. 欢迎语

☞ 欢迎光临上海通用汽车公司。
Welcome to Shanghai General Motors.

☞ 能有如此热情的团队参与我们的项目,我们深感愉快。
It's our great pleasure to have such an enthusiastic group to participate in our project.

3. 感谢语

☞ 感谢您为我们所做的如此精心的安排。

Thank you for such a thoughtful arrangement for us.

☞ 感谢各位专程远道到访本公司。

Thank you for coming all the way to our company.

4. 结束语

☞ 祝您参观一切顺利！

Wish you all the best in your tour/visit.

☞ 祝您访问圆满成功！

Wish your visit a complete success.

☞ 希望我们不久能再相会！

Hope to see each other again soon.

☞ 期待能有机会再次作为东道主接待您。

I am looking forward to the opportunity to host you here again.

☞ 一路平安。

Have a safe trip home.

Section C Further Exploration

将以下文中小标题译成中文，填入空格。

Welcome to the 105th Canton Fair

The 105th Canton Fair has optimized the layout of the exhibition-area, brought in the service concept and mechanism of being professional and people-oriented, and improved its service in an all-round way. 第105届广交会优化展区布局，引入专业化、市场化的服务理念和机制，以人为本，全面提升展览服务水平。

1. Customer Service Center

We integrate the on-site service system and provide the buyers and exhibitors with quality, highly efficient and one-stop service.

全面整合现场服务保障体系，为客商、展商提供优质、高效、顺畅的一站式服务。

2. VIP Service

All the VIP customers can enjoy such services as hotel reservation, person-to-person information consulting, conference arrangements, and many other customized services free of charge.

为广交会 VIP 客商免费提供酒店预订、专人信息咨询、会议安排等各种个性化服务。

3. International Pavilion Service

Invitation of domestic buyers is mainly conducted by trade delegations, supplemented by Foreign Trade Center's own invitation and nominations of overseas exhibitors of International Pavilion.

国内采购商继续采取以交易团定向组织邀请为主,外贸中心自主招商,进口参展商提名邀请为辅的方式。

4. Digital Venue

We install a wireless network covering all the exhibition areas and public area offering free and fast Internet access for all buyers and exhibitors.

建立覆盖全馆展览区域和公共区域的无线网络体系,为客商、展商免费提供便捷的上网服务。

5. Complex Guiding System

We further optimize the complex guiding system on the basis of the features of the venue and the layout of the exhibition sections.

根据新展馆构造特点和展区布局进一步调整优化导向系统,全方位加强导向指引。

6. Food and Beverage

The organizer has brought in over 30 restaurants and canteens, improved the distribution of the dining areas, and introduced a bigger variety of cuisines. With more than 30,000 square meters, the dining area can accommodate over 13,000 customers at the same time.

主办方引进了30多家各具特色的餐饮经营单位,完善设点布局,丰富餐饮品种。逾3万平方米的就餐区域可供13000多人同时就餐。

UNIT 2

Shopping

购物消费

Learning Objectives

1. To understand the differences between Chinese and western shopping practices;
2. To know how to translate with the technique of amplification;
3. To learn how to identify the key words of the sentences that you hear;
4. To learn how to translate/interpret passages or dialogues in the situation of shopping;
5. To learn useful words and expressions related to online and offline shopping.

Lead-in

● *Quiz* (True or False)

_____ 1. A shopaholic is a person considered to be addicted to shopping.

_____ 2. B2C is short for business-to-customs, a type of commerce transactions between businesses and the customs.

_____ 3. "Window shopping" refers to the browsing of goods by a consumer with no intention of purchase, either as a recreational activity or to plan a later purchase.

_____ 4. At airport duty-free shops, you usually buy products at a very high price.

_____ 5. Most French retailers and stores except those in tourist areas are still strictly forbidden from opening on Sundays and after 9 p.m. on weekdays.

_____ 6. Always keep the receipt in case you would like to return the goods and ask for refund.

_____ 7. When it comes to shopping, there is no difference between "paying tax" and "paying duty".

● **What are they? Fill in the blanks with English words.**

fitting room   discount   drugstore   vending machine   coupon
cashier   AliPay   price tag   fruit stand   shopping mall

1. _____   2. _____   3. _____   4. _____   5. _____

6. _____   7. _____   8. _____   9. _____   10. _____

Section A Translation

Translation Technique

增译

由于英汉语表达方式和遣词造句习惯不同，翻译时，有时需要增加必要的词，使译文意思明白，通顺易懂。一般在下面三种情况下需要增词：

1. **把原文句子里隐含的或上下文意思清楚而没有写出来的词增补出来**

原文：普通老百姓在不久的将来圆<u>私家车之梦</u>。

译文：The common people will be able to realize their <u>dream of owning a car</u>.

分析：这句中的"私家车之梦"其实指的是拥有私家车，因此增加了"own"这个词，使译文清晰易懂。

2. **由于句法需要，把原文中省略的句子成分补充完整**

原文：天色已晚，我得赶快回家。

译文：It is getting dark, <u>so</u> I must hurry home.

分析：这句话中，添加了连接词"so"，显化译文因果逻辑关系，符合英文表达习惯。

3. **为了能让读者了解带有特定文化色彩的词汇，需要对一些专用名词增加注解文字**

原文：在他面前大谈股票，那简直是<u>班门弄斧</u>。

译文：Talking too much about stock before him will be like <u>showing off one's proficiency with the axe before Lu Ban—an ancient Chinese master carpenter</u>.

分析：这句话中的鲁班是具有中国文化特色的专有名词，因此有必要在翻译时适当加词简单介绍下鲁班其人，便于读者理解译文。下面篇章翻译中有的句子也需要增译。

Passage Translation 1

Vocabulary

1. 可支配收入
2. 物质消费文化
3. 住房
4. 日常必需品
5. 消费习惯和态度
6. 名牌
7. 大幅度增长
8. 文化和自然遗产
9. 绿色消费
10. 年总支出
11. 最盛大的网络购物节日
12. 剁手族
13. 消费能力
14. 大牌奢侈品
15. 奢侈品消费市场

　　随着中国经济和社会的快速发展,近年来中国的消费结构变化显著。拥有更多可支配收入的人们正步入物质消费文化,这使得他们可以将更多钱用于旅游、信息技术产品、住房、医疗保险、娱乐和教育。这完全改变了人们喜欢把钱花在购买日常必需品上的消费习惯。

　　这些新的消费习惯和态度使社会变化很多,尤其体现在几代人之间的代沟问题上。当今年轻人关注的焦点是国内外的名牌。拥有这类产品的欲望使这些产业有大幅度增长。另外一个有趣的现象是中国旅游业及其相关产业的崛起。越来越多的中国旅游者开始开发探索国内旅游,游览中国的文化和自然遗产景观,因此环境保护和绿色消费不断兴起。其次,教育已经成为人们消费的一大部分。普通城市家庭的教育支出约占了年总支出的30%。与此同时,中国消费者网络购物方兴未艾。2014 年,在全世界最盛大的网络购物节日"双十一"那天,阿里巴巴以 571 亿元的创纪录销售额画上句号。淘宝方面表示,在其 5 亿注册用户中,可以称为"剁手族"的已达 108 万。

　　中国游客还是重要的海外消费群体。英国旅游 2014 年度前 10 个月的数据表明,中国与中东国家仍然是最强劲的高消费群之一,占总消费的 25%。由于中国顾客消费力很强,中国人所消费的Burberry，LV，Gucci等大牌奢侈品占整个奢侈品行业销售额的三分之一。有分析指出，中国人已经取代俄罗斯人和阿拉伯人，成为英国奢侈品消费市场的最大买家。随着中国国际化程度的加强，所有这些新的消费态度正改变着中国的面貌。

Notes

1. "这使得他们可以将更多钱用于旅游、信息技术产品、住房、医疗保险、娱乐和教育。这完全改变了人们喜欢把钱花在购买日常必需品上的消费习惯。"在这两句翻译中，由于后句中的"这"实际指代的是前句的内容，因此可以用合并法翻译这两句话，将后句译成前句的非限制性定语从句。此外，第一句中的"这"在句子中指代的是人们收入的增多，因此有必要增加词，译为"this new excess"。

2. "当今年轻人关注的焦点是国内外的名牌。"这句中的"名牌"确切地说是指具有著名商标的商品，因此不能简单译成"famous brand"，而应增译成"products with famous brand names"。

3. "中国消费者网络购物方兴未艾。"汉语中的成语翻译往往只能根据上下文释义。此句中，成语"方兴未艾"用来说明网络购物正在蓬勃发展，因而可以用"is gathering momentum and is there to stay"。汉语中许多四字格的翻译也大多用释义的方法翻译。

4. "2014年，在全世界最盛大的网络购物节日'双十一'那天，阿里巴巴以571亿元的创纪录销售额画上句号。"这句话里出现了较大的数字"571亿元"，译成了"57.1 billion yuan（\$9.34 billion）"。在这里，除了要把"571亿"正确转换为英语里的"51.7 billion"外，还在括号里把相应的美元价值标注出来，属于增译。增译往往是为了让读者更容易理解译文内容。

5. "淘宝方面表示，在其5亿注册用户中，可以称为'剁手族'的已达108万。"这句话中的"剁手族"是个新兴词汇，在翻译时可以直译，保留原语的语言特色，但也要在括号中加注，让读者更好理解其含义，因此宜译成"hands-chopping people"（big online spenders who self-mockingly say that they would like to chop their hands off after buying too much online）。

Passage Translation 2

Vocabulary

1. Black Friday
2. Christmas shopping season
3. discount
4. go from the red into the black
5. stampede
6. bargain
7. Panic Saturday

8. accrue revenue

9. slash price

Black Friday is the day after Thanksgiving. As Thanksgiving Day revolves around eating, Black Friday revolves around shopping. It has become the biggest day of the year for American retailers as they discount thousands of products, kick-starting the Christmas shopping season. According to one story, the name thus refers to shops doing such booming trade that they go from the red into the black. It might equally be named so because of the casualty rate. Shoppers got hurt in the stampede for bargains. Some even died.

Since Brits do not celebrate Thanksgiving, they had never taken to Black Friday until last year. The rhythms of Christmas used to be so simple, buying presents in December, eating and drinking too much, returning unwanted gifts, and then hunting bargains in the January sales. Such habits were altered by the arrival on British shores of Black Friday, an American retail phenomenon.

In the United Kingdom, Black Friday was a historic nickname within the emergency services for the last Friday before Christmas, as this is the most popular night for office Christmas parties, which consequently makes it one of the busiest nights in the year for ambulances and the police. In most of the United Kingdom, the Friday is referred to as Black Eye Friday, due to extremely high number of fights that break out in bars, pubs and clubs. In 2013, it started to be named Mad Friday, probably to avoid confusion with the American shopping phenomenon at the end of November called Black Friday, as this began to be adopted by many UK retailers.

Panic Saturday or Super Saturday is the last Saturday before Christmas, a major day of revenue for American retailers, marking the end of the shopping season which they and many customers believe begins on Black Friday. Panic Saturday targets last-minute shoppers. Typically the day is ridden with one-day sales in an effort to accrue more revenue than any other day in the Christmas and holiday season. Shoppers across Britain went looking for late Christmas bargains on Dec. 20, 2014 as high street spending reached £1.2 billion on what was being branded "Panic Saturday". Some of the country's biggest high street brands slashed prices for what was expected to be one of the busiest shopping days of the year.

Notes

1. "According to one story, the name thus refers to shops doing such booming trade that they go from the red into the black." 句中画线部分如果只是简单译成"从红变成黑",显然是不妥的,为了能让读者更加明白句子意思,在译文中进行加注,译为"转亏为盈"(红色记录赤字,黑色记录盈利),解释了何为"转亏为盈"。

2. "Such habits were altered by the arrival on British shores of Black Friday, an American retail phenomenon." 这句话中画线部分是同位语。英语中的同位语视长短不同和表达习惯不同,可以译成前置的"……的"结构,也可以译成"这一……"结构。这儿可以

译成"黑色星期五这一美国零售现象"。

3. "In the United Kingdom, Black Friday was a historic nickname within the emergency services for the last Friday before Christmas, as this is the most popular night for office Christmas parties, which consequently makes it one of the busiest nights in the year for ambulances and the police." 这句话翻译的难点是定语从句的处理。这是一句结构较复杂的长句,既有定语从句,也有状语从句,翻译时,将定语从句译成分句,译成"这也使之成了令救护车和警察最忙碌的夜晚"。

4. "Panic Saturday targets last-minute shoppers." 此句话中,"last-minute shoppers"根据上下文语境要增译成"熬到最后一刻才出手购物的顾客",而不是简单地译成"最后一刻的顾客"。

Sentences in Focus

1. 随着中国经济和社会的快速发展,近年来中国的消费结构变化显著。

2. 这使得他们可以将更多钱用于旅游、信息技术产品、住房、医疗保险、娱乐和教育。

3. 教育已经成为人们消费的一大部分。普通城市家庭的教育支出约占了年总支出的30%。

4. 中国消费者网络购物方兴未艾。

5. 由于中国顾客消费能力很强,中国人所消费的大牌奢侈品占整个奢侈品行业销售额的三分之一。

6. Black Friday has become the biggest day of the year for American retailers as they discount thousands of products, kick-starting the Christmas shopping season.

7. Such habits were altered by the arrival on British shores of Black Friday, an American retail phenomenon.

8. In the United Kingdom, Black Friday was a historic nickname within the emergency services for the last Friday before Christmas, as this is the most popular night for office Christmas parties, which consequently makes it one of the busiest nights in the year for ambulances and the police.

9. In 2013, it started to be named Mad Friday, probably to avoid confusion with the American shopping phenomenon at the end of November called Black Friday, as this began to be adopted by many UK retailers.

10. Panic Saturday or Super Saturday is the last Saturday before Christmas, a major day of revenue for American retailers, marking the end of the shopping season they and many customers believe begins on Black Friday.

Exercises

Ⅰ. Fill in the blanks with English words according to the given Chinese.

1. We will explore and generalize the _____(消费习惯) of Chinese women in terms of cosmetic products.
2. According to a recent survey conducted on Chinese consumers, it is found that people are willing to pay more for _____(名牌) and high-quality products.
3. The government may try to stimulate the economy as total fixed asset _____(支出) is expected to decelerate in the next few years.
4. The committee has established an _____(网购) for grains, and it plans to promote the whole industry by introducing favorable policies on taxation.
5. Taobao calls the group the "_____"(剁手族) who are extremely passionate about shopping online.
6. Overseas tourist destinations extend warm welcome to Chinese people with amazing _____(购买力).
7. Walmart is one of the largest _____(零售商) in the world which runs chains of large discount department stores and warehouse stores.
8. The market, he said, can serve as a bridge between sellers and buyers to offer the very latest _____(便宜货).
9. Black Friday was followed by _____(恐慌星期六) as shoppers poured into town centers preparing to spend an estimated £1.2 billion on gifts before Christmas Day.
10. The _____(大减价) of oil has negative effect on the economy of Russia which voiced its opposition to the sanction of the European Union and the U.S. government.

Ⅱ. Translate the following shopping terms into English or Chinese.

1. time-honored brand _____
2. shelf life _____
3. mortgage _____
4. installment payment _____
5. expiration date _____
6. 环保袋 _____
7. 旗舰店 _____

8. 条形码_____

9. 营业时间_____

10. 购物车_____

III. Translate the following sentences.

1. The shopping mall is spacious and clean with comfortable environment, mainly catering to medium and high-end clients who pursue good quality.
_____

2. You can't miss it when you arrive in Shanghai. Take Metro Line 1, get off at South Huangpi Road Station and exit from Gate 2.
_____

3. You can also find traditional handicrafts with distinctive eastern style in the many business streets and markets.
_____

4. New Yaohan was formerly known as Yaohan(八佰伴) and was established in 1992 by a Japanese firm.
_____

5. An increasing number of tourists are taking backpack tours, bringing more diversity to the tourism and retailing markets.
_____

6. 在过去的十年里,电子商务已极大地改变了人们的生活方式。(dramatically)
_____
_____

7. 与网购相比,某些物品在实体店买更简单方便。(item)
_____
_____

8. 今年,比利时是最受国际购物者欢迎的第二大目的地。(shopper)
_____
_____

9. 该百货店以其先进的设施、舒适的环境为顾客提供愉快的购物体验。(advanced)
_____
_____

10. 淘宝网说所谓的"剁手族"数量已达到108万。(so-called)
_____
_____

IV. Translate the following paragraphs.

1. Showrooming is the practice of going to a conventional store to look at a product and then buying it online for a cheaper price. There are certain things we may want to see before we buy, because any written description or image on the web, no matter how detailed, is just no substitute for looking at the real thing.

This is where showrooming kicks in.

2. 随着电子商务的迅猛发展,网购已然成了人们主要的消费方式之一。中国消费者发现网购既方便又便宜,因此去实体店购物的人越来越少。在这个不断变化的信息时代,新的消费习惯正改变着中国的面貌。

Section B Interpretation

Interpretation Technique

口译技能:如何找出句中的关键信息

  口译的成败在很大程度上取决于听辨的过程。听辨关键词是听辨句子关键信息的重要一步。所谓关键词,是指能体现说话者的说话意图和中心思想的词语,往往是句子的焦点信息。一个句子的关键词可以从词汇、句法、语意和语气四个层面来判断。

  在词汇层面上,名词、动词、代词等实词为关键词。如:"This year, we will lower borrowing rates and improve efficiency in order to further enhance business relations with developing countries." 这句话中的关键词是:lower, borrowing rates, improve, efficiency, enhance, business relations。

  在句法层面上,关键词可以是句子的主语,也可以是宾语或表语。如在"一个好老师必须做到德才兼备"中,"老师"和"德才兼备"是关键词。

  从语意层面上来说,可以根据句子的新旧信息,把句子理解为"已知信息 + 新信息"这样一种信息结构。如在"Now, let's toast to the everlasting friendship and cooperation between our two countries"这句话中,"now, let's toast to..."是一种固定的祝酒套话,是已知信息,这样在记忆时就可以把关键词定位在下面要祝酒的对象上,即"to the everlasting friendship and cooperation between our two countries"中的"friendship"和

"cooperation"。

在语气层面上,关键词是说话者重读、强调和重复的词汇。如"我现在的心情可以说是既高兴又惶恐"中,"高兴"和"惶恐"是关键词。

当然,由于每个人的认知和记忆方式不同,在听辨时要结合句子语境和背景知识,找到适合自己记忆模式的关键词,从而有效地理解说话人的意思。

练习建议:听中英文句子,辨别出句子中的关键词并复述原句。

Passage Interpretation 1

上海是个购物天堂,各式各样的商业街和购物中心迎接八方来客。上海作为当代中国的窗口城市,其购物中心是最时尚的。

无论你是否是购物狂,上海的顶级购物中心都值得一逛。这些购物中心大多位于繁华的商业中心。例如位于浦东陆家嘴地区的正大广场是上海最具影响力的商业和金融中心之一。这座13层楼的购物综合体具有完备的娱乐和购物设施,聚集了数百个商家以及70家饭店。正大广场是上海历史最悠久也是最好的购物中心之一,每天迎接数十万的顾客。来上海你一定不要错过正大广场。

紧邻豫园的豫园商城也叫城隍庙商城,是体验上海当地生活的绝佳去处。如果你想回顾上海过去的岁月,豫园商城可以带领你回味100年前的上海生活。在这儿,近百家的商店出售包括中药、拐棍、真丝雨伞、竹制家具、金鱼等各类物品,当地人很喜欢在这儿购物,他们能买到别处买不到的物品,上他们最喜欢的馆子吃饭。

Passage Interpretation 2

The largest and most popular shopping mall in the United States is the Mall of America in Bloomington, Minnesota. It cost 650 million dollars and opened in 1992, boasting more than 520 stores as well as more than 50 places to eat. Each year about 40 million people visit the Mall of America. Mall officials say 4 out of 10 visitors traveled long distances to shop here from more than 32 countries.

When the investors designed the mall, they not only wanted it to be a place for shopping and eating, but they also made entertainment a big part of their plan. The Nickelodeon Universe is an indoor theme park. It has more than 25 rides including several roller coasters. Another popular part of the mall is the Underwater Adventures Aquarium with 5,000 sea animals. When visitors walk through a 91-meter glass tube, sharks and other ocean animals swim above and beside them. Some visitors have other things on their minds besides sharks, shopping, food and roller coasters. These people go to the Chapel of Love to be married. Over 5,000 couples have had their weddings at the Mall of America.

More than 650 million people have visited the Mall of America since it opened 18 years ago. Now the investors have plans for a large addition. The "Phase Two" plan will nearly double the size of the mall. When it is completed, there will be enough room for up to 900 stores.

Dialogue Interpretation

A: Hello! Can I help you?

B: 嗯,我想帮我的未婚妻买冬衣。

A: Oh, it's high time you purchased in our clothes shop. We are now having a pre-season sale on all our winter apparel.

B: 真的吗? 怎么促销?

A: Everything for winter is 20% off.

B: 我想我的未婚妻会喜欢商店橱窗里的那件羊毛衫的。你能帮我挑一下和这件羊毛衫相搭配的裙子吗?

A: Sure, we have both skirts and trousers that would look well with the sweater. Look at this section.

B: 我特别喜欢这件花纹短裙。这条裙子会让我未婚妻看上去非常优雅。

A: You have a good taste. It's very much in style this year.

B: 我觉得绿色的不适合她的肤色。有没有裙子是浅色或者棕褐色的呢?

A: Look on the rack to the right.

B: 噢,我想买这件。我可以用旅行支票支付吗?

A: It's OK.

B: 太好了,给你。

Exercises

I. Interpreting technique practice.

You will hear 10 sentences. Please try to take notes of key words in each sentence by using the technique learned in this section and retell each sentence based on the key words.

1. _____
2. _____
3. _____
4. _____
5. _____
6. _____

7. _____

8. _____

9. _____

10. _____

Ⅱ. Spot dictation.

What's the biggest online shopping day in the world? Not Valentine's Day. Not Cyber Monday or (1) _____. They are the days that follow Thanksgiving in the U.S. and usher in the start of the holiday shopping season. The winner is China Singles' Day, (2) _____ on November 11, or 11.11.

Singles' Day in China is the biggest (3) _____ day in the world. It was created in 2009 by Alibaba's CEO Daniel Zhang to increase online sales. Since then, it has grown into a (4) _____.

Last year, Alibaba sold more than $1 billion worth of products in the first three minutes of the sales, reported Bloomberg. Total sales on Singles' Day soared to (5) _____ within 24 hours. That's four times bigger than Cyber Monday in the U.S., which is the Monday after Thanksgiving and (6) _____ a big shopping day. Today, Singles' Day is a retail blockbuster. Analysts predict that this year, sales on China Singles' Day will soar to a (7) _____.

In the U.S., Dealmoon is a shopping site targeting Chinese-Americans. Jennifer Wang, (8) _____ of the company, said, "We expect to have 3 million people coming to our site for the Singles' Day launch."

Some observers think Singles' Day could (9) _____ globally. In West Hollywood, California, a group launched an American version of the event on (10) _____, 2014, reported Atlas Obscura. They want to make 1.11 an official American holiday, "a day of recognition for those who find themselves on the other side of the couple's fence", according to the website.

Ⅲ. Sentence listening and translation.

1. _____

2. _____

3. _____

4. _____

5. _____

IV. Paragraph listening and translation.

_____

V. Dialogue interpretation.

A: Hi. What can I do for you?
B: 我可以试穿一下这个吗?
A: Of course. The fitting rooms are that way. I will show you over there. But let me know if you need any other sizes or colors. We also have this in green and red.
B: 太好了,谢谢!
A: How did this work out for you?
B: 很好,我要买两件,一件红色,另一件黑色。
A: OK. The total comes to 180 yuan.
B: 可以用信用卡吗?
A: Yes.
B: 给你。
A: Thank you. Here is your card back. I just need you to sign here. I wish you enjoy your stay in Wuxi.

VI. Interpreting in groups.

Role-play the following situation with your partners, acting as the Chinese speaker, English speaker and the interpreter respectively. One group will be invited to perform in class.

Characters: 1. Mr. Bill Anderson
2. Li Wei
3. A vendor

Location: flea market

Task: Bill Anderson, a tourist from the U.S., wants to buy some traditional handicrafts as gifts for his children. Li Wei, Bill's tour guide, works as his interpreter to help him make a deal with a Chinese-speaking vendor at the flea market.

Ⅶ. 3-minute talk on the given topic.

Talk on the following topic in three minutes based on the given reference questions.

Topic: **Shopping online and offline**

Questions for Reference:

1. Where do you recommend your guests to do shopping in Wuxi?
2. Which do you prefer, shopping online or offline?
3. What do you think are the most popular e-commerce platforms in China? Share your experience of online shopping with others.

Ⅷ. Theme-related expressions.

传统的实体商店	bricks-and-mortar stores
免税店	DFS (Duty Free Shop)
旧货市场,跳蚤市场	flea market
连锁店	chain store
小吃摊	snack stand
货架	shelf
减价	on sale
现金红包	cash voucher
双十一	Double Eleven
一年一度的购物狂欢会	annual shopping gala
限时抢购,闪购	flash sale
节日包裹焦虑症	holiday package anxiety

Section C Further Exploration

1. 将以下网页中的文字翻译成中文。

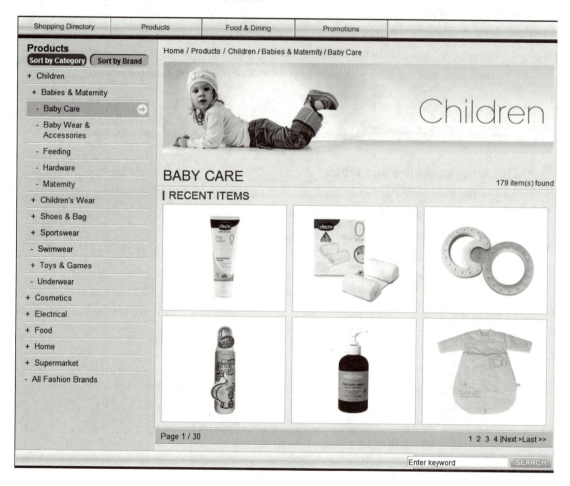

2. 学习以下流行热词。您还能找到更多与购物有关的流行词吗？

webroom	**Webrooming** is the practice of using the web to research a product and then purchase the product in an offline store. webrooming 指利用网络对某产品进行研究，再在线下商店购买此产品的行为。
click-and-mortar	With the "**click-and-mortar**" grocers, stores that have both a local presence and online shopping capability, customers can get the best of both worlds. "线上线下相结合"的模式让你既能在当地实体店亲身体验，又能在网上进行购买，从而让消费者鱼和熊掌兼得。

海淘	Amazon.com Inc., the e-commerce giant, said yesterday "it will offer direct delivery service for Chinese consumers who buy products on six overseas Amazon sites."电子商务巨头亚马逊昨日宣布,将为中国消费者开通海外六大站点的直邮服务。"海外购"俗称"海淘",英文为"buy products from overseas websites"。
orange-collar	The term **orange-collar** refers to the theme color of China's largest online shopping website, Taobao.com, and has been generalized to include people who make a living by doing jobs related to e-commerce."橙领"的橙,取自淘宝橙色系,"橙领"指通过淘宝联盟赚取收入的人,后泛指一切电商相关从业者。

UNIT 3

Catering Culture

饮食文化

Learning Objectives

1. To understand Chinese and western catering cultures;
2. To know how to translate and interpret menus;
3. To learn how to identify the structures of the sentences that you hear;
4. To learn how to translate / interpret passages or dialogues in the situation of banquet reception;
5. To learn useful words and expressions related to Chinese and western catering cultures.

Lead-in

- **Quiz** (True or False)

    In China,

    _____ 1. Ma Po tofu traditionally contains plenty of red chili, tofu and other related ingredients.

    _____ 2. *Zongzi* is traditionally wrapped with calamus leaves before it is boiled.

    _____ 3. For Chinese, it is considered impolite to point with chopsticks during a conversation over the meal.

    _____ 4. Lotus root is absolutely necessary to make the popular Chinese dish Kung Pao chicken.

    _____ 5. Don't stick your chopsticks upright in the rice bowl because it indicates that the food is for the dead.

    In the U.S.,

    _____ 6. When you have finished eating, place your knife and fork together on your plate.

Unit 3　Catering Culture 饮食文化

_____ 7. If your fork falls on the floor, apologize to everyone at the table, pick it up, clean it properly with your napkin, and continue using it.

_____ 8. You should always pass both the salt and pepper even if only one is asked for.

_____ 9. You should excuse yourself if you must leave the table during a meal.

_____ 10. If there are two forks on the table, you should start using the fork nearest to your plate first.

● **What are they? Fill in the blanks with English words.**

mat	chopsticks	chopstick rest	tofu	napkin
dumpling	hot dog	fork	green pepper	cheese
spoon	ginger	toothpick	tea pot	

plate　　1. _____　　2. _____　　3. _____

4. _____　　5. _____　　6. _____　　7. _____

8. _____　　9. _____　　10. _____　　11. _____

12. _____　　13. _____　　14. _____

Section A　Translation

Translation Technique

在介绍中国烹饪文化时，不可避免地要碰到形形色色的菜肴名称翻译，这是个不小的挑战。其实，除了要熟悉各种食材和调料的英文翻译外，中国菜名的翻译还要掌握以下几点：

35

（1）菜名前可写明烹饪方法，一般用过去分词形式。如，煎 pan-fried，炒 stir-fried，爆 quick-fried，炸 deep-fried，炖 stewed/braised，熏 smoked，烘 baked，煮 boiled，蒸 steamed，烤 roast，煨 simmered，腌 preserved，等等。

（2）菜名前也可加切菜方法，一般用过去分词形式，如切片 sliced，切丝 shredded，切丁 diced，磨碎 ground，切柳 filleted，等等。

（3）菜的配料和酱汁前用不同的介词，一般和主料分开或后浇到主料上的配料前用介词 with，酱汁前介词用 in。

例如：shredded pork **with** green peppers 这道菜中，配料和主料是分开的，所以用介词 with 连接。

又如：braised beef ribs **in** black bean sauce 这道菜中，主料是浸在汤汁或配料中的，用介词 in 连接。

在掌握以上内容后，中餐菜单翻成英文就不那么复杂了。一般来说，可以总结为以下四大类方法。

1. 以主料开头的翻译方法

（1）介绍菜肴的主料和辅料：主料（形状）+（with）辅料

例如：杏仁鸡丁　　chicken cubes with almond
　　　牛肉豆腐　　beef with beancurd
　　　西红柿炒蛋　scrambled egg with tomato

（2）介绍菜肴的主料和味汁：主料（形状）+（with, in）味汁

例如：芥末鸭掌　　duck webs in mustard sauce
　　　葱油鸡　　　chicken in scallion oil

2. 以烹饪方式开头的翻译方法

（1）介绍菜肴的烹法和主料：烹法 + 主料（形状）

例如：软炸里脊　　soft-fried pork fillet
　　　烤乳猪　　　roast suckling pig
　　　炒鳝片　　　stir-fried eel slices

（2）介绍菜肴的烹法和主料、辅料：烹法 + 主料（形状）+（with）辅料

例如：仔姜烧鸡条　braised chicken fillet with tender ginger

（3）介绍菜肴的烹法、主料和味汁：烹法 + 主料（形状）+（with, in）味汁

例如：红烧牛肉　　braised beef in brown sauce
　　　鱼香肉丝　　fried shredded pork in sweet and sour sauce
　　　清炖猪蹄　　stewed pig hoof in clean soup

3. 以形状或口感开头的翻译方法

（1）介绍菜肴的形状（口感）和主料、辅料：形状（口感）+ 主料 +（with）辅料

例如：芝麻酥鸡　　crisp chicken with sesame
　　　陈皮兔丁　　diced rabbit with orange peel

时蔬鸡片　　　sliced chicken with seasonal vegetables

（2）介绍菜肴的口感、烹法和主料：口感＋烹法＋主料

　　例如：香酥排骨　　crisp fried spareribs

　　　　　水煮嫩鱼　　tender stewed fish

　　　　　香煎鸡块　　fragrant fried chicken

（3）介绍菜肴的形状（口感）、主料和味汁：形状（口感）＋主料＋（with）味汁

　　例如：茄汁鱼片　　　sliced fish with tomato sauce

　　　　　黄酒脆皮虾仁　crisp shelled shrimps with rice wine

4. 以人名或地名开头的翻译方法

（1）介绍菜肴的创始人（发源地）和主料：人名（地名）＋主料

　　例如：麻婆豆腐　　Ma Po bean curd/Ma Po tofu

　　　　　四川水饺　　Sichuan boiled dumpling

（2）介绍菜肴的创始人（发源地）、烹法和主料：人名（地名）＋烹法＋主料

　　例如：东坡肉　　　Dongpo stewed pork

　　　　　北京烤鸭　　Peking roast duck

当然，为体现中国餐饮文化，有时使用汉语拼音命名或音译的翻译原则。

（1）具有中国特色且被外国人接受的传统食品，本着推广汉语及中国餐饮文化的原则，使用汉语拼音。例如：*Jiaozi*；*Baozi*；*Mantou*；*Huajuan*；*Shaomai*。

（2）具有中国特色且已被国外主要英文字典收录的，使用汉语方言拼写的菜名，仍保留其拼写方式。例如：tofu；Wonton；Kung Pao chicken。

（3）中文菜肴名称无法体现其做法及主料的，适用汉语拼音，并再标注英文注释。

　　例如：驴打滚儿 *Lüdagunr*（glutinous rice balls stuffed with red bean paste）

　　　　　锅贴 *Guotie*（pan-fried dumplings）

事实上，在中餐菜名翻译成英文的过程中，可以采用多种不同的方法，而且每一道菜都可以从不同的角度入手进行翻译。例如，川菜中的"宫保鸡丁"这道菜就有以下几种译法：

- sautéed chicken cubes with peanuts
- Kung Pao chicken
- diced chicken with chili and peanuts

Passage Translation 1

Vocabulary

1. 饮食文化

2. 民以食为天。

3. 色、香、味、形俱全

4. 佐料的调制

5. 切菜的刀工

6. 适时的烹调

7. 装盘的艺术

8. 四大风味

9. 八大菜系

10. 南淡北咸,东甜西辣

11. 代表菜

12. 清、鲜、嫩、脆

13. 食疗

14. 阴或阳

15. 保健

16. 延缓衰老

17. 酒逢知己千杯少

18. 白酒

19. 黄酒

20. 不可缺少的饮料

21. 乌龙茶

22. 花茶

23. 茶艺

24. 精美茶具

25. 敬茶礼仪

中餐文化

饮食文化是中国传统文化的重要组成部分。中国悠久的历史、广袤的疆土、好客的习俗,这些都孕育了中餐烹饪的独特艺术。

"民以食为天。"中国人非常重视吃。中餐烹饪以其"色、香、味、形"俱全而著称于世,讲究原料的选配、食物的质地、佐料的调制、切菜的刀工、适时的烹调,以及装盘艺术。

由于各地不同的气候、资源物产以及生活习惯,造就了各具特色的地方菜系,素有四大风味和八大菜系之说。四大风味指的是"南淡北咸,东甜西辣"。八大菜系指的是鲁菜、川菜、湘菜、粤菜、闽菜、苏菜、浙菜和徽菜。

鲁菜讲究调味纯正,具有"鲜、嫩、香、脆"的特色,最著名的菜有黄河糖醋鲤鱼和德州扒鸡。川菜特别注重调味,以麻辣著称,代表菜有火锅、回锅肉、鱼香肉丝和麻婆豆腐。粤菜强调选料珍奇,装饰精美,口感重清、鲜、嫩、脆,代表菜有白切鸡和红烧大群翅。苏菜咸中带甜,追求食物的本味,选料讲究,烹饪精细,菜品风格雅丽,代表菜有金陵盐水鸭、狮子头、松鼠鳜鱼等。

中餐也注重食疗。中国人认为食物都或阴或阳。中餐重视食物阴阳的平衡,以保持身体的健康。一般阴性食物性凉,热量低;而阳性食物性热,辛辣,高热量。同时,根据不同的症状,中国人擅长把加工过的药草加入食材中,制作出味道鲜美同时又具保健、防治疾病和延缓衰老功效的菜肴。

"酒逢知己千杯少。"只要是聚会场合,大都离不了酒。酒已经成为中国饮食文化的重要组成部分,渗透于社会生活的各个领域。中国酒主要分为白酒和黄酒两种。

中国也是茶的故乡。茶是中国人不可缺少的饮品。茶常常是中国人待客的佳品。中国茶主要分为绿茶、红茶、乌龙茶和花茶等。中国茶艺世界闻名,注重沏茶方法、精美茶具以及敬茶礼仪。

Notes

1. "中国悠久的历史、广袤的疆土、好客的习俗,这些都孕育了中餐烹饪的独特艺术。"此句的翻译难点是"孕育"。根据上下文,这个词在这儿的意思应该是"促成"的意思,所以,可以翻译为"contribute to";全句也可理解成"中餐烹饪的独特艺术"归功于"中国悠久的历史、广袤的疆土、好客的习俗",此时可以用"owe... to..."这个短语翻译。

2. "民以食为天。"这句谚语的翻译重点是"天"。此处,该句的确切意义是"食物对百姓来说是最重要的"。因此,要译出"天"的确切意思,即"最重要的必需品"。全句可以译成:"Food is the first necessity of the people."

3. "中餐烹饪……讲究原料的选配、食物的质地、佐料的调制、切菜的刀工、适时的烹调,以及装盘艺术。"这句话中"装盘艺术"需要增译成"装食物到盘子的艺术",即摆放食物的艺术,所以译成"the art of laying out food on plates"。

4. "鲁菜讲究调味纯正,具有'鲜、嫩、香、脆'的特色,最著名的菜有黄河糖醋鲤鱼和德州扒鸡。""黄河糖醋鲤鱼"这道菜强调了菜的出处地名和酱汁,所以可译成"Yellow River carp in sweet and sour sauce"。"德州扒鸡"则根据菜的出处地名和烹饪方法,译成"Dezhou stewed chicken"。全文中其他菜名翻译皆可参照本章介绍的菜名翻译技巧翻译。

5. "中国酒主要分为白酒和黄酒。"此句中,"白酒和黄酒"译成"liquor and yellow rice wine",而不是简单译成"white wine and yellow wine",因为"white wine"在酒类中属于白葡萄酒,对饮食文化的不了解会导致较大的偏差。

Passage Translation 2

Vocabulary

1. easy as pie
2. Thanksgiving turkey
3. ethnic food
4. Mexican taco
5. Cajun cuisine
6. savory
7. Tex-Mex treat
8. grab a quick bite
9. microwave dinner
10. instant food
11. all-time American favorite
12. home-maker
13. prepackaged meal
14. culinary art
15. casserole

"You are what you eat." Nutrition experts often use this saying to promote better eating habits. What we put in our mouths does become a part of us. But we can look at this statement another way. If you want to understand another culture, you ought to find out about its food. Learning about American food can give us a real taste of American culture.

What is "American food"? At first you might think the answer is easy as pie. To many people, American food means hamburgers, hot dogs, fried chicken and pizza. If you have a "sweet tooth", you might even think of apple pie or chocolate chip cookies. It's true that Americans do eat those things. But are those the only kind of food you can find in America?

Except for Thanksgiving turkey, it's hard to find a typically "American" food. The United States is a land of immigrants, so Americans eat food from many different countries. When people move to America, they bring their cooking styles with them. That's why you can find almost every kind of ethnic food in America. In some cases, Americans have adopted foods from other countries as favorites. Americans love Italian pizza, Mexican tacos and Chinese egg rolls. But the

American version doesn't taste quite like the original!

As with any large country, the U. S. A. has several distinct regions. Each region boasts its own special style of food. Visit the South and enjoy country-style cooking. Journey through Louisiana for some spicy Cajun cuisine. Take a trip to New England and sample savory seafood dishes. Travel through the Midwest, "the breadbasket of the nation", for delicious baked goods. Cruise over to the Southwest and try some tasty Tex-Mex treats. Finish your food tour in the Pacific Northwest with some gourmet coffee.

Americans living at a fast pace often just "grab a quick bite". Fast food restaurants offer people on the run everything from fried chicken to fried rice. Microwave dinners and instant foods make cooking at home a snap. Of course, one of the most common quick American meals is a sandwich. Americans probably make a sandwich out of anything that can fit between two slices of bread. Peanut butter and jelly sandwich is an all-time American favorite.

If you think American cooking means opening a food package and throwing the contents into the microwave, think again. On the one hand, it's true that Americans thrive on cold cereal for breakfast, sandwiches for lunch and instant dinners. From busy home-makers to professionals, many Americans enjoy the convenience of prepackaged meals that can be ready to serve in less than 10 minutes. On the other hand, many Americans recognize the value of cooking skills. Parents see the importance of training their children, especially daughters in the culinary arts.

Most Americans will admit that there's nothing better than a good home-cooked meal. But with cooking, as with any other skill, a good performance doesn't come by accident. Probably every cook has his or her own cooking style. But there are some basic techniques and principles that people follow. For example, baking is the primary method of preparing food in America. The dinner menu often has casseroles, roast meats and other baked goods. For that reason, Americans would find it next to impossible to live without an oven. American cooks give special attention to the balance of foods, too. In planning a big meal they try to include a meat, a few vegetables, some bread or pasta and often a dessert. They also like to make sure the meal is colorful, believing that several different colors of food on the plate usually makes for a healthy meal.

Notes

1. "You are what you eat." 此句不能望文生义,应该是指食物对人和文化方面的影响。所以,此句可以译成:"一方饮食养一方人。"

2. "If you have a 'sweet tooth', you might even think of apple pie or chocolate chip cookies." 此处的"sweet tooth"根据后面的"apple pie or chocolate chip cookies"两种甜味食物,可以理解成"喜欢吃甜食"。全句要译成:"如果你是好吃甜食的人,你可能会想到苹果派或巧克力片饼干。"

3. "Americans living at a fast pace often just 'grab a quick bite'." 这句话中的"living at a fast pace"可以译成"生活节奏快"。

Sentences in Focus

1. 中餐烹饪以其"色、香、味、形"俱全而著称于世。

2. "酒逢知己千杯少。"只要是聚会场合,大都离不了酒。

3. 中餐烹饪讲究原料的选配、食物的质地、佐料的调制、切菜的刀工、适时的烹调,以及装盘艺术。

4. "八大菜系"指的是鲁菜、川菜、湘菜、粤菜、闽菜、苏菜、浙菜和徽菜。

5. 中餐重视食物阴阳的平衡,以保持身体的健康。

6. If you want to understand another culture, you ought to find out about its food.

7. Except for Thanksgiving turkey, it's hard to find a typically "American" food.

8. Americans probably make a sandwich out of anything that can fit between two slices of bread. Peanut butter and jelly sandwich is an all-time American favorite.

9. Most Americans will admit that there's nothing better than a good home-cooked meal.

10. Probably every cook has his or her own cooking style. But there are some basic techniques and principles that people follow.

Exercises

I. Fill in the blanks with English words according to the given Chinese.

1. A lot of Chinese foods are also symbolic, especially during _____ (传统节日).

2. The doctor prefers his patients not to _____ (喜好甜食).

3. Visit an Asian bakery during the Chinese New Year, and you're likely to find a wide assortment of snacks with _____ (各种类型的籽) in them.

4. As for pomelos, this large ancestor of the grapefruit _____ (意味着富足), as the Chinese word for pomelo sounds like the word for "to have".

5. Cakes such as _____ (年糕) have symbolic significance on many levels. Their sweetness symbolizes a rich and sweet life, while the layers

symbolize rising prosperity for the coming year.

6. You may visit _____ (唐人街) in the U. S. and enjoy some traditional Chinese food.

7. Shandong cuisine _____ (以……为特色) its emphasis on aroma, freshness, crispness and tenderness.

8. _____ (苏菜) developed from the local recipes of Yangzhou, Suzhou and Nanjing.

9. In Chinese herbal medicine culture, food is medicine, to some extent, which can account for why in China, _____ (调味品) like ginger, garlic and scallion are indispensable daily ingredients.

10. People in coastal areas prefer _____ (海鲜), whereas those in central and northwest China eat more domestic animals.

Ⅱ. **Translate the following menu into English or Chinese.**

1. 扬州炒饭 _____
2. 龙井虾仁 _____
3. 西湖醋鱼 _____
4. 青椒炒肉丝 _____
5. 咖喱牛肉面 _____
6. twice cooked pork _____
7. hot and sour soup _____
8. scallion pancake _____
9. steamed meat dumpling _____
10. egg dumpling _____

Ⅲ. **Translate the following sentences.**

1. The diversity of geography, climate, customs and products has led to the evolution of what are called the "four flavors" and "eight regional cuisines".
   _____
   _____

2. Cuisine in China is a harmonious integration of color, aroma, taste and appearance.
   _____
   _____

3. Among the many cooking methods are boiling, braising, frying, steaming, baking, and roasting and so on.
   _____
   _____

4. When chefs finish their masterpieces, the food is arranged on a variety of plates and dishes so that it is a real pleasure to view, to smell and ultimately to savor.

5. In some regions of China, the number of eggs prepared depends on the gender of new-born babies: an even number for a girl, and an odd number for a boy.

6. 人们认为吃鱼能帮助你来年实现愿望。(come true)

7. 在中国文化中,面条作为生日庆祝的一部分是长寿的象征。(longevity)

8. 中餐注重的是阴与阳之间的平衡。(attach importance to)

9. 各种各样的粥和点心有助于弥补炎热的夏日里流失的水分。(porridge and dim sum)

10. 闽菜以其清淡的口味和酸甜的风味而闻名。(be acclaimed for)

IV. Translate the following paragraphs.

1. Panda Express rhymes with Federal Express, but Panda does not send your mail packages around the world, and neither is FedEx a government agency. Panda Express is found in shopping malls, supermarkets, university campuses and airports. They serve fast food of Chinese style. To achieve the quick service concept, customers select from a variety of entrees displayed at the counter while the restaurant workers put together the meal. Everything is ready to go as soon as the customer makes the final decision. With more than 500 restaurants by the year 2003, Panda is now a successful enterprise.

2. 中国是筷子的故乡。中国筷子历史悠久。筷子作为餐具使用的传统传入了许多国家，如越南、朝鲜、韩国等。筷子的发明反映了中国古代人们的智慧。尽管看上去简单，一副筷子却可以捏、夹、剥和搅动食物。如今，筷子则被看作结婚和其他重要仪式上的幸运礼物。

Section B Interpretation

Interpretation Technique

口译技能：听辨句子主干

听辨决定了口译的成败。听辨关键词是理解句子意义的基础，但要想理解讲话人的思想，还要听辨这些词语在句子里是如何组织起来表达意义的。这时，可以通过听辨句子主干来实现。具体可以通过下面3个途径实现：

1. **词语顺序法，即主谓宾法**

掌握句子的主语、谓语和宾语，一般都能把握整句的主要信息。如："Shandong cuisine emphasizes purity of the seasonings, characterized by freshness, tenderness, aroma and crispness." 这句话的主谓宾语分别是"Shandong cuisine""emphasize"和"purity of the seasonings"。这样很容易理解这句话的主要意思，即山东菜强调调味的纯正。

2. **经验模式法**

有些句子，如被动句、形式主语句等，按照主谓宾法听并不能快速掌握说话人的意图，这时可以采用"参与者+过程"的模式，分析句子中的参与者是谁、经历了什么过程。

例如："It gives me great honor to host this banquet on this wonderful time of the year." 此句中，参与者是"me"，经历的过程是"honor to host this banquet"。可以按这样的结构来听辨记忆信息。

3. **信息结构法**

从信息结构来说，句子分为主位和述位。前者一般指已知信息，后者为与已知信息相关的新信息。

例如："Now let's warmly welcome Premier Li Keqiang to give us some opening remarks." 这句话是主持套话，所以"Now let's warmly welcome"是已知信息，可以把重点放在欢迎谁那儿，因此这里的新信息应该是"Premier Li Keqiang"。

只有在听辨了句子主干后，才能抓住句子的主要信息，按照自己的理解来组织听到的信息，顺利完成接下来的口译笔记和口译表达。

练习建议：听中英文句子，辨别句子主干，复述句子。

Passage Interpretation 1

北京烤鸭已是名扬世界的美食,历代美食家吃北京烤鸭,吃出了许多讲究来。要想品尝真正的烤鸭口味,我们必须遵循下列规则:

季节不同,北京烤鸭口感也不同。冬春季节,北京烤鸭往往口感又肥又嫩。但在夏季,由于天气炎热,北京烤鸭较瘦,品质不高。

好的片法能提升烤鸭口味。烤鸭烤制成后,及时片下皮肉装盘食用。此时的鸭肉吃在嘴里酥香味美。

吃烤鸭的佐料有三种类型,它们各具不同风味,适应不同宾客的口味偏好。一种是甜面酱加葱段,再配黄瓜或青萝卜等。一种是蒜泥加酱油。还有一种是以白糖为佐料,较受不喜葱蒜的顾客偏爱。

Passage Interpretation 2

The culture of food and dining in the west is a little different from that in China. You are expected to have knowledge of table manners such as what fork or knife to use as these are essential in western dining. The meal would consist of several courses including a soup or salad, an appetizer, the main dish, and a dessert. The atmosphere will be filled with light music that would only serve as background as people converse with each other. The decorations are usually sparse and are only meant to highlight the atmosphere that is being created by the music. This type of dining is different from the dining experience in most restaurants in China. However, with global integration, more western restaurants are opening. The Chinese people, now more affluent and knowledgeable about international customs, are beginning to join in this dining experience. This is not to say that people have given up the profound Chinese culinary culture, but means that more choices are becoming available to population, which represents a significant improvement, changing the perception that the essence of western dining is fast food. As cultural exchange expands, the knowledge of western food will be improved.

Dialogue Interpretation

Chinese and Western Table Manners

Mr. Robert: The other day, I had a Chinese friend who came up to me with a problem. The problem is how to use western tableware properly. You know, at a big banquet, there are all sorts of knives, forks, spoons, wine glasses, beer glasses, soup bowls and dessert bowls that are given in a proper order in order to be used in a proper way.

Mr. Li: 大多数中国人确实对这个问题很头疼。对我来说,各种大小不同的刀叉让我都不知道哪个是用来吃什么的。我只知道色拉叉。有一次吃西餐,我全程用色拉叉吃,甚至吃牛排也是用色拉叉!真的很尴尬!你能说说怎么用西餐餐具吗?

Mr. Robert: Actually, it is very easy. Spoon is always put on the right, and fork on the left. Dessert forks and spoons are always placed on top of the plate. The point is to start from the outside to the inside and work your way in. You should use the fork with your left hand and the knife with your right hand.

Mr. Li: 听上去挺简单的。

Mr. Robert: Yes. Besides, you should scoop the soup away from you. Hold stemware by the stem rather than by the glass. After you finish the dinner, there is a special way to put knives and forks so that the waiter can see you have finished. Often you put your knives and forks together on the right side of the plate.

Mr. Li: 明白了。在全世界,不同的文化有不同的礼仪标准。在中国,所有的菜都摆在转盘上以便共享。每个人都有一副餐具,包括一个小碟子、一把勺子和一副筷子。用筷时,不能把筷子笔直插在米饭上,不能指着别人,也不能放在嘴里吸吮。此外,就餐时,要避免始终握筷不放,暂时不吃时,要把筷子与盘子并排放。

Mr. Robert: Interesting! How to use tableware properly is important both in China and western countries.

Mr. Li: 确实是这样。我们应该了解中西餐桌礼仪的异同。如果我们能实践基本的餐桌礼仪,我们在宴会上会更受欢迎。

Exercises

I. Interpreting technique practice.

You will hear the following 10 sentences. Please try to take notes of the structure of each sentence by using the technique learned in this section and retell each sentence.

1. _____

2. _____

3. _____

4. _____

5. _____

6. _____

7. _____

8. _____

9. _____

10. _____

II. Spot dictation.

Now, the VOA Special English program WORDS AND THEIR STORIES. A listener from Brazil, Elenir Scardueli, sent us a list of popular expressions about food. So today we will talk about expressions that use vegetables and fruits.

For example, a cucumber is a long, green vegetable that people often eat in salads. You might say a person is as cool as a cucumber if he never seems to worry about anything and stays calm in a stressful situation. If you put a cucumber in a solution of vinegar and spices for a long time, it becomes a pickle. But if you are (1) _____, you are in trouble or a difficult situation. If two people are very similar, you might say they are (2) _____.

There are several expressions about beans. If someone is very energetic, you might say she is (3) _____. If you say something does (4) _____, you mean it is of little importance. I might say you (5) _____ if you do not know anything at all about it. But if you (6) _____, you tell something that was supposed to be a secret.

Potatoes are a popular food in many areas. But something is considered (7) _____ if it is not important. You probably would not want to (8) _____. This also means a problem or issue that no one wants to deal with. Someone might call you a (9) _____ if you sit and watch television all day and get little or no physical exercise.

Like potatoes, turnips are root vegetables that grow in the ground. Here is an old saying: "(10) _____." That means you cannot get something from a person that he or she is not willing or able to give.

III. Sentence listening and translation.

1. _____

2. _____

3. _____

4. _____

5. _____

IV. Paragraph listening and translation.

_____

V. Dialogue interpretation.

A: As a foreigner, I traveled around China and noticed that cuisines differ in the north and south. There is a great variety of food in China.

B: 不同地区的人有着不同的生活方式、饮食习惯和物产，那么，不同的原料、不同的烹饪方法就使得人们做出的食物也大不相同。

A: Well, what is the biggest difference between northern and southern food?

B: 或许是烹饪方法吧。即使用一样的原料做出来的食物也不会相同，因为烹饪方法不同。

A: Can you give me an example?

B: 就说鱼吧。北方人做鱼时要放很多佐料，然后把鱼放在料里炖。南方人煮鱼时，一般只放一些姜，这样做出的鱼更为清淡。

A: It sounds that cooking styles are quite different between the south and the north.

Ⅵ. Interpreting in groups.

Students will be divided into groups of three. In each group, two students will role-play a dialogue based on the following given topic, while the third one will work as an interpreter. Students should try to make use of the skills or the expressions introduced in this unit.

Participants: 1. Mr. Wang, a Chinese manager
2. Mr. Smith, an overseas visitor
3. An interpreter

Location: at a Chinese restaurant

Task: Mr. Wang is inviting Mr. Smith to dinner at a Chinese restaurant. Over the meal, Mr. Wang introduces some Chinese dishes and table manners to Mr. Smith who knows little about Chinese food culture. Finally, Mr. Wang proposes a toast to Mr. Smith.

Ⅶ. 3-minute talk on the given topic.

Talk on the following topic in three minutes based on the given reference questions.

Topic: **Fast food in China**

Questions for Reference:
1. How much do you know about fast food?
2. Why is fast food popular in China?
3. Which do you prefer, fast food or home-made food? Give your reasons.

Ⅷ. Theme-related expressions.

一次性筷子	disposable chopsticks
转基因食品	genetically modified food
午宴(附有情况介绍或专题演讲等内容)	luncheon
色、香、味、形俱全	perfect combination of color, aroma, taste and appearance
四大菜系:山东菜、四川菜、粤菜、扬州菜	four regional cuisines: Shandong cuisine, Sichuan cuisine, Canton / Guangdong cuisine and Yangzhou cuisine
南淡北咸,东甜西辣	the light southern cuisine and the salty northern cuisine, the sweet eastern cuisine and the spicy western cuisine

• 请各位随意用餐。	Help yourself please.
• 晚宴采取自助餐形式。	We will have a buffet dinner.
• 白酒太烈了,我恐怕喝不了。	I am afraid that Chinese liquor is too strong for me.
• 请各位举杯,并同我一起为所有在座的朋友们的健康干杯!	May I invite you to raise your glasses and join me in a toast to the health of all our friends present here?
• 今晚我们将在海湾酒店设宴欢迎阁下,敬请光临。	We will prepare a reception banquet in your honor at Gulf Hotel this evening. We are looking forward to seeing you.

Section C Further Exploration

1. 《红楼梦》译本欣赏:比较以下两种译本的区别有哪些。

第五十八回(选段)

一时小丫头子捧了盒子进来站住。晴雯麝月揭开看时,还是只四样小菜。晴雯笑道:"已经好了,还不给两样清淡菜吃。这稀饭咸菜闹到多早晚。"一面摆好,一面又看那盒子内却有一碗火腿鲜笋汤,忙端了放在宝玉跟前。宝玉便就桌上喝了一口,说:"好烫。"袭人笑道:"菩萨,能几日不见荤,馋的就这样起来。"一面说,一面忙端起,轻轻用口吹。因见芳官在侧,便递与芳官,笑道:"你也学着些服侍,别一味呆憨呆睡。口劲轻着,别吹上唾沫星儿。"芳官依言,果吹了几口,甚妥。

霍克斯《红楼梦》译本:	杨宪益《红楼梦》译本:
Presently junior maids carrying food-boxes came into the room and stood there while Skybright and Musk removed the covers and inspected the contents: a bowl of soup and the now familiar rice-gruel	The young maid came back with a hamper for their inspection. And Qingwen and Sheyue, opening it, found the usual four kinds of pickles inside.
"But he's better now," said Skybright. "How much longer has he got to go on eating gruel and vegetables in brine? Why can't they send him some proper food for a change?"	"He's better now, but they keep serving this rice gruel and pickle," grumbled Qingwen. "Why not send a couple of easily digested dishes instead?"

Musk had finished laying now. Taking the large bowl of soup (ham and bamboo-shoots) from the food-box, she put it on the table for Bao-yu to try. He bent down over the bowl and slurped up a mouthful.	Just then, however, at the bottom of the hamper, she discovered a bowl of ham-and-fresh-bamboo-shoot soup. She put this before Baoyu, who took a sip.
"Ow, hot!"	"It's too hot!" he exclaimed.
Aroma laughed.	Xiren laughed.
"Holy Buddha! You're not all that starved for meat, surely? I'm not surprised you burn yourself if you go at it so greedily."	"A few days without meat and you've grown so greedy!"
She picked up the bowl and gently blew on it, then, as Parfumee happened to be standing by, she handed it to her:	"You can do this," she said. "Time you learned to make yourself useful, instead of acting like a silly goose. Mind you blow gently though. Don't spit into the soup."
"Here, you can do it. You may as well make yourself useful, instead of mooning around all day doing nothing. But blow on it gently: we don't want you spitting in it."	Fangguan did as she was told, and was managing quite well.
Parfumee began blowing as instructed. She seemed to be managing very nicely.	

2. 阅读以下关于苦瓜的制作方法，根据上下文将所给的英语动词以正确的形式分别填入以下空格。自己试试用英语介绍一道菜肴的制作方法。

The bitter melon, rich in vitamin C and low in calories, contains various healthy nutrients that can prevent diseases and enhance one's health. Here is a simple and easy recipe that may help you beat the summer heat.

Recipe: (Serves 2)

  Ingredients:

  bitter melon 2

  red sweet pepper 1, sliced Garlic

  Step 1: (1) _____ the bitter melons.

  Step 2: (2) _____ out the pulps.

  Step 3: (3) _____ the melons.

  Step 4: (4) _____ the garlic, sugar, light soy sauce and vinegar together to make the sauce.

  Step 5: Bring the water to a (5) _____ and add some salt and oil. (6) _____ the bitter melons for 15 seconds and cool them by cold water.

  Step 6: Mix the melons with the sauce and the (7) _____ red sweet pepper.

  If you want to jazz up your dish a little bit, you can also (8) _____ several drops of chili oil.

a) spoon
b) mix
c) boil
d) clean
e) blanch
f) shred
g) add
h) slice

UNIT 4

Travelling

观 光 旅 游

Learning Objectives

1. To understand the differences between Chinese and western customs and travelling etiquette;
2. To know how to translate the names of tourist attractions;
3. To learn how to memorize what you hear (1);
4. To learn how to translate/interpret passages or dialogues on the topic of travelling;
5. To learn useful words and expressions related to travelling.

Lead-in

● *Quiz* (True or False)

_____ 1. In India, women who prefer wearing dresses or skirts should be sure the clothes cover the legs, ideally down to the ankles.

_____ 2. In China, people are likely to be offended if you ask them personal questions, such as where they're from, how old they are, what they do for a living, and whether they're married.

_____ 3. The right hand is considered unclean in India. Never pass objects, eat or signal with your right hand.

_____ 4. People from Latin countries tend to feel more comfortable standing closer to one another as they interact, while those from North America need more personal distance.

_____ 5. In Canada, vehicles should keep to the left side of the road.

_____ 6. Although eating with your fingers is fine in very informal surroundings and situations, generally it is considered to be a bad manner and should be avoided in France.

_____ 7. When attempting to converse in France, you should at least make a respectable attempt to speak some elementary conversational French since not many French people like to speak English.

● What are the following tourist attractions? Fill in the blanks with English words.

| peak | valley | city | pool | residence |
| pavilion | ruins | mosque | wonderland | grotto |

1. Mogao _____
2. _____ of Yuanmingyuan
3. Forbidden _____
4. _____ of Unique Beauty
5. Jiuzhaigou _____

6. Great _____
7. Erquan _____
8. Yaolin _____
9. Lu Xun's Former _____
10. _____ of Surging Waves

Section A Translation

Translation Technique

一、旅游景点名的翻译

1. 直译

例如：三峡 Three Gorges   Five Great Lakes 五大湖区
　　　黄山 Yellow Mountain   Grand Canyon 大峡谷

2. 部分音译 + 部分直译

例如：杜甫草堂 Du Fu Thatched Cottage　　Rocky Mountains 落基山脉
　　　少林寺 Shaolin Temple　　　　　　　Niagara Falls 尼亚加拉瀑布
　　　Lake Huron 休伦湖

3. 拼音 + 解释

例如：海子 haizi, which means "lake"

4. 意译

为了突出景点的性质、用途、主要特征，可用意译的方法。

例如：颐和园 the Summer Palace　　　避暑山庄 the Summer Resort
　　　天府之国 Land of Abundance　　　行宫 temporary regal lodges

当不知道某个景点的确切译法，英译汉时可采取方法 2，即"部分音译 + 部分直译"；而汉译英时可采用方法 3，即"拼音 + 解释"的方法。

二、中国朝代名称的翻译

1. 一般用"音译（拼音）+ 直译"的方法

例如：清朝 the Qing Dynasty　　　　蜀国 the Kingdom of Shu

2. 有时也用直译的方法

例如：西汉 the Western Han Dynasty

Passage Translation 1

Vocabulary

1. 天坛
2. 老字号商店
3. 人民大会堂
4. 紫禁城
5. 鸟巢
6. 水立方
7. 胡同
8. 颐和园
9. 雍和宫
10. 夜生活区

> 游览中国首都北京有许多方式。其中，较好的一种是把它当作吃冰糖葫芦，一口一颗山楂，慢慢地品味。同世界上任何一个城市一样，北京四日游可以覆盖那些最出名的景点。
>
> 第一天
>
> 这条出城的线路可以早些安排，因为需要大量的攀登。没有登上长城，北京之游就不完整。长城绵延万里，而北京段只是其中的一小部分，但最受游客青睐。根据你的身体状况及个人喜好，你可以去爬陡峭的台阶，也可以在相对平坦的地方漫步。
>
> 十三陵埋葬着13位明朝皇帝。你可以顺路去游览一下。
>
> 第二天
>
> 这一天主要在市区游玩。首先去的目的地是天坛，历代皇帝常在此举行祭天仪式。如今周末早晨，普通百姓聚集在天坛唱歌、跳舞、打太极，进行各式各样休闲娱乐活动，获得乐趣。
>
> 乘的士向北一小段，就来到了前门大街。这个购物中心于2008年因奥运会而修缮一新，重现了20世纪早期的繁忙景象。当时中国传统与西方元素汇聚于此。同时，这里还有一些老字号商店，比如著名的北京烤鸭馆。
>
> 向北漫步，穿过主街大道和地下通道，就来到了天安门广场——中国的政治中心。广场正中心是毛主席纪念堂，西面是人民大会堂，东侧是中国国家博物馆，但这些景点并不是全年都对外开放。

紫禁城位于广场尽头,现在官方称为故宫博物院。你要认真计划,因为花上一整天时间可能连一小部分也看不完。

奥林匹克森林公园的面积是纽约中央公园的两倍。但是因为时间不多,你的最佳选择是鸟巢和水立方,它们是必看景点。

第三天

在几天的观光游览后,如果觉得脚很痛,或许你可以在王府井闲逛。如果你想知道北京人过去的生活方式,你就得走进胡同。南锣鼓巷是个不错的选择。

往西北再走一小段,你就会看到什刹海,周围环绕着众多酒吧和胡同,是传统与现代的完美融合。这一天要是想以一场京剧收尾,我建议大家观看为国际游客量身打造的容易理解的剧目。

第四天

最后一天,你可以去位于西北市郊的颐和园,那儿有精致高雅的长廊以及宽广的昆明湖。

佛教是中国的一大宗教信仰。深入中国大地,你总是能见到寺庙的踪影。但在北京城内雍和宫作为藏传佛教的象征有着独特的吸引力。

你或许想在北京的三里屯度过最后一夜,因为这里是真正的夜生活区。

Notes

1. "十三陵埋葬着13位明朝皇帝。"这句话中的"明朝"译成"the Ming Dynasty",但在笔译时,宜再增译明朝的具体起止公元时间段,让读者可以对照了解下,所以译成"the Ming Dynasty (1368 – 1644)"。

2. "首先去的目的地是天坛。"景点名的翻译有多种方法,这句话中的"天坛"的翻译体现了天坛的用途:祭天的地方,因而译成"the Temple of Heaven"。

3. "同时,这里还有一些老字号商店。""老字号"指的是那些有较长经营历史、受人认可的店铺,因而"老字号商店"译成"the businesses with time-honored brand",强调历史悠久。

4. "广场正中心是毛主席纪念堂,西面是人民大会堂,东侧是中国国家博物馆。"这句话的翻译主要是有关地理方位的介绍,这在介绍景点时常碰到。句子中,由于人民大会堂和中国国家博物馆都处于毛主席纪念堂以外,可以用介词 to 而非介词 in 表示方位,译成:"There's the Chairman Mao Memorial Hall at the center, the Great Hall of the People to the west and the Chinese National Museum to the east."

5. "如果觉得脚很痛,或许你可以在王府井闲逛。"这句话中,"王府井"直接音译成"*Wangfujing*",类似的还有"胡同"译成"*Hutong*","什刹海"译成"*Shichahai*","三里屯"译成"*Sanlitun*"。但也有采用"部分音译+部分直译"的方法的,如"前门大街"译成"*Qianmen* Street","天安门广场"译成"*Tian'anmen* Square"。文中也有用意译方法翻译的地名和景点名,如"紫禁城"译成"the Forbidden City","颐和园"译成"the Summer Palace"。

Passage Translation 2

Vocabulary

1. vacation destination
2. romantic getaway
3. the London Eye
4. literature lover
5. the Eiffel Tower
6. archaic edifice
7. sun bather
8. flaunt
9. pilgrimage
10. ardent art lover

In Europe, the rich history and scenic landscape make it the No. 1 vacation destination among tourists from all over the world. Be it for a romantic getaway, a family picnic or a teenagers' world tour, Europe holds an indispensable position among travel locations. Enlisted below is a list of the 6 best places to visit in Europe.

London

London, the capital of the United Kingdom, is a beautiful city that offers a plethora of scenic meadows, spectacular cathedrals, astonishing palaces and close-to-impossible architectural feats like the London Eye. Besides that, it has several museums and historic houses that recite the tale of this city's past. If you are a literature lover, then London is a must destination for you.

Paris

Paris, the paradise of fashion, culture and entertainment, is the most visited city in the world. It is also held as the most popular tourist destination due to the presence of the Eiffel Tower and several other historic buildings, museums, cathedrals and churches.

Rome

A talk about Europe is incomplete without a mention of Rome. Held as a place where one of the oldest civilizations of the world prospered, Rome is where you'd get to see numerous castles, palaces, archaic edifices, fountains, squares and well-manicured parks. Some tourists come here especially to have a look at the Renaissance architecture that this city boasts.

Barcelona

Barcelona, a major city in Spain, is regarded among the 10 best beach cities of the world. The city's coastline has clear waters and a temperate climate which make it a favorite destination among sun bathers. Besides that, Barcelona has a glorious past to flaunt. You may stroll through its bustling streets and take a look at the historic buildings, castles, churches, parks and museums.

Berlin

Berlin is a reputable place among the most visited places in Europe. This is because, just like several other European cities, Berlin has a rich and profound history and culture. A visit to this city will acquaint you with stately castles, exquisite palaces, museums, zoos and some of the best universities of the world.

Vienna

If you are a music lover and a steadfast devotee of Beethoven or Mozart, then a visit to Vienna is like going on a pilgrimage. This is because Vienna is the birthplace of these revered artists. You'd find their houses there and also find their memorial graves. Besides that, Vienna is known for castles, palaces, museums and historic monuments. If you are an ardent art lover, Vienna is the place for you. It has nearly one hundred museums dedicated to art!

Intrigued by whatever you read? Go, travel and have an experience of a lifetime.

Notes

1. "Be it for a romantic getaway, a family picnic or a teenagers' world tour, Europe holds an indispensable position among travel locations. Enlisted below is a list of the 6 best places to visit in Europe." 句中"Be it for a romantic getaway, a family picnic or a teenagers' world tour"译成"无论是作为情侣旅行的浪漫之地,抑或作为全家人一起野炊的地方,还是青少年环球旅行的去处"。

2. "London … is a beautiful city that offers a plethora of scenic meadows, spectacular cathedrals, astonishing palaces and close-to-impossible architectural feats like the London Eye." 句中的"the London Eye"译成"伦敦眼"也很形象,其实它是个巨型摩天轮。

3. "Paris, the paradise of fashion, culture and entertainment, is the most visited city in the world." 句中的同位语"the paradise of fashion, culture and entertainment"和主语"Paris"一起译成"巴黎作为时尚、文化、娱乐的天堂"。

4. "It is also held as the most popular tourist destination due to the presence of the Eiffel Tower." 句中的"the Eiffel Tower"用"音译+直译"的方法,译成"埃菲尔铁塔"。

5. "Barcelona has a glorious past to flaunt." 句中的"flaunt"为"炫耀"的意思,根据上下文,不一定要翻译出来,只需译成"巴塞罗那有着辉煌的过去"。

Sentences in Focus

1. 没有登上长城,北京之游就不完整。

2. 你来到天安门广场——中国的政治中心。广场正中心是毛主席纪念堂,西面是人民大会堂,东侧是中国国家博物馆。

3. 但是因为时间不多,你的最佳选择是鸟巢和水立方,它们是必看景点。

4. 往西北再走一小段,你就会看到什刹海,周围环绕着众多酒吧和胡同,是传统与现代的完美融合。

5. 佛教是中国的一大宗教信仰。深入中国大地,你总是能见到寺庙的踪影。

6. In Europe, the rich history and scenic landscape make it the No. 1 vacation destination among tourists from all over the world.

7. London, the capital of the United Kingdom, is a beautiful city that offers a plethora of scenic meadows, spectacular cathedrals, astonishing palaces and close-to-impossible architectural feats like the London Eye.

8. It is also held as the most popular tourist destination due to the presence of the Eiffel Tower and several other historic buildings, museums, cathedrals and churches.

9. The city's coastline has clear waters and a temperate climate which make it a favorite destination among sun bathers.

10. If you are a music lover and a steadfast devotee of Beethoven or Mozart, then a visit to Vienna is like going on a pilgrimage.

Exercises

I. Fill in the blanks with English words according to the given Chinese.

1. Nanjing Road is the _____ (游客最多的) shopping street in Shanghai every day, with crowds of pedestrians shopping and sightseeing.
2. China has become a major _____ (旅游目的地) following its reform and opening up to the world since the late 1970s.
3. China _____ (对……引以为豪) numerous tourist attractions including scenic spots, historical and cultural heritages.
4. The spectacular Danxia landform in Taining, Fujian Province, is a _____ (必看景点) created by Mother Nature over a long time.
5. Travelers who are _____ (日程紧的) often pack several destinations into a limited amount of time.
6. Despite the cultural conflicts between the east and the west, the newcomers have found their ways to _____ (融入) the new society so well that they have made many friends in China so far.

7. Retreating from the _____ (喧闹) of Shanghai City, he found himself comfortable living in a small city which is quiet and beautiful.

8. In the Confucius Temple of Qufu, people _____ (举行仪式) yesterday to commemorate the 2,558th birthday of Confucius, a great philosopher and educator in ancient China.

9. From January 1, 2013, Beijing offers 72-hour visa-free transit for _____ _____ (国际游客) with third-country visas and transit at Beijing.

10. Explore the best of Taiwan on a _____ (五日游) of its natural splendors and you will find it hard to leave this place.

II. Translate the following tourist attractions into English or Chinese.

1. mountain resort _____
2. Sun Moon Lake _____
3. Crescent Spring _____
4. Temple of the Town God _____
5. Museum of Qin Terracotta Warriors and Horses
   _____
6. 夫子庙_____
7. 趵突泉_____
8. 南禅寺_____
9. 龙门石窟_____
10. 黄山_____

III. Translate the following sentences.

1. Dragon-Tiger Mountain (Longhu Mountain) is the birthplace of the Taoist religion and a scenic and tourist resort.

2. Crystal clear waters, beautiful white sand beaches, swaying palm trees and fabulous dive sites make Maldives the best tropical holiday destination in the world.

3. The Temple of Heaven is the largest existing architectural complex.

4. The British Museum is full of the treasures the soldiers brought back from distant shores, such as the earliest known image of Jesus Christ.

5. In the first three quarters of 2013, the number of outbound trips rose 18 percent to 72.55 million.

6. 乌镇有6万人口，其中只有12000人是常住居民。

7. 中国的出境旅游市场变得越来越多元化，为各年龄阶层的游客提供适合的产品。(outbound tourism)

8. 如果不需要申请签证，到泰国旅游的中国游客会更多。(visa)

9. 来自全国各地的数万名学生在暑期涌入北京名校参观游览。(leading university)

10. 御花园是一个古典园林，有着400多年历史。(Imperial Garden)

IV. Translate the following paragraphs.

1. Tibet lies on the Qinghai-Tibet Plateau of the southwest border of China. The average height of the whole region is more than 4,000 meters above sea level, for which Tibet is known as "Roof of the World". The highest peak of the whole world is Everest Peak, which is as high as 8,846.27 meters above sea level.

2. 日月潭是台湾省最大的天然湖泊。湖的东部呈圆形，犹如太阳；而湖的西部则形如一轮弯月，由此而得名"日月潭"。日月潭始终是游客最多的台湾旅游目的地之一。每年，大量的国际游客都会到此观光并被其美景所折服。

Unit 4　Travelling 观光旅游

Section B　Interpretation

Interpretation Technique

口译技能：记忆信息（1）——逻辑分层记忆

口译的标准是准确传达源语的信息。要做到这一点，必须准确理解原文。理解是做好口译的前提和基础。在口译中，由于时间限制，我们不可能像做笔译那样，反复思考，寻求对原文的正确理解。我们必须在瞬间把握住源语的信息意义，然后用目的语表达出来。如何迅速理解并记住讲话内容对译员来说是一个挑战。

我们在听他人讲话时，如果只将注意力放在字、词上面，那么这些语言内容符号一旦消失，我们对内容的理解就会变得模糊，这是因为人脑的短时记忆能力很难将数百个单词一个一个地按顺序储存在大脑中。这时，可以通过把信息按照逻辑来分层，记忆信息。

逻辑分层记忆就是对信息的点（具体的信息）、线（各点之间的逻辑联系）和面（整体概念）进行全面的纵向的把握。这样把看似散乱的信息点按照逻辑层次组成较大的记忆单位，能大大提高短期记忆的容量。英语的逻辑关系，主要有先后、递进、转折、让步、因果、对照、对比、解释、条件、举例和归纳总结关系。

如：Not everybody reads the daily newspaper. People who don't read newspapers are sometimes referred to as non-readers. Early research has shown that the non-readers are generally low in education, low in income, either very young or very old. In addition, non-readers are more likely to live in rural areas and have less contact with neighbors and friends.

这段信息以"in addition"为线，按照递进的逻辑线索组织在一起。信息的开头指出了信息的面："People who don't read newspapers are sometimes referred to as non-readers."而信息的点则为"low in education""low in income""either very young or very old"和"live in rural areas and have less contact with neighbor and friends"。这样，在脑中记下的不是单个的词的总和，而是有逻辑关系的意义整体。在口译时，从脑中提取的信息也变得简单了。

而汉语的逻辑关系一般是隐含的，因此不能仅依靠逻辑关系词，有时还要依靠上下文。

例如："中国人在就餐时也用特殊的方式对他人表示尊重。首先，座位安排就很讲究。首席面朝大门，通常是留给最年长、最重要或头衔最高的客人。此外，中国人在餐间总是把最好的食物先给家里长辈吃。"

这里，只要记住信息的面是餐间"用特殊的方式对他人表示尊重"，线是"首先"和"此外"，点是"座位安排"和"最好的食物"。以点、线和面为基点，就能回忆起基本信息了。

练习建议：听较长中英段落，并分析段落中的点、线、面，概括逻辑分层并复述信息。

Passage Interpretation 1

据中国旅游研究院的数据，中国人的旅游偏好开始发生改变，有更多的中国人到国外旅

63

游。但就在中国游客探索更远的国度之际,也带去了各种不良习惯。例如,有些人在埃及古代神庙上刻字,在公共场合大声喧哗,随地吐痰,中国游客的口碑变得很差。中国游客在海外的不文明行为有损国家形象。

旅游者应自觉遵守社会公共秩序和社会公德,尊重当地宗教信仰和风俗习惯,注意公众场合特别是涉外场合的言谈举止,爱护旅游资源,保护生态环境。中国游客应成为中国形象的展示者。

中国国家旅游局发布了一套新的旅游出行指南,目的就是要纠正游客的不良行为。尽管这本指南是针对中国人在国内旅行提出的建议,但其主要的目的却是提升中国游客在海外糟糕的声誉。

有了最新的旅游出行指南,中国游客应该没有借口再继续不雅行为了,至少从理论上来说是如此。

Passage Interpretation 2

When you travel abroad you need to know how to tip in the country that you're in.

In Brazil, there will always be a standard service charge added, 10% of the bill, and you won't have to tip. If you do feel like being generous, an extra 5% −10% will really make your server very happy. Just remember to do this as privately as possible. Brazilians don't make a big show of this.

In Dubai it's a rule to charge 10% tip on all restaurant and bar bills. Waiters are not paid very much in Dubai, so it is always very appreciated if you can add a couple of dirhams.

In Thailand a tip will be appreciated, but never asked for. Leave the loose change after you've paid your bill, or you can leave a dollar at the table.

If the country you're visiting doesn't customarily practice tipping your servers, they will not expect a tip even if you've enjoyed really extraordinary service. Countries where tipping is not usually practiced include Italy, Japan, Vietnam, New Zealand, Australia, Belgium, France, Norway, Singapore, Malaysia and China.

Dialogue Interpretation

Tourist: Excuse me, is this the Gusu Travel Agency?
Agent: 是的。先生,要我为您做什么吗?
Tourist: I'm David Stone from America. This is my first trip to Suzhou. Would you please tell me something about the city?
Agent: 当然可以,斯通先生。苏州是座美丽的城市,由于河道密布,因而被称为"东方威尼斯"。苏州尤其以园林闻名于世,约有 150 个园林,有的园林已经有上千年的历史。苏州园林虽不大,但设计奇特,集自然美、建筑美和绘画美于一体。
Tourist: That's wonderful. I'd like to take a one-day tour around the city.
Agent: 好的,我们有几条线路。这些是旅游手册。它们能给您提供更详尽的说明。
Tourist: Thank you. Oh, I really want to see these places: Humble Administrator's Garden, Lion Grove Garden, Hanshan Temple and Tiger Hill. Do you have

any tours that include all of them?

Agent: 这条路线有的。你可以上午游览拙政园和狮子林。午饭后,到寒山寺游玩。整个下午游览虎丘。

Tourist: How long does the tour take?

Agent: 大约 8 小时。早上 8 点半巴士车从我们这儿出发。下午 4 点半返回。

Tourist: What is the cost of the tour?

Agent: 400 元,包括午餐。

Tourist: Are there any English-speaking guides?

Agent: 没有。但我们有这个中英双语的免费导游册子,上面介绍了所有你要去的地方。

Tourist: Oh, that'll be very helpful. Thank you very much.

Exercises

Ⅰ. Interpreting technique practice.

You will hear 10 paragraphs. Please try to memorize each paragraph by finding out the logic relationship among the sentences in it and retell each paragraph.

Ⅱ. Spot dictation.

China is looking to stop cheap (1) _____ that force tourists into expensive shops. The tourists buy the tours at low cost, but then they are expected to make expensive purchases at stores while (2) _____. The shops then give money back to the travel company that sold the low-cost trip. Sometimes, such (3) _____ lead to conflict between tour guides and tourists.

China's National Tourism Administration said Sunday it is looking at new fines for tourists that sign up for the (4) _____ trips. Before, Chinese officials (5) _____ travel companies that offer such trips. But that action did not reduce the number of tourists tricked into going to (6) _____. The Chinese tourism officials say they hope that fining tourists will stop this kind of discounted travel.

The new (7) _____ follows the death last week of a 54-year-old Chinese mainland tourist in Hong Kong. Chinese officials said he was beaten up outside a jewelry store last week. He reportedly (8) _____ a heart attack. The tourist reportedly was trying to calm a fight that resulted when two of his fellow tourists refused to make purchases, (9) _____ the tour guides.

In many other countries, including the United States, tour buses commonly stop at "tourist traps". These shops focus on selling goods to vacationers not from the area. The goods are often over-priced and of (10) _____.

Ⅲ. Sentence listening and translation.

1. _____

2. _____

3. _____

4. _____

5. _____

IV. Paragraph listening and translation.

_____

V. Dialogue interpretation.

A: Today is the day we see dolphins and I could barely sleep last night.

B: 我也是,很激动。既然今天的行程紧张,我们现在就开始青岛之旅吧。

A: OK. Our first stop is Zhanqiao Pier, isn't it?

B: 是的。栈桥建于1892年,用作军用码头,如今则是青岛的象征。

A: It sounds great. But when will we visit Qingdao Underwater World? You know, I can't wait to see the performance of dolphins.

B: 午饭后吧。我们整个下午参观青岛海底世界。

A: Great. What is the plan for tonight?

B: 我强烈推荐五四广场,那可是啤酒爱好者们去的好地方。

A: Thank you.

VI. Interpreting in groups.

Role-play the following situation with your partners, acting as the Chinese speaker, English speaker and the interpreter respectively. One group will be invited to perform in class.

Participants: 1. Ms. Lin, a Chinese tour guide
2. Mr. Smith, an overseas visitor
3. An interpreter

Location: Wuxi

Task: Ms. Lin, a Chinese speaker works as the local tour guide for Mr. Smith who would like to pay a visit to Wuxi, the famous tourist destination. Ms. Lin introduces the city and takes photos with Mr. Smith there.

Ⅶ. 3-minute talk on the given topic.

Talk on the following topic in three minutes based on the given reference questions.

Topic: Travelling alone or in a group

Questions for Reference:

1. Do you prefer to travel alone or in a group? Why?
2. Have you ever been in a difficult situation while travelling? What happened?
3. What was your best trip?

Ⅷ. Theme-related expressions.

自然景观、建筑

长廊	long corridor
殿	hall
拱顶	vault
祭坛	altar
角楼	watchtower
水榭	pavilion on the water
塔	pagoda; tower
亭台楼阁	pavilions, terraces, and towers
钟楼	bell-tower
碑林	the forest of steles; tablet forest
壁画	murals; fresco
八方来客	tourists from all parts of the world
苍松翠柏	green pines and cypresses
姹紫嫣红	a blaze of bright colors; colorful
雕梁画栋	carved beams and painted pillars

金碧辉煌	splendid and magnificent
惊涛拍岸	raging waves pound on the banks
景色如画	picturesque views
流连忘返	linger on; too delighted to leave
迷人	enchanting; bewitching; fascinating
奇珍异宝	rare treasure
鱼米之乡	a land of milk and honey
郁郁葱葱	luxuriantly green
上有天堂，下有苏杭。	In heaven there is the paradise, and on earth there are Suzhou and Hangzhou. / As there is the paradise in heaven, so there are Suzhou and Hangzhou on earth.
五岳归来不看山，黄山归来不看岳。	Trips to China's five great mountains render trips to other mountains unnecessary, and a trip to Huangshan renders trips to the five great mountains unnecessary.
桂林山水甲天下，阳朔山水甲桂林。	Guilin landscape tops those elsewhere, and Yangshuo landscape tops that of Guilin.

Section C Further Exploration

1. 对香港迪士尼乐园的门票说明，你能明白多少呢？仔细阅看，翻译一下。

1-Day Ticket: Standard Day

Standard Day Tickets are valid on all days, except Designated Days. Valid for one visit during the 6-month period beginning on the date of the purchase.

Prices:

General Admission (Ages 12-64) HK$499

Child (Ages 3-11) HK$355

Senior (Ages 65+) HK$100

1-Day Ticket: Designated Day

Designated Day tickets are valid for one visit on the date you select only.

Prices:

General Admission (Ages 12-64)	Child (Ages 3-11)	Senior (Ages 65+)
HK$499	HK$355	HK$100

2-Day Ticket

Visit on any 2 days within a 7-day period. First visit must be on or before the last day of the validity period printed on the back of the ticket.

Prices:

General Admission (Ages 12-64)	Child (Ages 3-11)	Senior (Ages 65+)
HK$680	HK$480	HK$170

2. 请找出下列公示语翻译中的错误并予以纠正。

(1) _____   (2) _____   (3) _____

(4) _____   (5) _____

UNIT 5

Ceremonial Speech

礼仪致辞

Learning Objectives

1. To understand ceremony etiquette and speech etiquette;
2. To learn Chinese idiom translation and the translation of zero-subject sentences;
3. To learn how to memorize what you hear(2);
4. To learn how to translate/interpret ceremonial speeches;
5. To learn useful words and expressions related to ceremonial speeches.

Lead-in

- *Quiz* (True or False)

　　　　　1. At a business banquet in China, you are not supposed to start eating until the person with the highest status has made a toast and begun to eat.

　　　　　2. After-dinner speech is a tradition which stretches back thousands of years, with speakers saying a few words after meal, so the content of the speech is expected to be formal all the time.

　　　　　3. Nodding has the meaning of "YES", but in countries like India it actually stands for "NO".

　　　　　4. Black color is the only choice for all kinds of formal ceremonies.

　　　　　5. An audience should show respect to the speaker by maintaining eye contact with him or her, which is considered as a crucial part of an audience's speech etiquette.

　　　　　6. It is always acceptable for an audience to answer the phone in a low voice at his seat while attending a concert.

● What are the events? Fill in the blanks with English words in the list.

Canton Fair   National People's Congress   Olympic Games
World Expo   Oscar Ceremony   Spring Festival Gala
Boao Forum for Asia   Confucius Memorial Ceremony

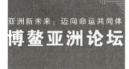
1. _____

2. _____

3. _____

4. _____

5. _____

6. _____

7. _____

8. _____

Section A Translation

Translation Technique

一、成语和四字格结构的译法

汉译英礼仪致辞中,常常碰到一些四字格和成语,一般翻译时,只要转述语义即可。如,"良辰佳时"译成"wonderful time","珠联璧合"译成"an excellent match",等等。但如果四字格之间有隐性的逻辑关系,通常要转换成显性的逻辑关系。如:"我们应该相互尊重,相互学习,取长补短,共同进步。"句中的四个四字格结构除了能体现并列关系以外,也体现了目的关系。本句可理解为:"我们应该相互尊重,相互学习,(以便我们)取长补短,共同进步。"可以译成:"We should respect and learn from each other so as to draw upon others' strong points to offset one's own deficiencies for achieving common progress."

二、无主句的译法

汉译英时,主语的确定也很重要。这是因为汉语句子可以没有主语,也可以有多个主语。汉语中出现在句子开头的词语不一定是句子的主语。无主句主语的主要处理方法如下:

1. 增补主语

活到老,学到老。**One is never too old to learn.**

学习外国的经验,必须有分析、批判地学。**We must learn foreign experiences with an analytical and critical eye.**

下雨了。**It is raining.**

2. 转成被动句

各民族之间建立了平等、团结、互助的新型关系。A new type of relationship of equality, solidarity and mutual assistance between different ethnic groups **has been established.**

3. 转换词性

采用新工艺大大降低了产品的成本。The **adoption** of the new process has greatly cut the cost of production.

4. 用 There be 句型

桌子上有一盆花。**There is** a bunch of flowers on the table.

Passage Translation 1

Vocabulary

1. 春和日丽
2. 博鳌亚洲论坛年会
3. 智库
4. 在论坛之上畅所欲言
5. 人均 GDP
6. 国际贫困线
7. 改善民生
8. 亚洲利益共同体
9. 经济全球化
10. 荣辱相依

尊敬的各位嘉宾,女士们,先生们,朋友们:

很高兴在春和日丽的季节,和来自 52 个国家的朋友们汇聚在中国美丽的海南岛,一起出席 2014 博鳌亚洲论坛年会。在此,我代表中国政府,对年会的召开表示热烈的祝贺!对远道而来的嘉宾表示诚挚的欢迎!

博鳌亚洲论坛已举办十二届,成为聚焦亚洲、放眼世界的一个重要平台。出席本届论坛的有亚洲和非洲多位政府首脑,也有众多的商界领袖和智库、传媒界的杰出人士,老友新朋汇聚一堂,大家都为亚洲与世界的发展大计而来。思想越辩越新,朋友也就会越交越真。我希望各位畅所欲言。

今天的亚洲正处在发展的关键时期。亚洲是全球最具活力的地区之一,经济规模占世界的 1/3,劳动力供给充足。同时,亚洲大多是发展中国家,人均 GDP 不高,地区发展水平很不平衡,还有 7 亿多人生活在国际贫困线以下,发展经济、改善民生的任务依然艰巨。发展仍然是亚洲国家的第一要务。在此,我愿提出几点看法,与大家交流。

第一,坚持共同发展的大方向,结成亚洲利益共同体。在经济全球化背景下,亚洲各国的发展,不可能独善其身,而是你中有我、我中有你的互利合作。

　　第二,构建融合发展的大格局,形成亚洲命运共同体。中国有句谚语,"单丝难成线,独木不成林。"创造亚洲的美好未来,要靠各国的自身发展,更要靠地区的共同进步。

　　第三,维护和平发展的大环境,打造亚洲责任共同体。远亲不如近邻,近邻可成友邻。实现亚洲的和平与稳定,需要地区国家共同担当起应尽的责任。

　　女士们,先生们！我们生活在一个相互依存的时代。亚洲各国应密切合作把我们共同的家园建设好,也为世界和平、发展、合作做出更大贡献。中国将永远与亚洲各国一道,荣辱相依,休戚与共,共同开创亚洲发展新未来！

　　最后,预祝本次年会取得圆满成功！谢谢！

Notes

1. "很高兴在春和日丽的季节,和来自52个国家的朋友们汇聚在中国美丽的海南岛,一起出席2014博鳌亚洲论坛年会。"这句话中"春和日丽"是典型的汉语中的四字格。对于这类词语,汉译英时往往只要翻译其意义就可,不必拘泥于四字格的形式。这儿"春和日丽"译为"lovely spring"。

2. "思想越辩越新,朋友也就会越交越真。"这句话中,难点是"新"和"真"这两个字。翻译时,不可望文生义,理解为"辩论后思想变成新的,朋友变成真的",而是按上下文,理解成"辩论后产生新的想法,朋友之间的关系也变得更加亲密",因此译成:"Exchange of views will create new vision, and more interactions bring friends closer."

3. "亚洲各国的发展,不可能独善其身,而是你中有我、我中有你的互利合作。"这句话中,出现了"独善其身"这个成语,成语的翻译只能舍弃形式,只要把成语的意义表达出来即可。这儿,"独善其身"指的是亚洲各国不能独自发展。其次,"你中有我、我中有你"这样的四字格的意思和句子中的"互利"其实是同一个意思,因此可以减译。所以,全句可以译成:"No Asian countries can achieve development in isolation from each other. Rather, with our interests closely entwined, Asian countries need to seek mutually beneficial cooperation."文中还有类似的句子,例如在倒数第二段中的一句话:"中国将永远与亚洲各国一道,荣辱相依,休戚与共,共同开创亚洲发展新未来！"这句话中的成语"荣辱相依,休戚与共"是难点。不仅要按照上下文正确理解,而且要分辨出此处两个成语是几乎同样的意思,因此需要减译一个,只要译一个成语的意思即可,译成"share weal and woe with other Asian countries"。

4. "亚洲是全球最具活力的地区之一,经济规模占世界的1/3,劳动力供给充足。"这是一句长句。长句的翻译可以按句意折或分。这儿,亚洲的经济规模和劳动力说明亚洲是个最具活力的地区之一,在句意上是有因果逻辑关系的,因而全句译成一句话:"Asia is one of the most dynamic regions in the world, boasting one third of the global GDP, and an ample supply of labor force."

5. "第一,坚持共同发展的大方向,结成亚洲利益共同体。"这句话是典型的汉语无主句。翻译这类句子时,要结合具体情况给句子补充主语。在这儿,显然主语是指我们亚洲,所以,添加主语"we"。全句译成"First, we should stick to the overarching goal of common

development and build an Asian community of shared interests."类似的句子还有"构建融合发展的大格局,形成亚洲命运共同体""维护和平发展的大环境,打造亚洲责任共同体",都可以这样处理。

6. "创造亚洲的美好未来,要靠各国的自身发展,更要靠地区的共同进步。"此句中主语词性要转换一下,从动词转为名词。全句译为:"Building Asia's beautiful future hinges upon not only the development of each and every country but, more importantly, the common progress of the whole region."

Passage Translation 2

Vocabulary

1. pay tribute to
2. Secretary of State
3. mutual respect
4. democracy
5. perspective
6. reverence
7. Chinese immigrant
8. Chinese American
9. dazzle
10. prosper

Good evening, everybody. Please have a seat. On behalf of Michelle and myself, welcome to the White House. And thank you for joining us as we host President Hu and the Chinese delegation, and as we pay tribute to the bonds between two great nations and two proud peoples.

There are too many distinguished guests to mention all of you tonight. But I do want to acknowledge a few who have championed relations between our nations: First of all, President Jimmy Carter and his wonderful wife Rosalynn Carter are here. As well as President Bill Clinton and my outstanding Secretary of State, Hillary Clinton.

President Hu, we have met today in a spirit of mutual respect: the United States—the oldest democracy in the world, and China—one of the oldest civilizations in the world. And while it's easy to focus on our differences of culture and perspective, let us never forget the values that our people share: A reverence for family; the belief that, with education and hard work and with sacrifice, the future is what we make it; and most of all, the desire to give our children a better life.

Let's also never forget that throughout our history our people have worked together for mutual progress. We've traded together for more than 200 years. We stood together in the Second World War. Chinese immigrants and Chinese Americans have helped to build America, including many who join us here tonight.

I'm told that there is a Chinese proverb that says: If you want one year of prosperity, then grow grain. If you want 10 years of prosperity, then grow trees. But if you want 100 years of prosperity, then you grow people.

And so I propose a toast,

To our people, the citizens of the People's Republic of China and the United States of America.

May they grow together in friendship!

May they prosper together in peace!

And may they realize their dream of the future for themselves, for their children, and for their grandchildren!

Cheers!

Notes

1. "And thank you for joining us as we host President Hu and the Chinese delegation, and as we pay tribute to the bonds between two great nations and two proud peoples." 这句话中,如果按照原句的结构,把 as 从句翻译成:"当我们欢迎胡锦涛主席和中国代表团,并且对中美两国和两国人民的紧密关系致意时",全句翻译腔会很浓,所以,为符合汉语表达,在不改变句意的前提下,全句译成:"感谢各位与我们一道欢迎胡锦涛主席和中国代表团,向中美两国和两国人民的紧密关系致意。"

2. "But I do want to acknowledge a few who have championed relations between our nations." 这句话中的"acknowledge"和"champion"这两个词的翻译是要结合句子语境的,此处不能生译成"承认"和"拥护"。这儿,总统提到的几位嘉宾,一定是特别介绍的,而且是对两国关系的发展不仅仅是拥护,而且是做出过特殊贡献的,因此全句译成:"但是,我想特别介绍一下对我们两国关系起到关键作用的人。"

3. "We have met today in a spirit of mutual respect: the United States—the oldest democracy in the world, and China—one of the oldest civilizations in the world." 这句话中,"the United States—the oldest democracy in the world, and China—one of the oldest civilizations in the world" 两个同位语的翻译是关键。这儿的同位语译成"we"的修饰语显得头重脚轻,可以和主句分开,分别译成两句话:"美国是世界上最悠久的民主制国家,而中国是世界上最古老的文明古国之一"。

4. "... let us never forget the values that our people share: A reverence for family; the belief that, with education and hard work and with sacrifice, the future is what we make it; and most of all, the desire to give our children a better life." 英译汉时,名词转动词是较为常见的。此句中的"reverence""belief"和"desire"可以译成动词,更符合汉语表达,译成:"重视家庭,相信教育、勤奋和牺牲可以创造未来,更重要的,想要为子女提供更好生活"。

5. "I'm told that there is a Chinese proverb that says: If you want one year of prosperity, then grow grain. If you want 10 years of prosperity, then grow trees. But if you want 100 years of prosperity, then you grow people." 英译汉时,由于被动语态在英语中较常使用,常常要处理被动语态的句子。此句中"I'm told that"显然不能直接译成"我被告知",根据汉语表达习惯,可以译成"我知道"。

Sentences in Focus

1. 很高兴在春和日丽的季节,和来自52个国家的朋友们汇聚在中国美丽的海南岛,一起出席2014博鳌亚洲论坛年会。

2. 我代表中国政府,对年会的召开表示热烈的祝贺!对远道而来的嘉宾表示诚挚的欢迎!

3. 老友新朋汇聚一堂,大家都为亚洲与世界的发展大计而来。思想越辩越新,朋友也就会越交越真。希望各位畅所欲言。

4. 创造亚洲的美好未来,要靠各国的自身发展,更要靠地区的共同进步。

5. 中国将永远与亚洲各国一道,荣辱相依,休戚与共,共同开创亚洲发展新未来!

6. On behalf of Michelle and myself, welcome to the White House. And thank you for joining us as we host President Hu and the Chinese delegation, and as we pay tribute to the bonds between two great nations and two proud peoples.

7. There are too many distinguished guests to mention all of you tonight. But I do want to acknowledge a few who have championed relations between our nations.

8. Let us never forget the values that our people share: A reverence for family; the belief that, with education and hard work and with sacrifice, the future is what we make it; and most of all, the desire to give our children a better life.

9. I'm told that there is a Chinese proverb that says: If you want one year of prosperity, then grow grain. If you want 10 years of prosperity, then grow trees. But if you want 100 years of prosperity, then you grow people.

10. I propose a toast,
    To our people, the citizens of the People's Republic of China and the United States of America.
    May they grow together in friendship!
    May they prosper together in peace!
    And may they realize their dream of the future for themselves, for their children, and for their grandchildren!
    Cheers!

Unit 5　Ceremonial Speech 礼仪致辞

Exercises

I . Fill in the blanks with English words according to the given Chinese.

1. On behalf of my colleagues, I'd like to _____ _____（对……表示热烈欢迎）to you and sincerely wish you a pleasant stay in Shanghai.
2. China is now _____（处于如此关键的时期）that without structural transformation and upgrading, we will not be able to sustain economic growth.
3. _____（地区发展）plays a vital role in the modernization of all countries, and is of great significance in the implementation of the scientific outlook on development and the construction of harmonious society in China.
4. Beijing police have made the security of the APEC meeting their _____ _____（当务之急）, with ample preparations for this event considered as important as the 2008 Olympic Games.
5. _____（经济全球化）can be compared to a two-blade sword or a coin with two sides. Advantages and disadvantages exist side by side.
6. Chinese Foreign Minister Wang Yi said China and Africa have always been a _____（命运共同体）and that neither side can grow without the other.
7. We sincerely welcome friends _____（远道而来的）to learn more about China and more about Sanmenxia, the city of swans.
8. To begin with, _____（相互尊重）is a basic principle governing contemporary international relations and the bedrock of stable state-to-state relations.
9. The ongoing urbanization process in China, or called new urbanization, will not only benefit China but also _____（为……做出贡献）the whole world.
10. China will continue _____（改善民生）with necessary and timely support, especially for those with low incomes.

II . Translate the following English expressions into Chinese idioms or translate the Chinese idioms into English.

1. colorful _____
2. in isolation from each other _____
3. direct and straightforward _____
4. fruitful achievements _____
5. be of significance _____

6. 汇聚一堂 _____

7. （历史）源远流长 _____

8. （文化）博大精深 _____

9. 突飞猛进 _____

10. 日新月异 _____

III. Translate the following sentences.

1. Here, on behalf of the members of the newly elected central leadership, I wish to express our heartfelt thanks to all other members of the Party for the great trust they have placed on us.

2. As China has forged partnerships with more than 60 countries around the world, China's global partnership network has "basically taken shape".

3. The launch of the Free Trade Area negotiations will be conducive to the economic integration of north Asia and the prosperity and stability of the region as a whole.

4. The purpose of the forum is to deepen communication, cooperation and economic exchange—between Asian countries, and between Asia and the rest of the world.

5. The opening ceremony on April 10 will be hosted by Chinese Premier Li Keqiang, with other world leaders in attendance including Australian Prime Minister Tony Abbott and Pakistan Prime Minister Nawaz Sharif.

6. 我们不仅关注自己国家的前途，也关注世界的前途。(concern)

7. 让我们共同努力，为下一代创造更美好的生活。

8. 不断变化的社会不仅给我们带来了问题，也给我们带来了机会。(ever-changing)

9. 真心希望各位能有机会去亲身体验一下欢乐的节日气氛。(festival)

10. 我们之间的关系是一种友好合作、平等互补的关系。

IV. Translate the following paragraphs.

1. Time flies! Year 2014 is coming to an end and 2015 is approaching. At this turn of the year, I now extend my best wishes to people of all ethnic groups in China, to our compatriots from Hong Kong and Macau Special Administrative Regions, to compatriots in Taiwan and overseas Chinese, as well as to friends in other countries and regions in the world.

2. 女士们,先生们,在过去的五年里,双方的合作可谓硕果累累。让我们共同努力,进一步加强伙伴关系并实现可持续发展。最后,我祝愿本次会议取得圆满成功。现在,我提议为我们之间的友谊及合作干杯。祝愿各位身体健康、合家幸福。

Section B Interpretation

Interpretation Technique

口译技能:记忆信息(2)——静态形象记忆

为了避免将精力放在字词上,我们在听描述性的语篇时,可以采用视觉化方法,边听边将听到的内容视觉化。静态形象记忆就是把空间结构说明想象成地图或路线图,把人物景象等在脑子里做简笔素描。这样,循着对信息的形象化理解,可以帮助我们记住讲话中的细节,把握住讲话的主要线索。形象记忆在口译中非常重要,它可以帮助我们丢掉语言形式,而将信息的意义提炼出来。

例如:"你去那儿找人领个表盖个章就好了。那儿有两个人办这个事情。一个男的,个子不高,白白净净的,说话很和气,他会给你一张表;另外一个女的是他们的领导,有点凶,短头发,戴个厚厚的眼镜,她负责盖章。"

听完这段话后,应该在脑子里有两张关于要去找的人的鲜明素描图:一男一女,男的个子不高,但白净和气,女的短发,戴眼镜,有点凶。通过这种对描写人物的形象化记忆,译者可以脱离原来的语言形式,直接抓住信息的主要意思。

又如:"武汉地处长江,乘船上可抵达重庆,下可达上海。武汉还是全国重要的铁路枢纽,京广、武九等铁路在此交汇,连接豫、湘、赣等省。"

如果有基本的地理知识,这段信息可以转换成一幅由两条横线和一条竖线构成的简单地图。长横线代表长江,短横线代表武九铁路,竖线代表京广铁路。这样武汉的地理位置在脑子里就非常清晰了。再结合自己对武汉和中国地理分布的背景知识,听完后译员能轻松记住这段话的意思。

Passage Interpretation 1

总统先生、奥巴马夫人、女士们、先生们、朋友们:

很高兴应奥巴马总统邀请,在一元复始的时节来到华盛顿,对美国进行国事访问。此时此刻,我谨代表13亿中国人民,向美国人民致以诚挚的问候和良好的祝愿!

我这次访问美国,是为增进互信、加强友谊、深化合作、推动21世纪中美关系继续向前发展而来。

中美建交32年来,两国关系已经成长为具有战略意义和全球影响的双边关系。

面对新形势新挑战,我们应该登高望远、求同存异,共同推动中美关系长期健康稳定发展。我希望通过这次访问,推进积极合作全面的中美关系,开启两国伙伴合作新篇章。

当今世界正处在大发展大变革大调整时期。让我们抓住机遇、携手前行,共同加强中美伙伴合作,同世界各国一道推动建设持久和平、共同繁荣的和谐世界。

再次感谢总统先生对我们的热烈欢迎!

Passage Interpretation 2

Mr. President of the People's Republic of China, Mr. Liu Qi, Members of the Organizing Committee, dear Chinese friends, dear athletes:

For a long time, China has dreamed of opening its doors and inviting the world's athletes to Beijing for the Olympic Games. Tonight that dream comes true. Congratulations, Beijing. You have chosen as the theme of these Games "One World, One Dream".

As one world, we grieved with you over the tragic earthquake in Sichuan Province. We were moved by the great courage and solidarity of the Chinese people. As one dream, may these Olympic Games bring you joy, hope and pride.

Athletes, the Games were created for you by our founder, Pierre de Coubertin. These Games belong to you. Let them be the athletes' Games.

Remember, they are about much more than the performance alone. They are about the peaceful gathering of 204 national Olympic committees, regardless of ethnic origin, gender, religion or political system. Please compete in the spirit of the Olympic values: excellence, friendship and respect.

Dear athletes, remember that you are role models for the youths of the world. Reject doping and cheating. Make us proud of your achievements and your conduct.

As we bring the Olympic dream to life, our warm thanks go to the Beijing Organizing Committee for its tireless work. Our special thanks also go to the thousands of gracious volunteers, without whom none of this would be possible.

I now have the honor of asking the President of the People's Republic of China to open the Games of the XXIX Olympiad of the modern era.

Passage Interpretation 3

Michelle and I are saddened to learn of the passing of Steve Jobs. Steve was among the greatest of American innovators—brave enough to think differently, bold enough to believe he could change the world, and talented enough to do it.

By building one of the planet's most successful companies from his garage, he exemplified the spirit of American ingenuity. By making computers personal and putting the Internet in our pockets, he made the information revolution not only accessible, but intuitive and fun. And by turning his talents to storytelling, he has brought joy to millions of children and grownups alike. Steve was fond of saying that he lived every day like it was his last. Because he did, he transformed our lives, redefined entire industries, and achieved one of the rarest feats in human history: he changed the way each of us sees the world.

The world has lost a visionary. And there may be no greater tribute to Steve's success than the fact that much of the world learned of his passing on a device he invented. Michelle and I send our thoughts and prayers to Steve's wife Laurene, his family, and all those who loved him.

Exercises

I. Interpreting technique practice.

You will hear 10 sentences. Please try to memorize each sentence by using the technique learned in this section and retell what you hear.

II. Spot dictation.

Director-general Bokova, ladies and gentlemen,

It gives me a great pleasure to join you for this important (1) _____ as the UN marks its 70th anniversary.

Education is very close in my heart. My father grew up in a very small village in China. In those days, not many villagers could read. So my father opened a night school to teach them how to read. With his help, many people learned to write their own names; with his help, many people learned to read newspapers for the first time; with his help, many women were able to teach their children how to read.

As his daughter, I know what education means to the people, especially those without it. After (2) _____, China has come a long way in education. I myself am a (3) _____ of that progress. Otherwise I would never become a soprano and a professor of music.

I am following my father's footsteps by teaching at China's Conservatory of Music to help continue China's success story. I want to thank Director-general Bokova and UNESCO for naming me the Special (4) _____ for Women and Girls Education. I am truly (5) _____ to work with the UN and do something about Global Education. I have visited many schools around the world. I've seen first-hand on how much we can do for education.

Education is about women and the girls. It is important for girls to go to school because they will become their children's first teacher someday. But women still (6) _____ over half of the world's poor population and 60% of adults who can't read.

Education is crucial in addressing (7) _____. In China, Spring Bud Education Program has helped over 3 million girls go back to school. Many of them have finished university education and they are doing well at work.

Education is about equality. In poor countries and regions, the number of school (8) _____ is astonishing. We call for more educational resources to these places.

Education is about the young people. Young people are the future. Education is important because it not only gave young people knowledge and skills but also helps them become responsible citizens. As the UNESCO special envoy and a mother myself, my (9) _____ to education for all will never change.

Many years ago, my father made a small difference in his village. Together we can make a big difference in the world. I was once asked about my Chinese dream. I said I hope all children, especially girls, can (10) _____ good education. This is my Chinese dream. I believe one day Education First will no longer be a dream, it will be a reality enjoyed by every young woman on this planet.

Thank you very much.

III. Sentence listening and translation.

1. _____

2. _____

3. _____

4. _____
   _____

5. _____
   _____

Ⅳ. Paragraph listening and translation.

_____
_____
_____
_____
_____
_____

Ⅴ. Dialogue interpretation.

Manager: 女士们，先生们，我很荣幸给各位介绍我们的来宾，通用汽车公司的史密斯先生。史密斯先生，我们很高兴您能来此参加工作并与我们的员工分享您宝贵的知识和经验。

Smith: I have been looking forward to meeting you for years. It is my pleasure and privilege to have received your gracious invitation and work with a distinguished group of people like you.

Manager: 我们会尽力使您在无锡期间过得舒适愉快。

Smith: Thank you so much for such a thoughtful arrangement for me.

Manager: 让我们共同举杯，为我们永久的友谊与合作，干杯！

Smith: Cheers! I believe that this visit to Wuxi will be significant to the cooperation between both sides.

Ⅵ. Interpreting in groups.

Role-play the following situation with your partners, acting as the Chinese speaker, English speaker and the interpreter respectively. One group will be invited to perform in class.

Participants: 1. Mr. John Williams
  2. Mr. Wang, general manager
  3. An interpreter

Location: Reception banquet

Task: You work as an interpreter at a reception banquet in honor of John Williams who is invited for personnel training of staff in your company. Introduce John to Mr. Wang, the general manager who extends warm welcome to John and makes a brief opening speech at the dinner. Mr. Wang speaks Chinese while John is an English-speaker.

VII. 3-minute talk on the given topic.

Talk on the following topic in three minutes based on the given reference questions.

Topic: Is public speech a great challenge to you?

Questions for Reference:

1. What are the qualities of a good public speaker?
2. How do you prepare for an opening speech?
3. Do you have any memorable experience of public speech? Describe it.

VIII. Theme-related expressions.

揭幕仪式	unveiling ceremony
奠基仪式	foundation laying ceremony
开工典礼	commencement ceremony
签字仪式	signing ceremony
剪彩仪式	ribbon-cutting ceremony
就职仪式	inauguration ceremony
请……发言	give the floor to … / let's welcome … to give a speech
请……颁奖	let's invite … to present the award
寄希望于本届大会	place our hopes on the current conference
促进友好合作关系	advance our friendly relations of cooperation
符合两国人民共同利益	accord with our common interests
携手合作	make joint efforts; make concerted efforts
预祝……圆满成功	wish … a complete success
出席今天招待会的有……	We have with us at the reception …
请全体起立,奏国歌。	Please rise and play the National Anthem.
请坐!	Please be seated.
有朋自远方来,不亦乐乎。	It's a delight to have friends coming from afar.
海内存知己,天涯若比邻。	Long distance separates no bosom friends.
十分荣幸能在美中两国之间的战略与经济对话首次会议开幕式上致辞。	It is a privilege to open this inaugural meeting of the Strategic and Economic Dialogue between the United States and China.

• 我愿借此机会,代表我们代表团的全体成员,对我们东道主的诚挚邀请表示真诚的谢意。	On behalf of all the members of the delegation, I would like to take this opportunity to express our sincere thanks to our host for their earnest invitation.
• 最后,让我们一起举杯,为阁下的健康,为各位贵宾的健康,为两国持久的友谊与合作,为这个世界的和平与繁荣,干杯!	In closing, I'd like you to join me in a toast, To the health of your Excellency, the health of all the distinguished guests. To the lasting friendship and cooperation of both countries. To the peace and prosperity of the world. Cheers!

Section C Further Exploration

Tips for Making a Good Presentation

Dress smartly. Don't let your appearance distract from what you are saying.

Smile. Don't hunch up and shuffle your feet. Have an upright posture. Try to appear confident and enthusiastic.

Say hello and smile when you greet the audience. Your audience will probably look at you and smile back: an instinctive reaction.

Speak clearly, firmly and confidently as this makes you sound in control. Don't speak too quickly in that you are likely to speed up and raise the pitch of your voice when nervous. Give the audience time to absorb each point. Don't talk in a monotone the whole time. Lift your head up and address your words to someone near the back of audience. If you think people at the back can't hear, ask them.

Use silence to emphasize points. Before you make a key point pause: this tells the audience that something important is coming. It's also the hallmark of a confident speaker as only these are happy with silences. Nervous speakers tend to gabble on trying to fill every little gap.

Keep within the allotted time for your talk.

Eye contact is crucial to holding the attention of your audience. Look at everyone in the audience from time to time, not just at your notes or at the PowerPoint slides. Try to involve everyone, not just those directly in front of you.

Walk around a little and gesture with your hands. Bad presenters keep their hands on the podium or in their pockets! Don't stand in one place glued to the spot hiding behind the podium! Good presenters will walk from side to side and look at different parts of the audience.

Try to involve your audience by asking them a question.

Refer to brief notes jotted down on small (postcard sized) pieces of card. Don't read out your talk, as this sounds boring and stilted. Don't look at your notes too much as this suggests insecurity and will prevent you making eye contact with the audience.

Use humor in moderation, but you'd better use anecdotes rather than rattle off a string of jokes.

Take along a wristwatch to help you keep track of time. The assessor may cut you off as soon as you have used the time allocated, whether or not you have finished.

Practise at home in front of a mirror. You can also record your presentation and play it back to yourself; don't judge yourself harshly when you replay this—we always notice our bad points and not the good when hearing or seeing a recording or ourselves! Time how long your talk takes. Run through the talk a few times with a friend.

It's normal to be a little nervous. This is a good thing as it will make you more energized. Many people have a fear of speaking in public. Practising will make sure that you are not too anxious. In your mind, visualize yourself giving a confident successful performance. Take a few deep slow breaths before your talk starts and make a conscious effort to speak slowly and clearly. Research by T. Gilovich (Cornell University) found that people who feel embarrassed are convinced their mistakes are much more noticeable than they really are. We focus on our own behavior more than other people do and consequently overestimate its impact. This is called the spotlight effect. If you make a mistake, don't apologize too much, just briefly acknowledge the mistake and continue on.

Build variety into the talk and break it up into sections. Apparently, the average person has a three minute attention span!

UNIT 6

Interview

交流访谈

Learning Objectives

1. To learn interview etiquette;
2. To learn how to translate people's names and proverbs;
3. To learn how to memorize what you hear(3);
4. To learn to translate/interpret passages or dialogues in the situation of interview;
5. To learn useful words and expressions related to interview.

Lead-in

- *Quiz* (True or False)

　　　　　1. Before a job interview, learning as much as you can about the company and about the position for which you're applying is a sign of respect.

　　　　　2. As long as you step out of the interview room, you may put your job interview to an end, only to wait for the call from the company in the following days.

　　　　　3. Being late for an interview or appointment tells others that you're self-centered, disorganized, rude or all three.

　　　　　4. Talk freely about your terrible experience with previous employer so as to please the interviewer by showing how eager you are to get the job.

　　　　　5. When asked about your weaknesses at the job interview, it is advisable for you to keep silent or tell a white lie.

　　　　　6. When you're offered a job, don't just say "yes" and take the job on the spot. Even if you know you want the job, take the time to evaluate the job offer to be absolutely certain that the position is right for you.

● What does each picture mainly refer to? Fill in the blanks with the words in the list.

job candidate　　　　　　job interview　　　　　　　job fair
college graduate　　　　　graduation ceremony　　　　diploma

1. _____

2. _____

3. _____

4. _____

5. _____

6. _____

Section A　Translation

Translation Technique

一、人名的翻译

英语和其他语言中的人名大多采用音译法进入汉语。现今较为规范的做法是：首先，必须确定名称持有者的国籍或民族身份，尽量遵从其所属民族语言的发音规律，按不同的音译表（如英汉音译表、法汉音译表、德汉音译表等）进行音译。例如，"Charles"译为"查尔斯"，"Francois"译为"佛朗索瓦"等。

尽管经过不少规范化的努力，汉语人名英译的方式仍然多样。

1. 汉语拼音广泛适用于当前中国大陆人名的汉英转换

例如，"王建国"译为"Wang Jianguo"。

2. 在汉语拼音未被采用之前，以及在当前的中国台湾、港澳地区和海外，威妥玛拼音（Wade-Giles Romanization）是汉语和英语之间名称转写的主要形式

例如，"钱学森"曾一度被音译为"Tsien Hsue-Shen"。

3. 某些华裔人名和港澳地名融合了非汉语的元素或本身就源自汉语以外的语言

例如，"李连杰"译为"Jet Lee"，世界级建筑大师美籍华裔"贝聿铭"的英文名是"Leoh Ming Pei"。

4. 汉语中还有些人名从表面上看是地道的汉语名称，实际上源自英语或其他外语

例如，20世纪为我国麻风病防治立下赫赫功勋的马海德先生，在英语中实为"George Hatem"。

要想正确翻译人名就要本着勤查勤看的态度去做好功课，积累这些知识，尤其是对当下各个领域的杰出人士、新闻人物要有所了解，否则只满足于通过传统的直译或音译获得译名的话，往往会造成误译。

二、谚语的翻译

1. 英汉谚语可分三种对应类型

(1) 语言形式与意义相同

例如：Constant dripping wears the stone（滴水穿石）
　　　Walls have ears（隔墙有耳）
　　　fish in troubled water（浑水摸鱼）

(2) 语言形式不同但意义相同

例如：like a drown rat（落汤鸡）
　　　a cat on hot bricks（热锅上的蚂蚁）
　　　blow cold and hot（朝三暮四）

(3) 语言形式相似但意义不同

例如：move heaven and earth（想方设法，千方百计）

2. 英汉谚语翻译通常采用以下四种方法

(1) 直译法：使用目的语的词组和句子，尽量保留原语的意义、形式和风格。

易如反掌 as easy as turning over one's hand/palm
君子动口不动手。A gentleman uses his tongue, not his fists.

(2) 增译法：当直译令人费解，而意译又使原有的比喻和内涵丢失时可用增译法，如翻译含有古代神话、寓言、历史故事、政策性词语时可用增译法。

例如：在他面前大谈股票，那简直是班门弄斧。If you talk much about stock before him, it will be like showing off one's proficiency with the axe before Lu Ban—the master carpenter.

三个臭皮匠，赛过诸葛亮。Three cobblers with their wits combined surpass Zhuge Liang, the master mind.

(3) 形象替代法：指在目的语中运用不同的形象来替代源语中的形象。这是两种文化中的不同哲学思想、宗教信仰等文化差异性造成的。

例如：这部电影在本届电影节上鹤立鸡群，大放异彩。Like a peacock among sparrows, this film was really a hit in this film festival.

爱屋及乌。Love me, love my dog.
覆水难收。It is no use crying over spilt milk.
千里之堤，溃于蚁穴。 A small leak will sink a great ship.

(4) 意译法：有许多谚语无法直译，也没有相应形象可以替代，此时先考虑"意"的准确完整，再考虑"形"的对应。

例如：你讲的这个例子很风趣，但是跟我讲的风马牛不相及。You have made a very vivid and interesting example. But I think it is dramatically different from the main part that I was talking about.

人人皆有得意之日。Every dog has his day.

通用口笔译

Passage Translation 1

Vocabulary

1. 资历
2. 主观性的决定
3. 应聘者
4. 无形的
5. 社交能力
6. 坦诚直率
7. 乐观友好
8. 过分亲密
9. 从容不迫
10. 海军蓝
11. 稍微有点暴露的服装
12. 少说多听

许多资历与工作经验几乎相同的求职人员竞聘同一职位，这是常发生的情况。那么招聘者如何做出选择呢？通常是通过面试来确定。

对于将面试作为一种选拔人才的流程，人们的意见褒贬不一。反对面试取人的主要理由是面试会导致完全主观性的决定。招聘者往往选择的不是最好的，而是给他们第一印象良好的应聘者。当然，对这种反对意见，一些招聘者会说他们自己在面试员工方面经验丰富，能够对每一个应聘者可能会有的表现做出合理的评估。赞同面试的主要理由（或许这还是一个很好的理由）是认为招聘者不仅看重应聘者的能力，还要看应聘者的个性是否能适应特殊的工作环境。比如，对于许多雇主来说，如果他们的秘书具有乐天的性格，偶尔的工作低效他们并不在意。因此，也许可以说面试的真正目的不是评价每一个应聘者可评估的方面，而是对其无形的方面进行推测，比如性格、个性及社交能力。

不幸的是，无论是雇主还是应聘者，许多人能力很强但面试表现不佳。当然，也有人面试很成功，但后来的工作表现并不令人满意。面试表现良好的求职者往往很自信，但从不自夸；提问和回答时，言语坦诚直率；乐观友好，但从不过分亲密；热情且乐观向上。

面试不佳的人往往会表现出人类行为的两种极端，他们或者非常羞涩，或者过于自信。他们或者缺乏热情，或者热情过度。他们或者只言片语，或者喋喋不休。他们或者过度礼貌，或者鲁莽粗鲁。

无论是求职面试还是初次约会，遵循下面的简单步骤，即使你实际上很普通，也能给人留下非常聪明的印象。

1. 说话从容不迫。说话要慢，从容不迫。说话语速慢的人被认为比说话语速快的人更容易解释清楚话题。

2. 多微笑。根据一项调查，参与者通过照片来猜测一个人是否聪明，他们认为微笑的人比不微笑的人更聪明。

3. 使用简单的语言。如果简单的词语足够表达清楚，不要使用不常见的词语。不必要地使用长词语会给人留下装聪明的印象。如果你会说一门外语，让他们知道。调查发现，人们通常认为会说多种语言的人更聪明。

4. 穿海军蓝。一项调查发现，人们认为，穿深蓝色服装的人比穿其他颜色服装的人更加博学、成功和独立。女性上班时应该穿比较保守的服装。根据另一项调查，即使稍微有点暴露的服装也会让人们认为女性职员的智慧和能力较差。

5. 倾听。人们认为少说多听的人比较聪明有趣。记住这个谚语：宁肯保持安静被别人怀疑很傻，也好过张开嘴巴证实这种怀疑。

Notes

1. "许多资历与工作经验几乎相同的求职人员竞聘同一职位，这是常发生的情况。"在这句话中，"这是常发生的情况"中的"这"指代的是前面整句话的内容，如用"it"指代另译一句或用"which"指代译成定语从句，都不如用"it is common that"这个句型并以"it"作形式主语来得言简意赅。全句译成："It is common that a number of applicants with almost identical qualifications and experience all apply for the same position."类似这样的句子都可以这样处理。例如，"我们要承认并尊重这些文化差异以免产生误解，这一点很重要。"可以译成："It is important for all of us to acknowledge and respect these cultural differences in order to avoid misunderstandings."

2. "他们自己在面试员工方面经验丰富，能够对每一个应聘者可能会有的表现做出合理的评估。"这句话中的"经验丰富"和"做出评估"之间并不是简单并列关系，而是因果关系，所以可以用"so... that..."句型，因此译成："They have become so experienced in interviewing staff that they are able to make a sound assessment of each candidate's likely performance."

3. "许多人能力很强但面试表现不佳。当然，也有人面试很成功，但后来的工作表现并不令人满意。"这两句话可以译成："There are many people of great ability who simply do not interview well. There are also, of course, people who interview extremely well, but are later found to be very unsatisfactory employees."分别将"能力很强"和"面试很成功"译成定语。事实上，定语从句和主句不一定是修饰语的关系，也可译成偏正关系，如这两句话中，都是转折关系，所以译成定语从句。又如，"The director had not thought it through and hired that off-beat singer, which was just meant to kill the time."译成："导演没有经过仔细考虑，随便找了一个跑调的歌手，只是为了能打发一下时间。"句中的定语从句和主句是目的关系。

4. "参与者通过照片来猜测一个人是否聪明，他们认为微笑的人比不微笑的人更聪明。"此句的难点是定语的翻译。"调查者"前的修饰语较长,是"参与通过照片来猜测一个人是否聪明",宜把修饰语后置。此外"不微笑的人"也要定语后置,译成定语从句。整句话译成:"Participants who were asked to guess a person's intelligence simply by looking at their picture rated those who were smiling as smarter than those who weren't smiling."

5. "记住这个谚语:宁肯保持安静被别人怀疑很傻,也好过张开嘴巴证实这种怀疑。"句中谚语直译成:"Better to keep quiet and be suspected a fool than to open your mouth and confirm the suspicion."

Passage Translation 2

Vocabulary

1. rapport
2. social skill
3. interaction
4. frame of mind
5. implement
6. slip into
7. stiff frame
8. "let's-get-to-the-point" kind of frame
9. weird
10. hang out with

Assuming rapport is definitely one of the best social skill tips I have ever learned about. Unfortunately I've forgotten a bit about it lately. Maybe you have too. So I think I'd bring it up again.

Now, what is assuming rapport? Basically, instead of going into a conversation or meeting nervously and thinking "How will this go?", you take different approach. You assume that you and the person(s) will establish a good connection (rapport). How do you do that? You simply pretend that you are meeting one of your best friends. Then you start the interaction in that frame of mind instead of the nervous one. I have found that this advice is surprisingly useful and easy to implement. Before the meeting, you just think that you'll be meeting a good friend. Then you'll naturally slip into a comfortable, confident and enjoyable emotional state. This also helps you and the other people to set a good frame for the interaction. A frame is always set in at the start of an interaction. It may be a nervous and stiff frame, a formal and "let's-get-to-the-point" kind of frame or perhaps a super relaxed one. The thing is that the frame that is set at the beginning of the conversation may stay on for a while. If it's a very stiff frame then it may very well continue to be so until the end. It can be quite difficult to change that frame into a more relaxed one. Breaking or changing that frame makes people feel uncomfortable or a bit weird. Therefore, you and the others become reluctant to do so, instead, just playing along.

First impressions last. So, setting a good frame at the very beginning can bring more enjoyment and better results out of any kind of meeting. That's why it's so useful to smile when you first meet someone. And it's also important to recognize that the impression made and frame set may not just last during the first conversation. It may continue throughout your relationship with this new friend, classmate or co-worker.

When you're with your friend, you don't think about what you should say next or what funny comment you could pull out of your sleeve. The conversation flows easily and naturally. I think this is what some people mean "Just be yourself". When your friends give you that advice, then they may mean that you should be "like you when you are hanging out with us". They want to see you bring out your natural and relaxed self in other interactions.

Notes

1. "Breaking or changing that frame makes people feel uncomfortable or a bit weird. Therefore, you and the others become reluctant to do so, instead, just playing along." 此句中,"play"这个词的翻译要放在句中判断,不能直译成"玩"。全句是指大家会继续交流,而不会改变原来的谈话氛围,所以,"play along"指的是继续交流下去,因而,全句译成:"破坏或者改变这种氛围可能会让人感到不适应或者有点奇怪。因此,你和其他人也不会这么做,而是继续在原来的氛围中交流下去。"

2. "It's also important to recognize that the impression made and frame set may not just last during the first conversation." 这句话在翻译时,要根据汉语表达习惯做语序的调整,把"It's also important"放到最后译。全句译成:"给人的印象和形成的交流氛围可能不仅仅只在第一次谈话中持续,认识到这一点也很重要。"一般带形式主语的句子的汉译都这样处理。

3. "When you're with your friend, you don't think about what you should say next or what funny comment you could pull out of your sleeve." 句子中的"pull out of your sleeve"要根据上下文确定具体的意思,不能直译成"从袖子里拿出来",而是和"comment"搭配译成"发表"。全句译成:"和朋友在一起的时候,你不会去思考接下来应该说什么或者发表什么有意思的评论。"

Sentences in Focus

1. 许多人能力很强但面试表现不佳。当然,也有人面试很成功,但后来的工作表现并不令人满意。

2. 面试表现良好的求职者往往很自信,但从不自夸;提问和回答时,言语坦诚直率;乐观友好,但从不过分亲密;热情且乐观向上。

3. 面试不佳的人或者非常羞涩，或者过于自信。他们或者缺乏热情，或者热情过度。他们或者只言片语，或者喋喋不休。他们或者过度礼貌，或者鲁莽粗鲁。

4. 说话语速慢的人被认为比说话语速快的人更容易解释清楚话题。

5. 记住这个谚语：宁肯保持安静被别人怀疑很傻，也好过张开嘴巴证实这种怀疑。

6. Before the meeting, you just think that you'll be meeting a good friend. Then you'll naturally slip into a more comfortable, confident and enjoyable emotional state.

7. A frame is always set in at the start of an interaction. It may be a nervous and stiff frame, a formal and "let's-get-to-the-point" kind of frame or perhaps a super relaxed one.

8. The thing is that the frame set at the beginning of the conversation may stay on for a while.

9. It's also important to recognize that the impression made and frame set may not last during the first conversation.

10. When your friends give you that advice, then they may mean that you should be "like you when you are hanging out with us".

Exercises

I. Fill in the blanks with English words according to the given Chinese.

1. Both countries need much better _____（互动）at the people-to-people level as that would change our perception of each other.
2. Stop complaining about the trifles. _____（言归正传）and tell us what happened to you.
3. During the second term of office, the President _____（被认为是）a decisive and resolute international leader.
4. The _____（理想的候选者）would have a university degree in journalism with rich related journalistic work experiences or teaching experiences.
5. Henry and I are here to teach you how to overcome fear and anxiety at a _____（工作面试）.
6. College graduates are expected to be well prepared in all respects so as to _____（给……留下好印象）interviewers.

7. Students are in need of more tutors at the remote village where the staff are calling on _____ (有经验的) teachers to volunteer their time.
8. _____ (开门见山) also makes things much easier when you need suggestions or if you did something wrong.
9. A recent survey found that Chinese youth today shows terribly poor _____ _____ (社交能力) as a result of fierce academic competition.
10. The security of online financing is _____ (与……有关) the economic security of the country as well as the integrity of individuals, companies and other entities.

Ⅱ. Translate the following names.

1. Jackie Chan _____
2. Sun Yat-sen _____
3. William Shakespeare _____
4. Jeremy Lin _____
5. Charles Kao _____
6. 李时珍 _____
7. 白求恩 _____
8. 郎世宁 _____
9. 霍英东 _____
10. 钱三强 _____

Ⅲ. Translate the following sentences.

1. Do you approve of people who become famous as a consequence of appearing again and again in the media, instead of having an artistic career?
   _____
   _____

2. Ranging from 1-10, 10 being the highest, how would you rate your career? Why?
   _____
   _____

3. If a group of overseas visitors just came to your country, what advice would you give them?
   _____
   _____

4. Have you looked at gay marriage from a different culture? If so, how are they different from those of your own culture?
   _____
   _____

5. Have you ever been in a situation where you felt you had to "do as the Romans do"?

6. 何为"双赢战略"？这对您来说有何意义？

7. 你为什么申请我们公司的这个职位？

8. 如果你一个目标都没实现会有何感受？

9. 自主创业阶段您需要考虑哪些事情？

10. 在我们结束采访之前您还有什么要说的吗？

IV. Translate the following paragraphs.

1. Q: How did you get your first role?
   A: Just auditioning. I was lucky enough to get an agent when I was 15. I just auditioned and auditioned and auditioned, and I got my first job when I was 16. When I was younger, I looked a lot older than I was. They have these working laws in England where you have to be 16: if you're over 16, you don't have to be restrained by working hours and things like that. In America, it's actually 18. So no one's going to hire a 15-year-old who's never actually done a job before to play someone who is 16 or above. They'll just get someone who's 16 or above, because it means they don't have to rest them every two hours and you don't have to school them. So I was going up for all these roles and getting none of them. But eventually I turned 16, so all those boundaries went away and that's when I got the first job.

2. 在美国和英国,工作经历是所有工作面试中最重要的话题。因此,详细解释你拥有哪些经历非常重要。一般来说,雇主想确切地了解你做过哪些事,任务完成得怎样。这不是谦虚的时候。要自信,随意地谈谈你在以往的工作中取得的成就。

___

___

___

___

___

Section B Interpretation

Interpretation Technique

口译技能:记忆信息(3)——动态形象记忆

当听到一些描述事件发展或一系列动作完成之类的信息时,动态形象记忆可以把信息形象化、生动化,就像视频重放一样,这在信息回忆时非常有效。

例如:"地震发生时我正开车路过现场,当时车辆在路面上来回晃动,路边山上有很多石头滚落,有的石头像小房子那么大,山谷中腾起很多灰尘,整个天空都暗了下来。"

为记住这段信息,可以把信息想象成一段视频。视频中,我在山谷开车,突然车摇晃,往车外看去,巨大的石头从山上滑落,然后看见腾起的灰把天空变暗。通过这一系列的动态形象记忆,信息很容易被理解和记忆。

又如:"I still remember when Deng Xiaoping visited America during my presidency. He was on the stage with a group of young children who sang Chinese songs. He kissed my daughter who was a little girl. He even wore a cowboy hat. That is very impressive to the Americans."

这段信息也很形象,可以结合个人对领导人出访的背景知识,把"on the stage with children, kissed my daughter"和"wore a cowboy hat"想象成电视里转播常看到的有关领导人出访的画面,就很容易理解记忆了。

Dialogue Interpretation 1

记者:你在短时间内就获得了很大的名气,这对你有什么影响?

Lady Gaga: It's been life-changing for me, but very exciting for my music.

记者:你也是歌曲创作者,你会写自己的歌。这样的创作过程是怎样开始的?

Lady Gaga: In all sorts of ways. Inspiration comes to me all day long, every day. Sometimes when I'm falling asleep, I have these visions. But it's not just music—it's music; it's the clothing; it's the stage performance.

记者：你会不会觉得与其说你是流行歌星，不如说你更像个行为艺术家？

Lady Gaga：I certainly am a performance artist. Yes.

记者：的确。你会不会担心你的音乐和这整套的艺术呈现是不是能够持续下去？我问的是演艺生涯，因为流行音乐事业，有时候弹指之间就结束了。你要怎么维系下去？

Lady Gaga：How am I going to stick around? Well, I just must remain prolific and relevant, as equally irrelevant, and continue to make great music. Longevity has a lot to do with discipline and ambition, which are two things that are certainly in my blood.

记者：你曾说安迪·沃霍尔对你的影响非常大。我是说，作为艺术家的他，作品流传相当久远，可为什么偏偏是他对你的影响特别大？

Lady Gaga：He made commercial art that was taken seriously as fine art.

记者：接下来再谈谈你的背景。我想要问一下小时候的你是怎样的，我猜应该不是个害羞的孩子。你小时候喜欢出风头吗？

Lady Gaga：No. I was a real pain in the ass.

记者：真的吗？怎么会？你做了什么事？

Lady Gaga：I just was very loud. I was always singing and dancing, and my father was always laughing with me, and I had a great childhood. I just was a very dramatic young woman. During free time, I was in the church playing some classical piece that I was learning or writing music. I just was a very creative young woman. And I'm just a very secluded person. I mean, just in all honesty, I only associate now even with the people that I work with. I don't really have many friends and it's the life that I choose.

Dialogue Interpretation 2

主持人：让我们大家用热烈的掌声欢迎美国总统奥巴马先生！

Obama：Good afternoon! It is a great honor for me to be here in Shanghai, and to have this opportunity to speak with all of you. So I'll start with this young lady right in the front.

学生1：我叫程熙，我是复旦大学的学生。上海和芝加哥从1985年开始就是姐妹城市，这两个城市进行过各种经济、政治、文化交流，您会采取什么措施来加深美国和中国城市之间的关系？谢谢！

Obama：Thank you very much for your question. It's wonderful to have these exchanges between cities. One of the things that I discussed with the Mayor is how both cities can learn from each other on strategies around clean energy.

学生1：总统先生，感谢您在就任第一年就访问中国并在中国与我们交流。我想知道此次中国之行您想收获什么。

Obama：The main purpose of my trip is to deepen my understanding of China and its vision for the future. In terms of what I'd like to get out of this meeting, having the wonderful opportunity to see the Forbidden City and the Great Wall, and meeting with all of you—these are all highlights.

学生2：总统先生，下午好！我来自同济大学。首先我想引用孔子的"有朋自远方来，不亦乐乎"这句话来欢迎您。中国推崇和而不同。我们知道美国文化的特点就在于多元性，请问您的这届政府会采取哪些措施去尊重各国不同的历史文化？谢谢您！

Obama: This is an excellent point. One of our strengths is that our culture is a very diverse culture. I think it's very important for the United States not to assume that what is good for us is automatically good for somebody else.

学生3：总统先生，我是来自于上海交通大学的一名学生。我想问一个有关于您得诺贝尔和平奖的问题。我们很好奇您的大学教育给您带来哪些影响，帮助您得到这个奖项。

Obama: Well, first of all, let me tell you that I don't know if there's a curriculum or course of study that leads you to win the Nobel Peace Prize. You know, successful people are those who are not only willing to work very hard but are constantly trying to improve themselves, to think in new ways, and not just accept the conventional wisdom.

主持人：谢谢奥巴马总统！也祝总统中国之行愉快！

Obama: I have had a wonderful time. I am so grateful to all of you.

Dialogue Interpretation 3

Host: Yang Lan is the chairwoman of Sun Media Group. I am very pleased to have her here at this table for the first time. Welcome.

杨澜：谢谢查理。谢谢邀请我来参加你的节目。

Host: Tell me how this started for you.

杨澜：这一切要从20年前大学即将毕业说起。那时候，中央电视台首次面向大学毕业生公开选拔《正大综艺》主持人。

Host: Have you thought about that kind of career before that?

杨澜：没有，完全没有。我在北京外国语大学主修英语语言文学。当我获得这个机会的时候，出于好奇就去了，我最后胜出，这为我在电视事业的发展奠定了很好的开端。

Host: So then you began to...

杨澜：之后我辞了工作来到美国，在哥伦比亚大学读研究生，主修国际关系。毕业后，我回香港加入凤凰卫视，开始制作自己的节目《杨澜访谈录》，这是当时中文电视的首个一对一深度访谈节目。

Host: Where did this entrepreneurial spirit that you have come from? The fact is that you have not just had a career, but you also have engaged in creating businesses and enterprises along with your husband.

杨澜：嗯，那是10年前，2000年。我们一起创立了阳光卫视，在大中华地区的第一个纪录片卫星频道。因为那时候，我非常沉迷于纪录片。但那个生意失败了。后来我们把频道卖了。

Host: Is there a website now that reflects the broadest understanding of who you are, what you are about and might even carry a blog from you?

杨澜: 我在中国几个领先的门户网站有博客,我也有推特。我们的天下女人网女性社区也有三四百万粉丝。

Host: Where is, you think, this remarkable career headed?

杨澜: 我不知道,我觉得中国现在有那么多令人兴奋的机遇。

Host: Finally, what brings you back to New York?

杨澜: 这次我是受邀参加在华盛顿举行的由《财富》杂志组织的全球最具权威女性大会,而且每次回纽约都让人感觉亲切。我在哥伦比亚大学住了3年,对这座城市有着深切的感情。

Host: We are glad to see you.

杨澜: 谢谢你,查理。

Exercises

I. Interpreting technique practice.

You will hear 10 sentences. Please try to memorize each sentence by using the technique learned in this section and retell each sentence.

II. Spot dictation.

Being prepared for a job interview will help you (1)_____ of answering questions and will help you make a (2)_____ on the interviewer. Here are some tips on how you can prepare ahead of time for the big day.

(3)_____ for the Interview

When you're looking for a job, it's important to always have one good suit to wear. That way you don't have to scramble, even if you get a last-minute call for an interview. Try everything on (4)_____ so you don't have any last-minute fashion disasters. Pay attention to details. Your hair, nails and shoes should all look polished and professional.

(5)_____ before the Job Interview

Use sites like Baidu and Bing.com to find information about the company, its management, and the positions the company typically offers. Use your connections to get (6)_____ that will help show the interviewer that you are knowledgeable about the company, its mission, and its employees.

(7)_____ the Interview

Plan your interview, request time off from work if you're employed, plan the logistics of getting to the interview with plenty of time (8)_____. Print out extra copies of your resumes and a list of references.

(9)_____

Do it by having a friend or family member run through typical questions with you. And also (10)_____ questions of your own, because you will be asked if you have any at the end of the interview. Stay calm and know that you're ready to do your best. You've spent time practicing and preparing, so you'll be ready to interview effectively.

Ⅲ. Sentence listening and translation.

1. _____
2. _____
3. _____
4. _____
5. _____

Ⅳ. Paragraph listening and translation.

_____

Ⅴ. Dialogue interpretation.

记者：From an employer's perspective, can you tell me specifically what makes it difficult to recruit workers?

用人单位1：招到合适的人员很难。更难的是招到研发人员。

用人单位2：我觉得困难就是大多数毕业生不去花时间了解公司，对企业文化也不了解就盲目地去投简历。

用人单位3：难就难在毕业生自己都不知道要找什么工作。

记者：What qualities do you value and expect from job applicants?

用人单位：态度、自我规划以及学习能力。

Ⅵ. Interpreting in groups.

Role-play the following situation with your partners, acting as the Chinese speaker, English speaker and the interpreter respectively. One group will be invited to perform in class.

Participants: 1. Mr. John Stevenson, a journalist
2. Student of Jiangnan University
3. Interpreter

Location: Jiangnan University

Task: John Stevenson, a journalist with an American newspaper, visited Jiangnan University. He made an interview with a first-year student on campus, asking him/her some questions about his/her study and college life.

VII. 3-minute talk on the given topic.

Talk on the following topic in three minutes based on the given reference questions.

Topic: **Meeting new people**

Questions for Reference:

1. Do you enjoy meeting new people? Why or why not?
2. What is the favorite topic for new acquaintances in your country?
3. What are some things you shouldn't ask people you have just met?

VIII. Theme-related expressions.

采访术语

大型电视系列片	maxi-series
自由撰稿人	freelance writer
特约撰稿人	guest writer
专栏作家	columnist
特派记者	special correspondent
消息灵通人士	well-informed source
权威人士/来源	authoritative source
新闻稿,通讯稿	news release
头条新闻	headline
独家新闻	exclusive news
抢先报道的独家新闻	scoop
内幕消息	inside story
花边新闻	box news
小道消息	grapevine news
时事	current news
专题报道	special report
狗仔队	paparazzi

访谈句型：

1. 你能说说中美两国商人在商务沟通方式上有何差异吗？
Could you tell us how you feel about the differences in business communication

style between Chinese and American businessmen?

2. 我们要承认并尊重这些文化差异以免产生误解，这一点很重要，不是吗？

It is important for all of us to acknowledge and respect these cultural differences in order to avoid misunderstandings, isn't it?

3. 刚才你提到了中国式的决策过程。您认为这种管理模式有无优点？将其与美国式的管理模式相比，您有何看法？

You mentioned the Chinese style of decision-making process earlier. Do you see any strength with this kind of management and how do you compare it with the American style of management?

4. 谈到员工的工作态度，中国人和美国人在这方面有何不同？

Talking about workers' attitude toward their work, how do the Chinese and the Americans differ in this respect?

5. 回到我们一开始的话题，您如何评价两种不同经营之道的利弊呢？

Returning to where we started, how do you comment on the merits and demerits of the two different approaches to business management?

6. 您如何看待在中国中西部地区进行长期投资的前景？

How do you view the prospects of making long-term investment in China's central and western regions?

7. 您认为应当建立一个什么样的世界新格局？

What in your view would be the kind of new international configuration of power that should be established?

8. 我要提的问题是，中美关系是否处在一个充满危险变数的十字路口？

My question is, do you believe that Sino-US relations are brought to the crossroads full of risky uncertainties?

9. 您能阐明一下贵国政府的环保政策吗？

Could you elaborate on your government policy with regard to environmental protection?

10. 谢谢您接受我的采访。

Thank you for sharing your time with me!

Section C Further Exploration

根据所给的中文填入所缺英文。

A: Mr. Chen, we often hear employers say it's not difficult to recruit people, but very difficult to (1) _____ _____. Why is that?

A: 陈先生，我们看到用人单位经常说招人并不难，但是<u>招到合适的人</u>特别难，这是什么原因呢？

B: That's the core of the problem. Every company needs capable people with (2) _____. But you will see those really dedicated employees only (3) _____ all workers. A US survey found the percentage lies between 20 percent and 30 percent. More than 50 percent of employees drift through each day and only do (4) _____. Another 20 percent don't fit into the workplace and feel pained to go to work. I think it applies to workplaces worldwide.

B：这个就是问题的实质所在。每一个企业都需要能人，都需要有经验、有专业知识、创造力和能动性的人。但是在职场上你会看到真正敬业的员工在整个职工队伍中只占一个很小的比例。美国的调查发现其百分比是20％到30％，但半数以上的员工是当一天和尚撞一天钟，你让我干什么我就干什么。还有20％的人根本不适应职场，来上班就很痛苦。我认为全世界的职场都是这样。

A: Some employers told us they believe (5) _____. They think many graduates never try to create value for their companies but think too highly of themselves by asking for (6) _____. What do you think of such complaints?

A：我们采访的一些雇主还告诉我们，他们认为现在的大学毕业生普遍存在一个问题，就是许多毕业生不去努力为企业创造价值，反而高估自己，向企业索要高薪、高职、高福利。您怎么看待企业对大学生的这种不满？

B: Companies and employers exercise "hard constraints". They are neither charity organizations nor schools offering compulsory education. (7) _____. That's why I call it "hard constraints", meaning employees are the ones to follow rules, not the other way round.

B：因为企业职场有"硬性约束"，它不是慈善机构，也不是义务教育制学校。它的首要目标就是创造利润。所以我就说这个叫"硬性约束"，意思是只有你服从它，没有它服从你的。

A: While employers might have complaints about college graduates, but are the latter the only party (8) _____?

A：招工者也许对大学毕业生有诸多抱怨，但只有后者应该受到指责吗？

B: It's natural for employers to maximize profits, but they also need to think about graduates' request on salaries. Without a win-win attitude, between employers and employees, it would be difficult to (9) _____. We can find there are a lot of unfair conditions for employees during recruitment. Many employers still (10) _____. This is in fact not helpful for the company's long-term development.

B：用人单位肯定选择企业利益的最大化，但也要考虑毕业生的薪资待遇的要求。因为只考虑单方面的利益没有一个双赢的态度，雇佣双方其实也很难形成长久的合作关系。我们注意到，现在在招聘过程中有很多霸王条款，还有很多单位还是将大学生当成廉价劳动力。这实际上不利于企业的长期发展。

UNIT 7

Sports
体育运动

Learning Objectives

1. To learn how to translate sentences with active voice and passive voice;
2. To learn how to take notes for interpretation (1);
3. To learn how to translate/interpret passages or dialogues on the topic of sports;
4. To learn useful words and expressions related to sports and games.

Lead-in

● *Quiz* (**Answer the following questions**)

1. What sport is played at Wimbledon? _____
2. In which city and country were the 2000 Summer Olympic Games held?
_____
3. What country does the soccer player Lionel Andrés Messi come from?
_____
4. In which sport was Muhammad Ali the world champion? _____
5. How many bases are there on a baseball field? _____
6. In which country were the 2014 Winter Olympic Games held? _____
7. Is baseball played with an oval ball? _____
8. How many holes are there in a typical golf course? _____
9. On what kind of surface is the French Tennis Open played, clay surface or hard surface? _____
10. What sport does the Houston Rockets play? _____

● **What are they? Fill in the blanks with English words.**

frisbee   snooker   wrestling   ice hockey
figure skating   baseball   diving   golf
rock climbing   surfing   rugby   fencing
pole vault   bungee jumping   balance beam

1. _____   2. _____   3. _____   4. _____   5. _____

6. _____   7. _____   8. _____   9. _____   10. _____

11. _____   12. _____   13. _____   14. _____   15. _____

Section A   Translation

Translation Technique

主动表达和被动表达

汉语表达往往突出动作和动作执行者，但动词没有形态变化。英语表达往往不必突出动作的执行者，但动词有复杂的形态变化。反映在句法形态中，汉语句子往往多用主动语态，而英语句子中则广泛使用被动语态。汉语句式在译成英语时常译为被动式。

1. 无主句

原文：装配和调试的时候应该把所有零件清洗干净。

译文：When being assembled and adjusted, all parts should be cleaned.

2. 泛指人称句（It is ... that ... ）

原文：众所周知，改革开放三十多年来经济发展取得了显著的成绩。

译文：It is well known that remarkable success has been attained in economic development since China implemented the policy of reform and opening-up over 30 years ago.

3. 话题评说句

原文：长江上已经建起了上百座大桥。

译文：Over 100 bridges have been built across the Yangtze River.

4. "由"字句

原文：这个任务由小刘完成。

译文：This task will be completed by Xiao Liu.

5. "把"字句

原文：你把她吓得哭起来了。

译文：She was scared to tears (by you).

英语的被动语态分为"结构被动"和"意义被动"两种，前者更为常见。结构被动指的是使用被动语态的结构（be + done）来表示被动的意思，而意义被动则是用主动形式表示被动的意义。英译汉时被动语态一般有以下几种常用方法：

1. 把英语的被动句直接转换成汉语的被动句，通常句中带有被动词（如"受""被""遭受""遭遇"等）

原文：During the wars, many national treasures were seized and taken away by foreign invaders.

译文：在战争期间，许多国宝遭到外国侵略者的掠夺。

原文：The play was widely-accepted by the Chinese, the theatres filled rapidly.

译文：该剧深受中国观众的青睐，剧院一下子就坐满了人。

2. 把英语的被动句转换成汉语的话题评述句或主动句

原文：The latest version of the vehicle was featured by the state-of-the-art technology in the industry.

译文：最新出来的这款车的特点是拥有行业内尖端的技术。

3. 把英语的特殊被动句转换成无主句或泛称句

原文：It is reported that China's economy growth will exceed 8 percent this year.

译文：据报道，中国的经济增长速度今年将超过8%。

4. 把某些"by+施动者"表示原因的英语被动句转换成汉语的"因为……"

原文：It is a long way from Beijing to London. The distance has sometimes seemed to be compounded by historical, philosophical and political gaps in our outlooks.

译文：北京和伦敦相距甚远。这距离有时似乎更遥远了，因为在历史、哲学和政治方面，我们的观点相去甚远。

Passage Translation 1

Vocabulary

1. 岩画

2. 陶俑

3. 马球

4. 文人墨客

5. 《醉打金枝》

6. 蹴鞠

7. 《水浒传》

8. 垂丸

9. 民族传统体育

10. 箭术

11. 踢毽球

12. 拔河

13. 赛牦牛

14. 荡秋千

15. 抛绣球

16. 跳板

17. 踩高跷

18. 打陀螺

19. 秧歌

20. 太极拳

21. 健身房

22. 健身设施

23. 新兴产业

24. 体育大国

25. 竞技体育

中国体育在秦、汉和三国时期开始真正成形。历朝以来，体育运动场景在岩画、陶俑和诗歌中都有记录。唐朝时马球在皇宫、军队和文人墨客中很流行，连妇女也很喜欢。著名中国古代戏剧《醉打金枝》中描写的公主就酷爱这项运动。宋朝时期，作为现代足球运动的最初形式，蹴鞠（一种内填毛发的皮球），非常受欢迎，上至皇帝下至普通百姓都参与这项运动。在《水浒传》中，高俅就曾因为擅长踢蹴鞠而官居高位。元朝时期，人们喜欢一种叫作垂丸的运动，它与现代高尔夫运动相似。人们用一根一端弯曲的棍子把球击入洞中。击中数目最多者胜出。除了球类运动，摔跤、舞蹈、下棋、赛马等都是当时人们的日常消遣。

当时中国少数民族的夏季运动包括箭术、打猎、摔跤和赛马。冬季他们喜爱滑雪、滑冰和滑雪橇比赛。新中国成立以后，中国政府大力发展民族传统体育。在多达 1000 多种的少数民族体育项目中，较为有名的是蒙古族的摔跤、赛马和箭术，回族的踢毽球和拔河,藏族的赛牦牛,苗族的荡秋千和赛龙舟,壮族的抛绣球,朝鲜族的荡秋千和跳板,满族的滑冰,侗族的踩高跷,以及瑶族的打陀螺。

赛龙舟、放风筝、秧歌、围棋、气功和太极拳是在各民族中都广为流传的传统体育项目。

如今中国人对健身日益重视,生活方式也随之发生了很大变化。在一些大中城市,花钱健身已日益流行。中国各地有许多健身房和体育馆,它们大多对公众开放,得到广泛使用。健身设施在社区和其他公共场所随处可见。人们用不同方式参与健身正日益成为一种趋势。体育作为新兴产业,近年来在中国发展迅速。体育用品行业总产值以每年约500亿元的速度增长。

中国已是一个体育大国。竞技体育得到了快速发展。特别是在北京奥运会上,中国运动员打破了43项世界纪录和132个奥运会纪录,获得了51枚金牌。

Notes

1. "历朝以来,体育运动场景在岩画、陶俑和诗歌中都有记录。"这句话的英译可以使用被动语态,体育运动场景有记录指的是体育运动场景被记录了下来,以"体育运动场景"为主题,译为:"Sporting scenes have been recorded over the dynasties in stone paintings, pottery figurines and poems."

2. "宋朝时期,作为现代足球运动的最初形式,蹴鞠(一种内填毛发的皮球),非常受欢迎,上至皇帝下至平民百姓都参与这项运动。"这句虽然是长句,但句子内部逻辑关系还是很明显的,"一种内填毛发的皮球"可以英译成同位语,修饰"蹴鞠";"非常受欢迎"与"上至皇帝下至平民百姓都参与这项运动"这两个部分可以用"so … that"句型,显化后者是前者的结果。因此,全句译成:"In the Song Dynasty, *cuju*, a primitive soccer game using a leather ball filled with hair, was so popular that everyone from the emperor to ordinary people participated in it."

3. "中国各地有许多健身房和体育馆,它们大多对公众开放,得到广泛使用。健身设施在社区和其他公共场所随处可见。"这两句话中,前句的主题是健身房和体育馆,它们并不是"对公众开放,得到广泛使用"的动作施动者,不能翻译成主语,翻译时可以避开施动者,使用被动语态。后句话中的"可见"在汉语带有被动意义,也可使用被动语态。因此,这两句话可以译成:"There are many gymnasiums and stadiums across China. Most of them are open to and widely used by the general public. Body-building equipment can be found everywhere in communities or other public places."

4. "中国已是一个体育大国。竞技体育得到了快速发展。"汉译英时,用来作修饰语的"体育"可以英译成"sports"或"sporting",如 sports/sporting event(体育比赛项目), sports celebrity(体育明星)。前句话中的体育大国可以译成:"sports/sporting power"。此外,这两句话可以用合句法翻译,译成:"China has become a sporting power, with its competitive sports developing rapidly."

109

Passage Translation 2

Vocabulary

1. play tag
2. arm wrestler
3. tumble
4. anguish
5. creative forces
6. competitive games
7. ruthless
8. sportsmanship
9. play fair
10. pep talk

When did sport begin? If sport is, in essence, play, the claim might be made that sport is much older than humankind, for, as we all have observed, the beasts play. Dogs and cats wrestle and play ball games. Fishes and birds dance. The apes have simple and pleasurable games. Young animals, particularly, tumble, chase, run, wrestle, imitate, and laugh to the point of delighted exhaustion. Their play, and ours, appears to serve no other purpose than to give pleasure to the players, and apparently, to remove us temporarily from the anguish of life. Some philosophers have claimed that our playfulness is the noblest part of our basic nature. In their general conceptions, to play harmlessly and experimentally permits us to put our creative forces, fantasy, and imagination into action.

First or second graders may be more eager to talk about the fun they have in sports. As they move into more competitive games, kids become more focused on winning. They often forget to have fun. Without constant reminders and good examples, they may also forget what behavior is appropriate before, during, and after a sporting event. If a child has a coach who cares only about being in the first place, the child picks up the message that it's OK to be ruthless on the field. If parents are constantly pressing them to play better, children will try any method of achieving one.

Adults who emphasize good sportsmanship, however, see winning as just one of the several goals they'd like their kids to achieve. They help young athletes take pride in their accomplishments, so that the kids see themselves as winners, even if the scoreboard doesn't show the numbers going in their favor. The best coaches and parents encourage their kids to play fair, to have fun, and to concentrate on helping the team. Remember the saying, "Actions speak louder than words". That's especially true when it comes to teaching your kids the basis of good sportsmanship. Your behavior during practices and games will influence them more than any pep talk or lecture you give them.

Notes

1. "If sport is, in essence, play, the claim might be made that sport is much older than humankind, for, as we all have observed, beasts play." 此句中的被动语态部分 "the claim might be made that" 可用泛指人称译成主动语态"我们就可以认为"。全句译成："如果体育运动的本质就是游戏的话，我们就可以认为体育运动比人类古老，因为正如我们所观察到的，野兽也进行嬉戏。"

2. "Young animals, particularly, tumble, chase, run, wrestle, imitate, and laugh to the point of delighted exhaustion." 这句话中的"delighted exhaustion"不要死译成"开心得筋疲力尽"，根据上下文，小动物们是玩得很开心，一直玩到筋疲力尽，因此可以译成"开开心心地玩到筋疲力尽"。全句译成："特别是小动物们，它们翻筋斗、追逐、奔跑、扭打、模仿、嬉笑，开开心心地玩到筋疲力尽。"

3. "Without constant reminders and good examples, they may also forget what behavior is appropriate before, during, and after a sporting event." 句中"without constant reminders and good examples"部分如果直译，应该是"如果没有人一直提醒他们，给他们树立榜样"，"提醒和树立榜样"都是对孩子树立体育精神的正确指引，所以也可意译为"在没有人正确指引的情况下"。全句可译成："在没有人正确指引的情况下，他们会忘记在赛前、赛中和比赛后保持良好的举止。"

4. "Adults who emphasize good sportsmanship, however, see winning as just one of the several goals they'd like their kids to achieve." "sportsmanship"意为"体育精神"，"good sportsmanship"根据上下文，译为"高尚的体育精神"。全句译为："那些强调高尚体育精神的成年人，却把获胜看作是希望自己孩子完成的众多目标之一。"

5. "Your behavior during practices and games will influence them more than any pep talk or lecture you give them." 句中的"influence"的意义不是简单的"影响"，根据上下文语境，是指在教育孩子体育精神时，父母的以身作则（behavior）相比较于鼓舞士气的讲话和说教（pep talk or lecture you give them）作用更大或效果更好。因此，全句译为："成年人在孩子训练和比赛时以身作则，效果要比任何鼓舞士气的讲话和说教都好得多。"

Sentences in Focus

1. 中国体育在秦、汉和三国时期开始真正成形。历朝以来，体育运动场景在岩画、陶俑和诗歌中都有记录。

2. 宋朝时期，作为现代足球运动的最初形式，蹴鞠（一种内填毛发的皮球），非常受欢迎，上至皇帝下至普通百姓都参与这项运动。

3. 在多达1000多种的少数民族体育项目中，较为有名的是蒙古族的摔跤、赛马和箭术，回族的踢毽球和拔河，藏族的赛牦牛，苗族的荡秋千和赛龙舟，壮族的抛绣球，朝鲜族的荡秋千和跳板，满族的滑冰，侗族的踩高跷，以及瑶族的打陀螺。

4. 赛龙舟、放风筝、秧歌、围棋、气功和太极拳是在各民族中都广为流传的传统体育项目。

5. 中国已是一个体育大国。中国竞技体育得到了快速发展。

6. If sport is, in essence, play, the claim might be made that sport is much older than humankind, for, as we all have observed, the beasts play.

7. Young animals, particularly, tumble, chase, run, wrestle, imitate, and laugh to the point of delighted exhaustion.

8. Adults who emphasize sportsmanship, however, see winning as just one of the several goals they'd like their kids to achieve.

9. They help young athletes take pride in their accomplishments, so that the kids see themselves as winners, even if the scoreboard doesn't show the numbers going in their favor.

10. The best coaches and parents encourage their kids to play fair, to have fun, and to concentrate on helping the team.

Exercises

I. Fill in the blanks with English words according to the given Chinese.

1. The Olympic motto is "_____"（更快、更高、更强）which means that one's focus should be on bettering one's achievements, rather than on coming in first.
2. Nearly 3,800 athletes _____（参与）the Nanjing 2014 Summer Youth Olympic Games.
3. A _____（技能娴熟的）*cuju* player could be highly valued by emperors in ancient China.
4. Playing Mahjong, a popular _____（日常消遣方式）is found effective in brain training of the elderly.
5. Mongolian wrestling, whistling archery, fireworks-snatching, horse wrestling, dragon dance, swinging, bar running race, stilt running race, are some of the _____（少数民族体育运动）that express their vigor and enthusiasm in special ways.
6. Students were required to play badminton at the _____（体育馆）due to heavy rain.
7. We have many modern _____（健身设施）catering to the

different needs of our members.

8. Chinese athletes won a total of 106 gold medals in 27 sports events in Olympic Games, World Championships and World Cups, of which 53 were Olympic golds in 17 events. In a word, in 2004 China made remarkable achievements in _____ _____（竞技体育）.

9. Climbers walked along the arch of the Sydney Harbour Bridge behind the Sydney Opera House on May 30, 2014, as they attempted to _____ _____（破纪录）for the number of people on the arch of the famous bridge at the same time.

10. James Cleveland Owens, the first American _____（运动员）to win four gold medals in one Olympics, was born in 1913.

II. Translate the following passive-voice sentences into Chinese.

1. This product is characterized by its durability and reliable function.
   _____
   _____

2. Dragon boat races are held at the festival while *zongzi* are consumed by the living.
   _____
   _____

3. It is predicted that the global population is expected to increase from six billion to eight billion over the next 25 years.
   _____
   _____

4. Significant achievements have been made in the field of environmental protection.
   _____
   _____

5. I was criticized by the manager for my inactivity in the team work.
   _____
   _____

III. Translate the following sentences.

1. Julien Absalon from France is a world-famous mountain bike cyclist who won two Olympic gold medals, four World Championships and 17 World Cups.
   _____
   _____

2. The Qatar women's basketball team gave up in a match at the Asian Games on Wednesday after being refused permission to wear the Islamic headscarf.
   _____
   _____

3. Coupling physical education with the national college entrance examination might encourage more schools to boost the time and quality of sports participation on campus.

4. Beijing announced at its work conference for sports on Feb 4 that it plans to develop winter sports and campus football when it is bidding for the 2022 Winter Olympics.

5. After the home team Brazil lost to Germany in the semifinals 1 to 7, many have cast the blame onto legendary rocker Mick Jagger（米克·贾格尔）.

6. 舞狮不仅是一种受欢迎的传统节日活动,也是一项竞技体育。

7. 2008年中国在北京主办了第29届奥运会,实现了亿万中国人民的梦想。

8. 人们花钱在健身房和体育馆健身正日益成为一种趋势。

9. 竞技体育的快速发展带来了体育产业总产值的增长。

10. 自巴西世界杯开幕以来,数千万的中国球迷聚集在客厅、学校的宿舍、酒吧以及餐厅观看比赛。

IV. Translate the following paragraphs.

1. China's two-time Grand Slam winner Li Na announced her retirement via Sina microblog on Friday morning and will hold a press conference on Sunday in Beijing, according to her agent company. Speculation over Li's retirement has been rife ever since the 32-year-old pulled out of the US Open and other hard-court tournaments afterwards due to knee injuries. But insiders thought she will not hang up her racket before playing in home tournaments.

2. 最近的一项调查发现,从第一夫人到学生和家庭主妇,在美国有2000多万人练习瑜伽。发生改变的不仅仅是热爱瑜伽的人多了,瑜伽的风格也多样化了起来。瑜伽源于印度并进而风靡世界。如今,中国的年轻人练习瑜伽也日益成为一种趋势。相信瑜伽产业在中国将成为一个值得投资的新兴产业。

Section B Interpretation

Interpretation Technique

口译技能:口译笔记(1)

常言道,好记性不如烂笔头。我们的短时记忆容量有限,不足以应付长段信息的记忆。因此,在口译时,我们需要借助于笔记将经过大脑综合分析过的信息提取出来。

口译笔记应记要点,切忌"全""乱"。口译笔记是记忆的延伸或补充,不应也不可能取代脑记。在口译中,我们没有必要将整段的信息完整地记录下来,过多地依赖笔记只会适得其反,导致注意力全在记录上,而忽视了对信息意义的总体把握。信息记忆还是应当靠大脑来完成,笔记只是一个辅助工具,帮助我们集中精力,将获取的信息意义有条理地储存在大脑中。笔记不是信息源语形式的简单再现,而是将理解的关键信息记录下来,这样笔记才可以成为帮助我们记忆的一个有效工具。

那么在笔记中,具体应当记什么呢?一是记主题词、关键词和逻辑线索词,它们是理解之后信息的主要内容。二是记不需要理解但又容易忘的内容,如数字、专有名词和列举的项目等。

例如:There is one more gold medal to award tonight. This gold medal belongs to all Greeks, because for 17 days we all represented Greece, on the track, in the pool and on the sea, at the venue gates and the Olympic lanes, on the courts and on the mats, in the stands, on the springboard and on the rings, in the Press Centers and the Olympic Village.

笔记示例:
```
          god mdl / →G°
∵    17 ds / △ G
          track          ⎫
          pool + sea     ⎪
          gates          ⎪
          O lanes        ⎪
          court + mat    ⎬
          std            ⎪
          S B + rings    ⎪
          P C            ⎪
          O V            ⎭
```

很显然,上面的笔记并没有把全部文字都记录下来,但是凭借这个笔记,在短时间里,我们可以结合短时记忆,轻松地回忆所听信息的大意。笔记中记下的都是一些关键词、专有名词和数字。逻辑线索词"because"用数学符号"∵"表示。此外,所有列举的项目都竖着排列,逻辑清楚。

Passage Interpretation 1

中国武术深受老百姓喜爱,因为它可以强身健体。武术练习强度不同,形式也多种多样,人们可以根据自己的年龄、兴趣和身体状况进行选择。而且,练武术不需要很大的地方和复杂的设备,易于推广。近几年来,武术辅导站遍及全国。很多身体欠佳的人通过长期练习武术得到益处。许多医院也利用武术作为治疗慢性病的方法。

武术还是一种表演艺术。在中国360多种地方戏中,武术的作用非同一般。有些戏专门表现精彩的武打动作。国内外的功夫片中也充满华人大师的武术动作,吸引了大量观众。

功夫和武术最早是一回事。但近三十年来武术已经成为一门具有竞技性、表演性和对抗性的体育项目。太极拳是一种徒手的武术,是练身、练意、练气三结合的整体运动。气功是中国独特的一种深呼吸健身术。

Passage Interpretation 2

Ball games have become an integral part of modern society. They give us entertainment, providing us a means to safely free ourselves from stress. There are many different ball games that can do this for us. Some people enjoy football, while others like basketball. These two ball games are the most popular in China. Other games such as baseball are growing in appeal, yet have not become popular. The development of these games is interesting. Football, or soccer, originally developed from ball games found in both China and Europe. It has grown to become the world's most popular sport. Football clubs were first established in Europe and then founded in the rest of the world. These football clubs train players who may later go play for their nations in the World Cup. This is the most-watched ballgame championship on the planet. Basketball is one of the few sports with a known date of birth. It was created in 1891 by James Naismith. The teams of the

National Basketball Association or NBA are becoming household names in China. The rise of such stars in China as Yao Ming highlights the creation of the Chinese Basketball Association, or CBA. This popularity of sports has led to the further development of the sports industry. It is important that these organizations were established so that people would have a safe way to relax and enjoy themselves.

Dialogue Interpretation

A: China is now a sporting power. Could you tell me more about sports in China?

B: 好的。为了增强人民体质,中华全国体育总会制订了国家体育锻炼标准和全民健身计划。目前体育运动在城乡普遍开展,全国有1/3的人经常参加体育运动。现在人民的健康状况有了很大改善,平均寿命超过70岁。

A: How do Chinese people participate in sports?

B: 许多社区都有便利的健身设备。除此之外,羽毛球馆、健身中心等活动场所也受到越来越多人的青睐。一些具有中国特点的传统体育项目也是人们喜爱的运动方式,例如武术、太极拳、气功等。

A: It seems that Chinese people are in favor of traditional sports. Do Chinese people like outdoor sports?

B: 我正想说这点。由于户外运动有助于缓解繁重工作和激烈竞争的压力,越来越多的中国人迷上了户外运动,攀岩、滑雪、漂流等户外运动日益火爆。

A: I guess the sports industry must be flourishing in China.

B: 完全正确。现在,体育消费在人们生活中所占的比重越来越大。电视转播、体育广告、体育彩票等相关体育产业发展迅速。

A: And I noticed China's quick rise in the Olympic medal rankings over the last two decades.

B: 是的,这很大程度上归功于举国体制。按照这种机制,运动员的训练费用、路费、出国比赛费用均由国家承担。

A: So, only the government sponsors the development of sports in China, right?

B: 也不完全是。近年来,一些企业、高等院校、商业性体育俱乐部甚至个人也会赞助专业运动队,培养高水平运动员。

Exercises

I. Interpreting technique practice.

Please try to take notes of key words and logic words in each sentence by using the technique learned in this section and retell each sentence based on the key words.

1. _____

2. _____

3. _____

4. _____

5. _____

6. _____

7. _____

8. _____

9. _____

10. _____

Ⅱ. Spot dictation.

　　Competitive video gaming—known as (1)_____—should be included in the Olympic Games, the creator of World of Warcraft has told the BBC. Rob Pardo, who until July was the chief creative officer at Blizzard Entertainment, said "sport" now had a broad definition. "Videogames are well positioned to be a (2)_____," he told Afternoon Edition on BBC 5 Live.

　　Professional e-sports (3)_____ currently attract audiences of millions. A recent (4)_____ held in Seoul, South Korea, filled a stadium of 40,000 people—with many more watching either online or at meet-ups around the world.

　　"There's a very good argument for e-sports being in the Olympics," Mr. Pardo, who was also lead designer on StarCraft: Brood War(《星际争霸：母巢之战》), a game often credited with (5)_____ the e-sports phenomenon.

　　"I think e-sports is a very (6)_____. You will see those (7)_____ who have to be lightning quick in reflexes and decision making." However, he conceded that video gaming faces a (8)_____ to win those who follow more physical sports.

　　"The point is how you define sport," he said, "If you want to define sport as something that takes a lot of (9)_____, then it's hard to argue that videogames should be a sport, but at the same time, when I'm looking at things that are already in the

Olympics, I start questioning the definition."

Having new sports admitted into the Olympic roster is a (10) _____ process and has become increasingly difficult since the International Olympic Committee (IOC) capped the number of sports allowed in the Games.

Even if e-sports were to be recognized as an Olympic sport, that does not mean it will be included in the Games. It merely means a case that can be presented to the IOC.

III. Sentence listening and translation.

1. _____
2. _____
3. _____
4. _____
5. _____

IV. Paragraph listening and translation.

_____

Ⅴ. **Dialogue interpretation.**

A: What sport is your favorite, Mr. Smith?
B: 网球。而且我知道李娜是来自中国的网球选手,两届大满贯得主。
A: Yes. But I feel regret to tell you that she announced her retirement via Sina Microblog last Friday.
B: 真遗憾。但我相信会有越来越多的人参与到这个流行的体育项目中去的。
A: Definitely. The government has laid down policies to encourage national fitness. It will, indirectly or directly, help people to maintain physical fitness and promote the development of sport industry.
B: 从这个层面来看,这对百姓以及国民经济都是一项重要举措。
A: I can't agree with you more. Now, many residential community centers are equipped with fitness facilities so that people can exercise or play sports free of charge. How about taking a look with me?
B: 好主意。

Ⅵ. **Interpreting in groups.**

Role-play the following situation with your partners, acting as the Chinese speaker, English speaker and the interpreter respectively. One group will be invited to perform in class.

Participants: 1. Jack, international student
2. Li Wei's father
3. Li Wei, interpreter

Task: Li Wei's father is a *kung fu* lover who has been into this sport for twenty years. Jack, an international student from Denmark, studies at Jiangnan University and takes great interest in this traditional Chinese sport. Li Wei introduces Jack to his father who tells Jack more about the history of *kung fu* as well as the *kung fu* stars well known in the world. Li Wei's father speaks Chinese while Jack is an English-speaker.

Ⅶ. **3-minute talk on the given topic.**

Talk on the following topic in three minutes based on the given reference questions.

Topic: **Find time to play sports**
Questions for Reference:
1. Do you often play sports? Why or why not?
2. What are the benefits of playing sports?
3. What is your suggestion for those who don't like playing sports?

VIII. Theme-related expressions.

• 世界纪录	world record
• 冠军	champion
• 亚军	runner-up/the 2nd place
• 季军	the 3rd place
• 取得决赛权的八名选手	the last eight
• 决赛名次	final placing
• 奖牌榜	medal tally
• 卫冕冠军	defend champion
• 颁奖仪式	victory and ceremony/awarding ceremony
• 风格奖	sportsmanship trophy
• 奖杯	cup/trophy
• 世界大学生运动会	World University Games
• 邀请赛	invitational tournament
• 锦标赛	championship
• 残疾人奥林匹克运动会(残奥会)	Paralympic Games
• 火炬接力/火炬传递	torch relay
• 吉祥物	mascot
• 水上运动	aquatics
• 田径	track and field
• 马术	equestrian
• 体操	gymnastics
• 现代五项	modern pentathlon
• 铁人三项	triathlon
• 举重	weightlifting
• 摔跤	wrestling

Section C Further Exploration

Read about the introduction of some popular sports in the world and translate the underlined words into Chinese with the help of the pictures and words.

1. <u>Aerial yoga</u>, a new fitness exercise in which practitioners hang from a hammock suspended from the ceiling, is becoming popular in Japan. 近日,一种名为"＿＿＿＿＿"的新型健身运动在日本悄然流行,练习者借助挂在房顶上的吊床悬在空中。

2. <u>Parkour</u> is a sport in which participants jump, vault, and climb over obstacles in a fluid manner. It is a non-competitive way to move fluidly in a complex environment. It was developed by the French. "＿＿＿＿＿",指参与者用跳跃、跨越或者攀爬等一系列流畅的动作通过障碍物的一种运动。这是用一种非竞技性的方式在复杂环境中自由移动的运动,是由法国人发明的。

3. A new fad is led by <u>figurerobics</u>, a training approach combining both muscular and aerobic training with rhythmic music. 最近流行一种名叫"＿＿＿＿＿"的塑身运动,这种运动配合有节奏的音乐进行肌肉有氧训练。

4. Michelle Obama managed to spin a <u>hula hoop</u> for 142 revolutions at a fair at the White House to promote children's health. America's First Lady hosted a group of school children to the White House for a Healthy Kids Fair on Wednesday. 日前,米歇尔·奥巴马在白宫举行的一个儿童健康推广会上转起了＿＿＿＿＿,共连续转了142下。美国第一夫人米歇尔于本周三邀请一群学生前往白宫参加一个儿童健康宣讲会。

UNIT 8
Education Home and Abroad
中外教育

Learning Objectives

1. To know how to translate long sentences;
2. To learn how to take notes for interpretation(2);
3. To learn how to translate / interpret passages or dialogues on the topic of education;
4. To learn useful words and expressions related to education.

Lead-in

● *Quiz* (True or False)

_____ 1. The imperial examination in ancient China, designed to select prospective officials for the royal court, was conducted at two levels, *xiangshi* (provincial level) and *huishi* (national level).

_____ 2. The candidate of imperial examination who won the first place was called *zhuangyuan*. The one who won the second place was called *tanhua* while *bangyan* went into the third one.

_____ 3. Children in the U.S. are usually divided by age groups into grades, ranging from kindergarten and first grade for the youngest children, up to tenth grade as the final year of high school.

_____ 4. China's 12-year compulsory education consists of two parts: 6 years in primary school and 6 years in high school.

_____ 5. Generally speaking, undergraduates are expected to complete 4 years of learning before they earn their bachelor's degree in China.

_____ 6. Ivy League colleges and universities refer to eight east-coast colleges and universities renowned for their high academic standards and significant history.

_____ 7. The "211" program was designed to develop about 100 key institutions of higher learning with key research projects poised to meet challenges in the 21st century.

● **Fill in the blanks with the top universities in English.**

1. 北京大学　　2. 牛津大学　　3. 悉尼大学　　4. 清华大学

5. 剑桥大学　　6. 麻省理工学院　　7. 耶鲁大学　　8. 帝国理工学院

9. 哈佛大学　　10. 普林斯顿大学　　11. 早稻田大学　　12. 香港大学

Section A　Translation

Translation Technique

拆句法和合句法

拆句法和合句法是两种相对应的翻译方法。

拆句法是把一个长而复杂的句子拆译成几个简单、简短的句子。这种方法常用于英译汉。例如：

原文：Keeping fit and leading a reasonable and regular life is the material basis for self-cultivation.

译文： 保持身体健康，生活方式合理而有规律，这是自我修养的物质基础。

合句法是把几个短句合并成一个长句。汉语强调意合，结构较松散，因此简单句较多。所以汉译英时要根据句意利用连词、分词、介词、不定式、定语从句、独立结构等把汉语短句连成长句。例如：

原文： 中国是个大国，百分之八十的人口从事农业，但耕地只占土地面积的十分之一，其余为山脉、森林、城镇和其他用地。

译文： China is a large country with four-fifths of the population engaged in agriculture, but only one tenth of the land is farmland, the rest being mountains, forests and places for urban and other uses.

原文： People are the same everywhere. They are born. They are babies. They are children. They are adults. They grow old. They die.

译文： 各地的人都是一样的。人生下来都要经历从婴儿、儿童、成年人直至衰老死亡的各个人生阶段。

原文： Pitcher was a quiet man who usually didn't let his face show his feelings.

译文： 皮切尔不爱说话，不轻易在脸上显露喜怒哀乐。

Passage Translation 1

Vocabulary

1. 希望工程
2. 春蕾计划
3. 国家助学奖学金
4. 勤工助学
5. 特殊困难补助
6. 学费减免
7. 国家助学贷款
8. 九年制义务教育
9. 扫盲
10. 素质教育
11. 德育、智育、体育和美育
12. 专业资格认证培训与考试
13. 继续教育
14. 终生教育

自1949年中华人民共和国成立以来,中国政府一向十分重视发展教育事业,实行以政府办学为主体,社会机构及个人共同办学的体制。除了教育投入逐年增加外,还实施了希望工程和春蕾计划。希望工程于1989年由中国青少年发展基金会发起,目的在于帮助贫困地区辍学少年儿童,向国内外社会力量集资助学。1992年发起的春蕾计划是为了帮助辍学女童重返校园。此外,为保证家庭经济困难的学生获得高等教育机会,中国政府采取有效措施,诸如国家助学奖学金制度、勤工助学制度、特殊困难补助制度、学费减免制度、国家助学贷款制度等。

中国教育的近期目标是在全国大部分地区基本普及九年制义务教育,在大城市试行普及高中阶段教育。我们要继续进行普通高等院校调整,优化高等教育的布局和专业结构。我们还要加强高等学校重点学科的建设,使博士生的培养基本立足于国内。我们坚持多种形式、多种途径的成人教育办学路子。国内的各个大学差不多都办夜大学或短训班。我们也重视扫盲工作,争取近期在全国基本上扫除青壮年文盲。

素质教育是要全面提高国民素质和民族创新能力。我们强调德育、智育、体育和美育有机结合,使我们的学生全面、健康地发展,成为创造性人才,同时具有团结、协作和奉献精神。

中国的教育消费市场发展迅速,各种专业资格认证培训与考试火爆。继续教育成为时尚,终身学习正在为越来越多的人所接受。教育的国际合作与交流活动越来越频繁。中国已经是世界上出国留学生最多的国家。同时,来中国的外国留学生数量也迅速增长。

Notes

1. "自1949年中华人民共和国成立以来,中国政府一向十分重视发展教育事业。"这句话里,"教育事业"容易被译为"education career"。其实这儿的"事业"不用翻译出来。在中文中有许多这样的词,如"问题""事业""力度"等,它们没有具体的意义,只是汉语的一种表达习惯。如"同情心理"只需译成"sympathy","心理"不必译出,"失业现象"只需译成"unemployment","现象"不必译出。翻译这类短语时需要仔细斟酌。全句译成:"Ever since 1949 when the People's Republic of China was founded, the Chinese government has always attached great importance to education."

2. "希望工程于1989年由中国青少年发展基金会发起,目的在于帮助贫困地区辍学少年儿童,向国内外集资助学。"这句话由3个分句组成,翻译时可以使用合句法,用分词短语合并。全句译成:"Project Hope was initiated by the China Youth Development Foundation in 1989, aiming at providing financial assistance for primary and junior high school dropouts in poor areas by raising funds from home and abroad."

3. "此外,为保证家庭经济困难的学生获得高等教育机会,中国政府采取有效措施,诸如国家助学奖学金制度、勤工助学制度、特殊困难补助制度、学费减免制度、国家助学贷款制度等。"这句话中,难点是各种"制度"如何翻译。由于这儿的各项措施不一定都是制度,翻译时不一定非要使用"system"这个词,因此"制度"一词不一定都需要翻译出来。全句译成:"Meanwhile, to ensure that students from low-income families have access to higher education, the government has adopted effective measures of financial assistance, including state stipends and scholarships, work-study programs, subsidies for students with special economic difficulties, tuition reduction or exemption and state loans."

4. "我们强调德育、智育、体育和美育有机结合,使我们的学生全面、健康地发展,成为创造性人才,同时具有团结、协作和奉献精神。"这句话也适用合句法显化逻辑关系,含有因果关系,因此可以使用"so that"从句。全句译成:"We lay emphasis on the reasonable integration of moral, intellectual, physical and aesthetic education to promote students' all-round and healthy development, so that they may become creative talents who attach great importance to solidarity, collaboration and dedication."

5. "中国的教育消费市场发展迅速,各种专业资格认证培训与考试火爆。"这句话也可以使用合句法翻译,用with独立主格结构把后半句译成前半句的伴随状况。全句可以译成:"The educational market is booming in China, with thriving training and tests for various professional qualifications."

Passage Translation 2

Vocabulary

1. laureate
2. the growing strength of the faculty
3. State Science and Technology Awards
4. be at the forefront in
5. be emblematic of
6. watch with great interest
7. human, physical, and informational resources
8. the proliferation of nuclear weapons
9. the all-around development of individuals

In its first century, Tsinghua has played an integral role in the development of China. Many of its 170,000 graduates have become leaders in their fields. The first two Chinese laureates of the Nobel Prize Chen-ning Yang and T. D. Lee were both educated at Tsinghua. Professor Qian Xuesen, Professor Zhu Guangya, and Professor Qian Sanqiang, among other Tsinghua graduates, have made important contributions to China's scientific development. We at Yale are especially proud of our role in your early history. Four of the first five presidents of Tsinghua studied at Yale.

Everyone who visits Tsinghua is impressed by the rapid pace of investment in new facilities and the growing strength of the faculty. Tsinghua's contributions in science, engineering, environment, and sustainable design are known around the world, and its efforts in educating leaders in business and public policy are much admired.

Tsinghua has been at the forefront in forging partnerships with institutions around the world. You have longstanding and successful collaborations with MIT, Johns Hopkins, the University of Michigan, and Columbia University. Tsinghua has also been a leader in forging collaborations with industry. You have joint research centers with more than 30 companies, including Toyota, United Technologies, and Boeing.

Yale is fortunate to be Tsinghua's partner in some of these important collaborations. The Yale-Tsinghua Program in International Healthcare Management, established in 2009 as part of Goldman Sachs' 10,000 women initiative, is providing advanced training to 500 women professionals from rural China. And a Yale-Tsinghua collaboration with the China Association of Mayors is helping municipal leaders meet the challenges of sustainable development in the 21st Century.

Universities around the world salute Tsinghua for its commitment to send its students overseas and to host students from abroad. Over 3,200 Tsinghua students go abroad annually, and each year Tsinghua hosts more than 800 visiting students, in addition to the nearly 2,000 who are pursuing their degrees. In this way, Tsinghua is contributing importantly to improving the understanding of China by future leaders around the world and to improving the understanding of the world by future leaders of China.

Tsinghua's extraordinary progress is emblematic of a major development that we who represent universities from around the world have been watching with great interest: the rise of China's universities. As barriers to the flow of people, goods, and information have come down, and as the economic development process proceeds, China has increasing access to the human, physical, and informational resources needed to move its universities to the higher level of excellence.

Increasing the quality of education around the world results in better-informed and more productive citizens. The fate of the planet depends on our ability to collaborate across borders to solve society's most pressing problems—the persistence of poverty, the prevalence of disease, the proliferation of nuclear weapons, the shortage of water, and global warming. Having better educated citizens and leaders will help us to confront these challenges.

I close by quoting from President Hu's speech at the National Conference on Education held in Beijing last July: "Education is the cornerstone of national rejuvenation and social progress, and the basic means to improve the all-around development of individuals. It carries hundreds of millions of families' expectations for a better life."

For 100 years, Tsinghua has been dedicated to fulfilling these expectations. On behalf of the world's universities, I offer heartfelt congratulations to Tsinghua University as it begins a second century in pursuit of a better life for its graduates, and a better world for all humanity.

Unit 8 Education Home and Abroad 中外教育

Notes

1. "The Yale-Tsinghua Program in International Healthcare Management, established in 2009 as part of Goldman Sachs' 10,000 women initiative, is providing advanced training to 500 women professionals from rural China." 这是个长句,不必译成一句话,根据拆句法,可以把"established"分词短语译成句子。全句译成:"2009年耶鲁大学与清华合作推出国际医疗管理课程,该项目是高盛集团万名女性资助计划的一部分,为500名来自中国农村地区的女性专业医疗人员提供先进的培训。"

2. "Tsinghua's extraordinary progress is emblematic of a major development that we who represent universities from around the world have been watching with great interest: the rise of China's universities." 这也是一句长句,根据句意,各国代表正在关注中国大学的崛起,而清华是其中的代表。所以,为了汉语表达习惯的需要,要用拆句法把原句拆分成两句表达。全句译成:"今天在座的各国大学代表都以极大的兴趣关注着中国大学的崛起,而清华非凡的进步正是中国大学飞速发展的一个象征。"

3. "The fate of the planet depends on our ability to collaborate across borders to solve society's most pressing problems—the persistence of poverty, the prevalence of disease, the proliferation of nuclear weapons, the shortage of water, and global warming." 汉语句子中常见动词的并列。句中,可以把"to collaborate across borders to solve society's most pressing problems"译成更符合汉语表达的两个并列动词短语。全句译成:"地球的命运取决于我们跨越国界,共同合作解决人类社会紧迫问题的能力。这些问题包括:持续的贫穷、疾病的蔓延、核武器扩散、水资源缺乏和全球变暖。"

4. "I offer heartfelt congratulations to Tsinghua University as it begins a second century in pursuit of a better life for its graduates, and a better world for all humanity." 根据汉语动词使用较多的特点,可以把句中的"in pursuit of"译成动词"为……而努力"。另外根据汉语表达习惯,把"as"从句拆分,独立译成汉语的简单句子。全句译成:"我想向清华大学表达最诚挚的祝贺。她即将走向新的百年,并继续为其毕业生的美好未来和整个人类社会的美好未来而不懈努力!"

Sentences in Focus

1. 中国政府实行以政府办学为主体,社会机构及个人共同办学的体制。

2. 为保证家庭经济困难的学生获得高等教育机会,中国政府采取有效措施,诸如国家助学奖学金制度、勤工助学制度、特殊困难补助制度、学费减免制度、国家助学贷款制度等。

3. 中国教育的近期目标是在全国大部分地区基本普及九年制义务教育,在大城市试行普及高中阶段教育。

4. 素质教育是要全面提高国民素质和民族创新能力。

5. 继续教育成为时尚，终身学习正在为越来越多的人所接受。

6. Everyone who visits Tsinghua is impressed by the rapid pace of investment in new facilities and the growing strength of the faculty.

7. Tsinghua's contributions in science, engineering, environment, and sustainable design are known around the world, and its efforts in educating leaders in business and public policy are much admired.

8. Tsinghua has been at the forefront in forging partnerships with institutions around the world.

9. Universities around the world salute Tsinghua for its commitment to send its students overseas and to host students from abroad.

10. On behalf of the world's universities, I offer heartfelt congratulations to Tsinghua University as it begins a second century in pursuit of a better life for its graduates, and a better world for all humanity.

Exercises

I. Fill in the blanks with English words according to the given Chinese.

1. Many students put in their best efforts to get admitted to colleges and universities and accept the highly intense exam-oriented _____ _____（教育体制）.

2. *Kong fu* star Jackie Chan attended a charitable concert in Beijing on Monday, as part of a nationwide charitable program in _____（筹款）to aid school dropouts.

3. China's higher education _____（旨在）achieving better quality, better structure, deeper reform and brighter prospects.

4. Cost rises of labor and raw materials have pushed China's textile industry to become _____（更多样化）.

5. To meet the challenge of reforming the education system, we need to _____ _____（采取措施）to train teachers and use better teaching methods.

6. Extending _____（义务教育）is a good policy to relieve parents of heavy economic pressure and promote education equality for the whole society.

7. It is reported that the Xinjiang Uygur Autonomous Region has decided to _____

_____ (普及双语教育) in its southern region and rural areas.

8. Efforts have been made to _____ (扫盲) among young and middle-aged people and the work in rural areas has made great advancement.

9. Nantong Development Zone voices stronger support to entrepreneurial talents by offering two to four million yuan of initial funding to _____ (高层次人才) who come to set up independent innovative technological enterprises in the area.

10. China's Ministry of Finance made public the catalogue of administrative approval items including government procurement, _____ _____ (税收减免), and foreign loans.

II. Translate the Four Books and the Five Classics into Chinese.

1. *The Great Learning* 《_____》
2. *The Doctrine of the Mean* 《_____》
3. *The Analects of Confucius* 《_____》
4. *Mencius* 《_____》
5. *The Book of Songs* 《_____》
6. *The Book of History* 《_____》
7. *The Book of Rites* 《_____》
8. *The Book of Changes* 《_____》
9. *The Spring and Autumn Annals* 《_____》

III. Translate the following sentences.

1. The Chinese University of Hong Kong is a comprehensive research university with over 150,000 outstanding graduates.
   _____

2. Our university has academic links and research collaboration with various institutions in mainland China.
   _____

3. Many of our research outputs have been put into practical use through technology transfer.
   _____

4. Since the implementation of China's 10th Five-Year Plan, our university has undertaken over 1,000 national, provincial or ministerial projects.

5. China will gradually exempt tuition and fees for secondary vocational education. Tuition and fees will also be waived for senior high school students from poor families.

6. 在食品科技、生物技术、工业设计及纺织技术领域，江南大学已逐渐成为国内最重要的国际交流中心之一。

7. 科举制度沿用了1300多年，直到清朝末年为止。

8. 一年一度的全国高考旨在选拔优秀高中毕业生进入大学。

9. 越来越多的中国学生选择留学，而在华留学的外国人人数也大幅增加。

10. 周六，人们举行各种文化活动来庆祝北京第一所孔子学院成立10周年。

IV. Translate the following paragraphs.

1. The outstanding achievement of our academics and researchers are well recognized with a number of prestigious national and international awards and fellowships. The list includes Fellow of the Royal Society in the UK, Foreign Associate of the National Academy of Sciences of the USA and Foreign Academician of the Chinese Academy of Engineering, the State Natural Science Award as well as the State Scientific and Technological Progress Award.

2. 为了支持孔子学院的发展，促进汉语言文化在全球的推广，培养合格的汉语言教师及优秀的汉语言学习者，孔子学院总部（又称"汉办"）启动了"孔子学院奖学金"计划,资助外国学生、学者及汉语言教师在中国相关大学学习汉语。

_____

_____

_____

_____

_____

Section B Interpretation

Interpretation Technique

口译技能:口译笔记(2)

口译笔记起到提醒和引导的作用。所以,典型的笔记以关键词和逻辑线索词为主,表明源语的内容和思维线路。

实际操作中,英语和汉语都有可能用到。经常是哪种语言记录更方便就用哪种。口译笔记除了用源语或目标语,还有几种方法需要掌握。

(1) 使用缩写。长单词都要缩略书写,以便提高效率。如"government"可以缩写成"gov","specilized"可以缩写成"specd",等等。

(2) 使用一些约定俗成的缩略语。如"UNESCO"代表"联合国教科文组织","UNICEF"代表"联合国儿童基金","IMF"代表"国际货币基金"。

(3) 使用各种符号。每个符号并不是简单对应一个字词,而可以代表几个意思,这样可以少记些字词。此外,各种符号可以组合创新运用。例如,如果用"d"代表今天,那么"..d"的组合运用,则是"前天"的意思。需要指出的是,用什么符号,每个符号有几个意思等都是因人而异的,没有统一的符号体系。

通常,口译笔记符号主要包括以下几类。

1. 数学符号

一些数学符号在笔记中被赋予丰富的意义。如:

∴ 所以   ≈ 大约,大概,左右
∵ 因为   > 大于,多于,比……大
= 等于或就是,意味着   < 小于,少于,比……小

2. 标点符号

标点符号也能表达丰富的意思。如:

? 问题,疑惑,难题   : 各种各样"说"的动词
! 惊叹,奇迹   ( ) 包括

3. 其他形象表意的符号

每个人都可以自创一些符号。只要自己记得清,不混淆,都是可以使用的。如:

□← 来访,进入,进口,引进外资,来华投资   《《 远小于,远弱于

□→ 出访,外出,出口,海外投资
＃ 停止,暂停
＆ 与,和,共同
∈ 属于
← 来自于
→ 导致,结果是
↓ 下降,减少,降低
↑ 增长,增加
∞ 接触,交往
～ 被替换为
⊕ 医院
⊙ 会议
☆ 杰出的,出众的

〉〉远大于,远强于
° 人
h° 主持人
$° 富人
⊥ 在压力下
* 重要的,优秀的
Σ 总
@ 关于
√ 正确,好
× 错误,不好,否定
© 版权
□ 国家
∥ 但是，然而

口译笔记符号设计方法有：

（1）一般逻辑关系词不用文字而只用符号记录。如："因为"用"∵","所以"用"∴",列举用"}"。

（2）高频词以大写字母为主,象形符号或汉字为辅。如：

工业：I 或 工
中国：中
男：♂
女：♀

总之，没有一套统一的符号可遵循，符号使用因人而异。同时也不要太迷信符号，刻意追求符号搜集，本末倒置。笔记只是脑记的辅助。只有结合笔记，用短时记忆储存听到信息的意义才是关键。但如果有可能，也可以试着总结常用的一些符号，固定每个符号都可以代表什么，并尝试自己创新组合使用已有的符号，这样将大大提高符号的使用效率。

Passage Interpretation 1

第四届全球孔子学院大会开幕已经两天了。各位代表以满腔的热忱投入会议活动，积极建言献策，广泛深入讨论，使大会各项议程进展非常顺利。在此，我谨代表中华人民共和国教育部和孔子学院总部，向你们表示诚挚的感谢！

明天上午，我们将举行大会闭幕式，校长和院长分论坛的召集人将与大家交流和分享大会的讨论成果。之后，中国教育部部长袁贵仁先生将作总结讲话。总部将认真听取各位代表的意见和建议，把明年的工作做得更好。

经过5年的努力，我们已在88个国家和地区建立了280多所孔子学院和270多个中学孔子课堂。各国朋友都认为，孔子学院就是一个大家庭，在世界各地有我们的兄弟姐妹。今晚，我代表中国教育部和孔子学院总部，在这里设宴，款待出席大会的中外朋友！希望大家这次中国之行心情愉快！

Unit 8 Education Home and Abroad 中外教育

Passage Interpretation 2

September is traditionally the end of summer and the beginning of autumn in the UK. It is also the month when children go back to school after their long summer holidays, but what do you actually know about British schools?

There are two types of school in England. State-run schools are paid for by the government, so are free to attend. Independent schools are private, which means you have to pay to attend. The school day usually starts at 9 in the morning and finishes around 4, with breaks for lunch of course. In many schools, you have to wear a uniform too. Children start school when they are 5 years old. This is called primary school, and lasts until the child is 11 when he or she will go on to senior school. Secondary school is compulsory from 11 to 16 years of age. At 16, students take national examinations for GCSE. After this, students can stay on that school for another 2 years and take A Level examinations. These examinations are necessary if they want to go on to university at 18. Some universities start in September, but others begin in October.

Courses normally last 3 years, but some, such as languages, engineering or medicine, can take much longer to complete. Students usually go to university in a different town, so they need to get used to living alone, paying bills and washing their own clothes. For many, this is a difficult time, but everyone soon becomes used to it! Universities in Britain used to be free, but many students now have to pay for part of their course. Similarly, students used to receive a grant-money from the government in order to live. Nowadays, they have to borrow money from banks or the government, called a student loan, or take part-time jobs.

School and university life are not just about studying, however. Many students take part in drama productions or play music. Others, of course, take part in a wide range of sports, such as football, rugby and cricket. Many of the friends British people make at school and university remain friends for life, so it seems true to say that your schooldays really are "the best days of your life".

Dialogue Interpretation

A: 我怎么申请美国的大学呢?

B: You should go to the library to find some information about American universities, and write to the Admission Office. Then the Admission Office will send you application forms and other related materials. From my experience, many applicants write to several universities instead of just one.

A: 据说申请学校会耗费掉很多时间和精力。

B: That is true. I'll list for you the requirements of almost all the universities. First of all, you need official transcripts of your undergraduate work, three letters of recommendation from your professors who know your competence, and the official TOEFL score. Then you need a financial guarantee and an application fee.

A: 然后是什么?

B: If they agree to enroll you, you can apply for a visa from the U.S. embassies.

A: 所有这些手续下来需要多久呢?

B: From 3 to 6 months if everything goes well.

A: 我在考虑申请哪一所学校。

B: Are you thinking about a public university or a private one?

A: 我也不知道,有什么区别?

B: Public universities are usually state-funded, whereas private universities usually get their funding elsewhere.

A: 那么哪一类更好呢?

B: One isn't necessarily better than the other. It depends a lot on the school administration and the teachers. There are many universities for you to choose from. Some famous universities such as Harvard, Yale, the University of Michigan, and Massachusetts Institute of Technology are really wonderful places to study, but they are very competitive and expensive. Some smaller universities or institutes are also very nice but less expensive.

M: 谢谢你的帮助。

W: You are welcome. Please feel free to ask if you have any more questions.

Exercises

I. Interpreting technique practice.

Try to collect some signs and abbreviations that you plan to use in note-taking and memorize the meanings that they signify.

II. Spot dictation.

The University of Hong Kong is the oldest university in Hong Kong. (1)_____ _____ under the Revolution of 1911, it incorporated the Hong Kong College of Medicine, which had been providing (2)_____ medical education in Hong Kong since 1887.

The University was established to provide a modern (3)_____ for Chinese students, and has built up a tradition of excellence. Since its foundation it has produced over (4)_____, many of whom have gone on to become leaders of society, occupying leading positions in education, the arts, industry, commerce, the (5)_____ _____, and the professions. Its honorary graduates include Hu Shih, Mother Teresa, and Nelson Mandela.

The University's main estate (6)_____ the north-western slopes of Hong Kong Island and overlooks Victoria Harbor. The University presently has (7)_____, a graduate school, and a number of independent centers of studies and learning. The University's School of Professional and Continuing Education is the largest tertiary-level provider of (8)_____ in Hong Kong. The University currently has a student population of over 27,400 including more than 15,550 undergraduates and

11,850 postgraduates, and an academic staff population of over 1,650.

The University (9) _____ playing its part on the international academic stage through leading-edge education and research. Through its unfailing (10) _____ the highest standards in the pursuit of scholarship, it seeks to serve China and the wider international community.

III. Sentence listening and translation.

1. _____

2. _____

3. _____

4. _____

5. _____

IV. Paragraph listening and translation.

Ⅴ. **Dialogue interpretation.**

A：这是您第一次来中国吗？

B：Yes. I come to study the Chinese language in Peking University.

A：您来中国之前对中国有多少了解？

B：I knew that China is an old civilization with a recorded history of over 5,000 years. And I also knew some *kung fu* stars like Jackie Chan, Bruce Lee, Jet Lee, etc. It's amazing that people can fly over walls, rivers or trees.

A：很有意思。不过只有在电影里你才能看到人们飞来飞去的。顺便问一下，您对这里的大学生活适应了吗？

B：Yes. I like my life here so much that I'd like to extend my stay in Beijing and apply for a degree program of international trade. As we know, our country established partnership with China two years ago, so many business people look forward to doing business with Chinese.

A：所以，这就是你来中国留学的主要原因吧？

B：Yes, it's true.

A：祝您在中国生活愉快！

Ⅵ. **Interpreting in groups.**

Role-play the following situation with your partners, acting as the Chinese speaker, English speaker and the interpreter respectively. One group will be invited to perform in class.

Participants：1. Mr. Jack Parker
　　　　　　　2. Zhang Min
　　　　　　　3. An interpreter

Location：Campus

Task：Mr. Jack Parker, a guest professor from the U.S., is doing research in Chinese education system. Zhang Min comes across Jack and his interpreter on campus. Zhang Min greets them and answers some questions asked by Jack on the topic of higher education. Zhang speaks Chinese while Jack is an English-speaker.

Ⅶ. **3-minute talk on the given topic.**

Talk on the following topic in three minutes based on the given reference questions.

Topic：**Differences in education systems between China and the U.S.**

Questions for Reference：

1. How much do you know about Chinese education system?
2. What do you know about American education system?
3. What do you think are the major differences in education systems between China and the U.S.?

Ⅷ. Theme-related expressions.

学年	academic year
学习成绩	academic record
在职培训	in-service training
注册人数	enrollment
专业课	specialized course
必修课	compulsory course
选修课	optional course/elective course
社会实践	social practice
博士后	post doctorate
博士	doctor (Ph.D)
硕士	master
学士	bachelor
旁听生	guest student (英)/auditor (美)
大学一年级学生	freshman
大学二年级学生	sophomore
大学三年级学生	junior
大学四年级学生	senior
试点项目	pilot project
填鸭式教学法	cramming/forced-feeding method of teaching

Section C Further Exploration

梅西大学是新西兰唯一的全国性大学。阅读以下入学申请须知，说说大意并尝试填写所附的申请表。

APPLICATION FOR ADMISSION AS AN INTERNATIONAL STUDENT

Decide what you want to study: **international.massey.ac.nz**
↓
Complete the application form, review the Checklist (in Part K) and send with supporting documents to: **international@massey.ac.nz**
↓
When all conditions have been met the University will issue an Offer of Place
↓
Accept the Offer of Place, pay the fees stated in the offer and apply for accommodation and a student ID card
↓
Massey will issue a Confirmation of Place (receipt of payment) after receiving payment
↓
Apply for a visa with New Zealand Immigration presenting your Confirmation of Place (receipt of payment)
↓
Arrive at Massey University
↓
Attend International Student Orientation
↓
Begin your programme of study

Academic year

Massey University operates:

Intake/Semester 1	February to late June
Intake/Semester 2	July to early November
Intake 3	August and September
Intake 4/Summer School	November to February

PhDs and English Language programmes can start at any time during the year. For details see **international.massey.ac.nz**.

Verification of documents

To verify documents photocopy both sides of each page of the original document and use an official company stamp (in English) including, "This is a true copy of the original", on the front of each page. To complete the verification, documents must be signed and dated by an authorised person, eg, a notary public, a justice of the peace, a solicitor, a commissioner of oaths, an official of the issuing authority or an approved Massey University agent. The signature and company stamp must be an original on the copies provided – the stamp and signature cannot be copied. Documents in languages other than English are to be translated into English by a certified translator and verified in English. Applicants who have had a name change must provide verified evidence of that change, e.g., a deed poll or marriage certificate.

Admission criteria

To be admitted into a Massey University programme applicants need to meet both the academic and English language requirements. The criteria listed here is for general admission only and some programmes have additional requirements and/or require a higher level of English language. For details please visit **international.massey.ac.nz**

ACADEMIC ADMISSION

PhD
Admission to Doctoral study requires a high calibre Masters or Bachelor with Honours degree with demonstrated research skills.

Postgraduate
Admission into a postgraduate programme requires an appropriate undergraduate degree from a recognised tertiary institution.

Graduate Diploma
Admission to a Graduate Diploma requires successful completion of a three year diploma or undergraduate degree from a recognised tertiary institution.

Undergraduate
Successful applicants will have achieved the equivalent to Year 13 in New Zealand (NCEA level 3 University Entrance). Refer to page 3 of this document for a guide to entry requirements by country.

Pre-degree
Successful applicants from outside New Zealand will have achieved the equivalent to successful completion of Year 12 in New Zealand. See page 3 of this document for a guide to entry requirements by country.

CREDIT ASSESSMENT (RECOGNITION OF PRIOR LEARNING)

Applicants may request an assessment for recognition of previous tertiary study by ticking the Credit section on the application form. There is no additional fee when the credit is assessed at the same time as the application for admission. Credit applies to undergraduate study only and course outlines must be provided.

ENGLISH LANGUAGE REQUIREMENTS

The minimum English language requirements for admission to Massey University are:

Postgraduate (including PhD)
Academic IELTS 6.5 (no band less than 6.0), **or**,
TOEFL 575 (paper), TWE 4.0, **or**,
iBT 90 (internet), with writing score of 20.

Undergraduate (including Graduate Diplomas)
Academic IELTS 6.0 (no band less than 5.5), **or**,
TOEFL 550 (paper), TWE 4.0, **or**,
iBT 80 (internet), with writing score of 19.

Pre-degree (including Certificate of Foundation Studies)
Academic IELTS 5.5 (no band less than 5.0), **or**,
TOEFL 525 (paper) **or**,
iBT 70 (internet), with writing score of 18.

NOTES:

1. English language test results are valid for two years only.
2. Applicants with TOEFL (paper) results please request ETS to send the results directly to Massey University. The institutional code is 9480.

Higher English language requirements are requested for some programmes.

PART A: Personal details of applicant

Student ID: (if known) ☐☐☐☐☐☐☐☐

Surname/Family name (as shown in passport):
_____

Given names (as shown in passport):
_____

Preferred name: _____

Date of birth: Day ☐☐ Month ☐☐ Year ☐☐☐☐

Gender: ○ Male   ○ Female

Citizenship (as shown on passport):
_____

Ethnic group: _____

PART B: When do you intend to begin study?

Year: _____

○ Intake/Semester 1 (February)
○ Intake/Semester 2 (July)
○ Intake 3 (August/September)
○ Intake 4/Summer School (November)

PREFERRED CAMPUS:

○ Albany (Auckland)
○ Palmerston North (Manawatū)
○ Wellington

Do you want to study full-time or part-time?

○ Full-time   ○ Part-time

PART C: English language programmes

Complete this section only if you intend to study English Language.

How long will you study (four weeks minimum): _____

Which month do you intend to start your English programme?
_____

PART D: Diplomas, degrees, doctoral study

LEVEL OF STUDY

○ Foundation Studies   ○ Pre-degree
○ Undergraduate   ○ Graduate Diploma
○ Postgraduate   ○ PhD

List programmes in order of preference.

1st choice: _____
    Major: _____
2nd choice: _____
    Major: _____

PART E: Senior High School/NZ Secondary School or Foundation Study

NSI number (if you have previously studied in New Zealand):
_____

HIGH SCHOOL QUALIFICATIONS

SCHOOL: _____
Country: _____
Qualification: _____
Year started: _____   Year finished: _____
SCHOOL: _____
Country: _____
Qualification: _____
Year started: _____   Year finished: _____

PART F: English language proficiency

Applicants who have completed an academic qualification in a country where English is the first language can be considered for an exemption from providing English language test results.

What was the language used for your overseas schooling?:
_____

I will take/have taken an English language proficiency test (Academic IELTS or TOEFL with TWE or ER):

Date to be taken: _____
Name of test: _____
Result (if known): _____

Have you studied English language in New Zealand?   ○ Yes ○ No

If 'Yes', please complete the following and include evidence of this study.

Name of School: _____
Date started: _____   Date finished: _____

PART G: Tertiary education

Have you studied at any New Zealand tertiary institution? ○ Yes ○ No

Have you studied at a tertiary institution other than Massey University since leaving high school?   ○ Yes ○ No

HIGHER EDUCATION/NEW ZEALAND INSTITUTION

INSTITUTION: _____
Country: _____
Qualification: _____
Year started: _____   Year finished: _____
INSTITUTION: _____
Country: _____
Qualification: _____
Year started: _____   Year finished: _____

Please provide verified official documentation of academic transcripts for all qualifications and study (including any study previously undertaken within New Zealand).

通用口笔译

CREDIT (FOR UNDERGRADUATE PROGRAMMES ONLY)

Do you wish to have previous study assessed for recognition of credit towards a Massey University degree? ○ Yes ○ No

Your application must include an official outline and course descriptions of all study.

PART H: Contact details

CURRENT ADDRESS:

Line 1: _____

Line 2: _____

Line 3: _____

Postcode: _____ Country: _____

Phone (day): _____

Phone (night): _____

Cellphone: _____

Email: _____

EMERGENCY CONTACT

Please advise the person you would like us to contact in an emergency.

Name: _____

What is this person's relationship to you? (eg parent, husband, brother)

Relationship: _____

Phone (day): _____

Phone (night): _____

Cellphone: _____

Email: _____

ALTERNATIVE ADDRESS

An alternative address that Massey can use to contact you (eg home, family member, or employer)

Line 1: _____

Line 2: _____

Line 3: _____

Postcode: _____ Country: _____

PART I: Additional questions

PLEASE SELECT YOUR MAIN ACTIVITY AS AT 1 OCTOBER

○ Not in paid employment
○ Student
○ Overseas
○ In paid employment

HEALTH AND DISABILITY

Do you have any disability, impairment (including learning disabilities), long-term injury, or chronic medical condition(s) that may impact on your ability to study and/or participate in university activities? ○ Yes ○ No

If 'Yes', please provide a report from a registered health professional so we can assess our ability to support you during your study in New Zealand.

CONTACT WITH OTHER STUDENTS

For study purposes, do you consent to your name, email address and phone number being shared with other students studying the same papers? ○ Yes ○ No

Name of Massey University academic staff contact (where applicable):

_____

Name of Institutional Agreement/Cohort (if applicable)

_____

What is you intended career? _____

Will your chosen Massey University programme help you achieve your career goals? ○ Yes ○ No

Do you intend to complete a Massey qualification? ○ Yes ○ No

FINANCING YOUR STUDY

How will your study be financed?
○ Personal funds
○ US Federal loan
○ Home government scholarship
○ NZAID
○ Other: _____

PART J: Agent stamp

Only relevant if applying through an agent

[Stamp box]

Agency name: _____

Agent's email address: _____

UNIT 9
Cultural Exchange
文化交流

Learning Objectives

1. To know how to translate culturally loaded words;
2. To learn how to take notes for interpretation(3);
3. To learn how to translate/interpret passages or dialogues on the theme of Chinese culture;
4. To learn useful words and expressions related to Chinese culture.

Lead-in

● *Quiz* (True or False)

_____ 1. Ox does not belong to 12 Animal Zodiac.

_____ 2. Uygur people like to treat guests with tea, naan and fruits before the main dishes are served.

_____ 3. Zhuang ethnic group is the largest minority group in China mainly living in Guangxi.

_____ 4. In A.D.130, Zhang Heng, an astronomer and literary scholar, invented the first instrument for monitoring tsunami.

_____ 5. In the Ming and Qing dynasties, painted clay figurines were very popular. The most famous were the Clay Figurine Zhang made in Tianjin and the Huishan clay figurines made in Wuxi, Jiangsu Province.

_____ 6. In the U.S., something old, something new, something borrowed and something pink refer to the items that a bride must wear on her wedding day in order to be blessed with a perfect ceremony.

_____ 7. The preserved egg is one of the most disgusting Chinese foods to most westerners.

● **What festival is each picture related to? Fill in the blanks with the words in the list.**

Trooping the Color   Halloween   Thanksgiving Day   Valentine's Day   Lantern Festival
Doll's Festival   Dragon Boat Festival   Double Ninth Festival   St. Patric's   Easter

1. _____   2. _____   3. _____   4. _____   5. _____

6. _____   7. _____   8. _____   9. _____   10. _____

Section A   Translation

Translation Technique

文化含义词的处理

汉语中的文化含义词有两大类：
● 第一类来自中国的历史传统。
　（1）文化名词：惊蛰 Waking of Insects　　春分 Spring Equinox
　（2）物品用词：旗袍 cheongsam　　　　　　饺子 *jiaozi* (dumpling)
　　　　　　　　粽子 *zongzi* (glutinous rice wrapped in reed leaves)
　（3）礼仪用词：叩头 kowtow　　　　　　　作揖 make a bow with hands folded in front
● 第二类来自中国的现代社会用语。
　如：个体经济 self-employed business
　　　社会主义精神文明 socialist cultural and ethical progress
　　　基本实现小康 build a moderately well-off society
　　　街道妇女 housewives working in the neighborhood
　　　"三高"农业 high-yield, cost-effective and high-tech agriculture
● 文化含义词的翻译通常采用以下三种手法：
　（1）替代（substitution）
　寺、庙、庵、观 temple　　　　　　　　　　红眼病 green-eyed
　（2）释义（paraphrasing）
　亲家 relatives by marriage　　　　　　　　连襟 husbands of sisters
　司马昭之心，路人皆知。Sima Zhao's ill intent is plain to all.
　（3）音译（transliteration）
　阴阳 *yin* and *yang*　　　　　　　　　　　风水 *feng shui*

● 此外,第一类文化含义词的翻译要注意以下情况:
(1)汉语中某些家庭成员的说法与英语中并不对等,如"姐姐"/"妹妹"和"sister"。
(2)汉语中一些词的联想意义与英语中也不一样,如"喜鹊"和"magpie",汉语中喜鹊象征好的预兆,是吉祥之物,而英语中"magpie"可用于形容饶舌的人,带有贬义。

第二类文化含义词,在翻译时往往是照字面直译,而要注意采取意译的方法,这样才能做到语用意义的对等。如以下两句中"化"的翻译要依据语境选取不同的表达方式。

美化环境 beautify the environment
干部队伍的年轻化、知识化、专业化。Make our rank of leaders younger, better educated and more competent professionally.

Passage Translation 1

Vocabulary

1. 农历新年
2. 腊八节
3. 除旧迎新
4. 守岁
5. 贴春联、年画和剪纸
6. 逛庙会
7. 走亲访友
8. 压岁钱
9. 游灯会
10. 猜灯谜
11. 舞龙
12. 舞狮
13. 踩高跷
14. 清明节
15. 二十四节气
16. 艾草
17. 七夕节

春节是中国的新年。传统意义上的春节是指从腊月初八的腊八节,一直到正月十五元宵节。春节来临,背井离乡的游子都纷纷回家团聚。除夕这一天对华人来说是极为重要的。这一天人们准备除旧迎新,吃团圆饭。春节期间的主要活动有:腊月初八喝腊八粥,除夕夜包饺子、包汤圆、做年糕,吃团圆饭守岁,另外还有贴春联、年画、剪纸,放爆竹和逛庙会。春节期间,人们穿上崭新的衣服,走亲访友,相互拜年,恭祝来年大吉大利。长辈还要给晚辈"压岁钱",寓意"压岁祈福"。

正月十五为元宵节。正月十五日是一年中第一个月圆之夜,也是大地回春的夜晚,人们对此加以庆祝。人们吃汤圆、游灯会、猜灯谜。有的地方还有舞龙、舞狮、踩高跷、扭秧歌等活动。

清明节是中国重要的传统节日之一,至今已有两千多年历史。公历4月5日前后为清明节,为二十四节气之一。除了扫墓,还有踏青、放风筝、荡秋千、娱乐游戏等活动。

农历五月初五,是中国民间的传统节日——端午节。这个节日是为了纪念在流放期间投江自尽的楚国大夫屈原。端午节的主要习俗有吃粽子、赛龙舟和挂艾草。

农历七月初七的夜晚,是人们俗称的七夕节,它是中国传统节日中最具浪漫色彩的一个节日,被称为"中国情人节"。如今有情男女都会在这个晚上祈祷姻缘美满。

农历八月十五日是中国的传统节日——中秋节。在这天,每个家庭都团聚在一起,一家人共同观赏象征丰裕、和谐和好运的圆月。此时,大人们尽情吃着美味的月饼,品着热腾腾的香茗,而孩子们则在一旁拉着明亮的兔子灯尽情玩耍。

Notes

1. "传统意义上的春节是指从腊月初八的腊八节,一直到正月十五元宵节。""腊八"指的是农历十二月初八。"腊八节"是节日名称,应该简短为好。因此,用解释的方法翻译不妥,这儿可以用音译的方法,直接译成"Laba Festival"。全句可以译成:"Traditionally, the Spring Festival starts from the Laba Festival which falls on the 8th day of the 12th lunar month to the Lantern Festival which occurs on the 15th day of the first lunar month."

2. "除夕夜包饺子、包汤圆、做年糕,吃团圆饭守岁。"这句话中,"饺子、汤圆和年糕"都是具有中国特色的春节美食,一般用音译法翻译,但也可结合释义法。但是"守岁"这个文化词则要具体解释意思,是指一直守到新年开始,译成"stay up late into the New Year"。全句译成:"People make *jiaozi*(dumplings), *tangyuan*(glutinous rice dumplings) and *niangao*(glutinous rice cake), have family reunion dinner on the New Year Eve and stay up late into the New Year."

3. "走亲访友,相互拜年,恭祝来年大吉大利。"这句话中的"拜年"是我国春节的传统习俗。古时是指晚辈给长辈叩头拜年。但是,现在随着时代的发展,拜年并不一定要跪下叩头。句子中的"走亲访友"其实就是相互拜年,因此句中"相互拜年"是意义重复,可以减译。全句译成:"Wearing new clothes, people also visit relatives and friends and convey auspicious New Year greetings."

4. "人们吃汤圆、游灯会、猜灯谜。有的地方还有舞龙、舞狮、踩高跷、扭秧歌等活动。"这句话里文化词很多,特别值得一提的是"秧歌"。秧歌是一种舞蹈,因此扭秧歌其实是一种舞蹈表演,因而译成"*yangko* dance"。全句译成:"People eat sweet dumplings, visit lantern shows and guess lantern riddles on the Lantern Festival. There are other activities such as dragon dances, lion dances, stilt walking and *yangko* dance in some parts of China."

Passage Translation 2

Vocabulary

1. rock and roll
2. blues
3. rhythm and blues
4. techno
5. hip hop
6. recorded music
7. music industry
8. community orchestra
9. promote and market
10. Billboard magazine

The music of the United States reflects the country's multi-ethnic population through a diverse array of styles. Rock and roll, blues, country music, rhythm and blues, jazz, pop, techno, and hip hop are among the country's most internationally-renowned genres. The United States has the world's largest music industry and its music is heard around the world. Since the beginning of the 20th century, some forms of American popular music have gained a near global audience.

Native Americans were the earliest inhabitants of the United States and played its first music. Beginning in the 17th century, immigrants from the United Kingdom, Ireland, Spain, Germany and France began arriving in large numbers, bringing with them new styles and instruments. African slaves brought musical traditions, and each subsequent wave of immigrants contributed to the melting pot.

The United States has produced many popular musicians and composers in the modern world. Beginning with the birth of recorded music, American performers have continued to lead the field of popular music, which, out of all the contributions made by Americans to world culture, has been taken to heart by the entire world.

The American music industry includes a number of fields, ranging from record companies to radio stations and community orchestras. Total industry revenue is about $40 billion worldwide, and about $12 billion in the United States. Most of the world's major record companies are based in the United States; they are represented by the Recording Industry Association of America (RIAA).

The major record companies produce materials by artists who have signed with them. Record companies may also promote and market their artists, through advertising, public performances and concerts, and television appearances. Commercial sales of recordings are tracked by *Billboard* magazine, which compiles a number of music charts regularly.

Notes

1. "African slaves brought musical traditions, and each subsequent wave of immigrants contributed to a melting pot." 句中的"wave"不能直译成"波浪",在句中指的是一拨一拨的移民潮为美国的音乐大熔炉做出了贡献。所以,全句译成:"同时,非洲奴隶也带来了他们的音乐传统,并且后来的每次移民潮也为这个大熔炉做出了贡献。"

2. "Beginning with the birth of recorded music, American performers have continued to lead the field of popular music, which, out of all the contributions made by Americans to world culture, has been taken to heart by the entire world." 这句话的定语从句较复杂,主要是对"out of"短语的处理,它分隔开了定语从句中的关系代词和动词,翻译时需厘清关系。全句译成:"从唱片音乐开始,美国的音乐人一直在流行音乐领域里处于领先地位,有人说在美国对世界文化做的贡献中,音乐真正赢得了全世界的青睐。"

3. "Most of the world's major record companies are based in the United States; they are represented by the Recording Industry Association of America (RIAA)." 这句话主要是被动语态的处理,英译汉时一般是被动转主动。全句可以译为:"世界上大多数主要唱片公司都是在美国,美国唱片业协会(RIAA)是这一行业代表。"

4. "Commercial sales of recordings are tracked by *Billboard* magazine, which compiles a number of music charts for various fields of recorded music sales." 这句话同样是被动语态句的处理,被动转主动,"which"引导的定语从句译成分句。全句译成:"有一家名叫《公告牌》的杂志会追踪纪录唱片的销量,定期发布一系列音乐排行榜。"

Sentences in Focus

1. 春节期间的主要活动有:腊月初八喝腊八粥、除夕夜包饺子、包汤圆、做年糕、吃团圆饭守岁,另外还有贴春联、年画、剪纸、放爆竹和逛庙会。

2. 春节期间,人们穿上崭新的衣服,走亲访友,相互拜年,恭祝来年大吉大利。

3. 除了扫墓,还有踏青、放风筝、荡秋千、娱乐游戏等活动。

4. 农历七月初七的夜晚,是人们俗称的七夕节,它是中国传统节日中最具浪漫色彩的一个节日,被称为"中国情人节"。

5. 这一天,每个家庭都团聚在一起,一家人共同观赏象征丰裕、和谐和好运的圆月。

6. The music of the United States reflects the country's multi-ethnic population through a diverse array of styles.

7. Rock and roll, blues, country music, rhythm and Blues, jazz, pop, techno, and hip hop are among the country's most internationally-renowned genres.

8. The United States has produced many popular musicians and composers in the modern world.

9. The American music industry includes a number of fields, ranging from record companies to radio stations and community orchestras.

10. Record company may also promote and market their artists, through advertising, public performances and concerts, and television appearances.

Exercises

I. Fill in the blanks with English words according to the given Chinese.

1. The Spring Festival witnesses the spring rush when huge crowds of migrant workers hurry home for _____(全家团圆).
2. As the air quality of the city continues to give rise to concerns, many non-governmental organizations are asking the public to refrain from _____(燃放烟花) during the coming Spring Festival.
3. People who observe *Longtaitou* (traditional Chinese Dragon Head Raising Festival) usually follow a folk belief that people should not have a haircut during _____(正月).
4. A _____(阳历) is a calendar whose dates indicate the position of the earth on its revolution around the sun or equivalently the apparent position of the sun moving on the celestial sphere.
5. Children wearing traditional costumes joined a ceremony to _____(纪念) Qu Yuan at Dragon Boat Festival.
6. People have dreamed of leaving their home planet and exploring other worlds _____(自古以来).
7. _____(随着……的来临) the 2016 Olympic Games, the Chinese Tennis Association unveiled a new national team logo, creating a fresh image on the international stage.
8. If you wish to _____(走亲访友) in Sweden and are a citizen of a country outside the EU, you will in most cases need a visa.
9. Longmen Grottoes boasts over thousand statues of lion which has been viewed as an _____(吉利的) animal in Chinese culture.
10. The ethnic groups of China are distinguished by their different _____(传统与习俗) in marriage, childbirth, funerals, festivals, food, housing, costume and recreational activities.

II. Translate the following terms into English or Chinese.

1. scented tea _____
2. *The Peony Pavilion* _____
3. clay figurine _____
4. cross-talk _____
5. shadow play _____
6. 昆曲_____
7. 丝绸之路_____
8. 庙会_____
9. 山水画_____
10. 小品_____

III. Translate the following sentences.

1. With an increasing awareness of the importance of taking care of mothers and newborns, maternity matrons see a growth in demand and income.

2. As Tomb Sweeping Festival and Cold Food Festival are on the same day, people in some places still have the custom of eating cold food on that day.

3. Chiness knot, an ancient knotting art in China has been one of the most fashionable things recently all over the world.

4. *The Drunken Beauty*, also known as *The Hundred-Flower Pavilion*, is the representative play of the Mei School and one of the most outstanding works of Peking Opera master Mei Lanfang.

5. By depicting Naxi deities, legendary Naxi ancestors and animals, Dongba paintings convey the harmony between human and nature.

6. 这座古镇在正月十五举办了各种比赛来庆祝元宵节。

7. 最早的汉字是商代的甲骨铭文。

8. 丝绸之路将中国的丝绸引入了中亚、西亚和欧洲，极大地促进了中西方之间的贸易往来。

9. 书法艺术在东南亚国家很受欢迎。

10. 在中国，茶有着悠久的历史并且在人们的生活中发挥着重要的作用。

Ⅳ. Translate the following paragraphs.

1. Events celebrating Chinese New Year and Beijing's successful bid for hosting the 2022 Winter Olympics were staged in Helsinki, capital of Finland, Feb. 18, 2015. More than 40,000 people took part in the Ninth "Happy Chinese New Year" Beijing Cultural Temple Fair, which was co-organized by the municipal government of Helsinki and Beijing Municipal Government. The temple fair featured fascinating parades, cultural performances, exhibitions, intangible cultural heritage shows and gourmet food items. A photo exhibition, themed "Charming Beijing, Passionate Winter Olympics" was also held.

2. 正月十五元宵节标志着春节的结束。在这一天，人们吃汤圆，逛灯展，猜灯谜。因此，元宵节也是家人团聚的重要时刻。人们互相表达对彼此的美好祝愿。和谐的家庭氛围意味着在新的一年家人幸福、健康。

Section B Interpretation

Interpretation Technique

口译技能：口译笔记（3）

除了用上一章口译技能提到的符号和缩略语外，一般口译笔记总体还遵循以下记录原则：

（1）记下一个独立且完整的意义后，马上画"/"。

（2）勤换行。一行最多记 4 个意义，即最多 3 个"/"。否则，口译时，信息太多，读取和组织信息很累。

（3）并列的信息要纵向排列。然后用大括号把并列的信息括起来。

（4）遇到之前已经记录下的信息时，就用箭头或直线把上面已经记录的信息符号拉下来，无须重新写。

例如：除夕之夜，一大家子一定会在一起会餐，最受欢迎的食物是饺子，人们认为它能带来好运和吉祥。

笔记示范：

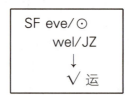

这个笔记中"饺子"最后被再次提到，但不用再记，为节约时间，只要用线直接拉下来就可以了。

那到底该如何练习口译笔记呢？为了熟练掌握笔记技能，可以先单独练习笔记，也就是先将笔记练习与口译练习分开。

（1）视记练习。找来一段文字，边看边记录内容。这样，练习者不必在听与译上分神，而是专门练习笔记方法，如笔记格式设计、符号的使用等，从而达到熟练掌握笔记技巧的目的。

（2）听记练习。视记练习进行一段时间后，当对笔记方法的掌握达到一定熟练程度后可以转而进行听记练习。顾名思义，听记练习就是播放一段讲话录音，练习者边听边记。这种练习的目的是将听辨过程引入笔记训练中来，使练习者逐渐学会将脑记与笔记相结合。

（3）综合练习。笔记练习的最后阶段就是模拟口译训练，即边听讲话，边记笔记，然后译出。

但是，笔记无论如何都不能喧宾夺主，口译时应该主要运用大脑短时记忆记住所听信息的意义，笔记只是起辅助作用。

Passage Interpretation 1

中国戏曲综合了对白、音乐、歌唱、舞蹈、武术和杂技等多种表演方式。它与希腊戏剧和印度梵剧并称为世界最古老的戏剧形式。中国戏曲的起源可追溯到原始社会的歌舞和宗教仪式,直到宋元时期才形成比较完整成熟的艺术体系。据统计,我国各地约有三百六十多种戏曲剧种,其中昆曲是现存最古老的剧种之一。

昆曲发源于元朝的昆山腔,至今已有六百多年的历史。它逐渐从昆山传播到全国各地,成为从16世纪到18世纪末中国影响最大的剧种。包括京剧在内的很多剧种都是在昆曲的影响下发展而来,因而昆曲素有"百戏之母"的雅称。2001年,昆曲被联合国教科文组织命名为"人类口头非物质遗产代表作"。

昆曲尽管在20世纪初濒临灭绝,现又再度兴盛。现存著名的剧目包括与莎士比亚同时期的明代戏曲大家汤显祖的《牡丹亭》、孔尚任的《桃花扇》。

Passage Interpretation 2

Chinese expect friendships to be lasting. For Chinese a true friendship endures throughout life changes. Chinese are still friends even if they haven't been in contact for 20 years. In North America, even the relationship in which people feel close and tell each other personal problems may not survive life changes such as moving to another city, graduation from a university, a change in economic circumstances, or marriage.

In China, the friendships are formed by people who work or go to school together. You may or may not like the person, but if he or she can do something for you because of his position or job, you can be friends. But in North America, business and friendship are kept separate. A person may have friends at work and at leisure time. Also friends tend to have similar financial circumstances, because friendship in the west is based on equality. Besides, westerns expect friends to be independent. Their friendship is mostly a matter of providing emotional support and spending time together.

A westerner will respond to a friend's trouble by asking "What do you want to do?" The idea is to help the friend to think out the problem and discover the solution he or she really wants and then to support the solution. Chinese friends give each other more concrete help. A Chinese will help a friend get a job, or arrange an appointment with a good doctor. Chinese friends give each  other money and might help each other out financially over a long time. Chinese usually expect more from their friends. You can feel free to tell your friend what he/she can or should do to help or please you.

Dialogue Interpretation

A: Did you see the statue of Confucius launched by the China Confucius Fund?

B: 看到了。孔子是中国古代的思想家、教育家、政治家,也是儒学的创始人。他对今天中国人的生活和思想依然有着重大的影响。

A：Confucianism seems to be back in fashion again. As far as I know, about five to six million Chinese students are currently studying *The Analects of Confucius*. The government is promoting the Confucian values as a way to address the social problems that have emerged as a result of the accelerated economic growth.

B：儒家思想是中国传统文化的主干,强调的是公正、人际关系的和谐以及个人对国家的社会责任感。

A：Some American scholars did a comparative study of Confucius with Greek and Roman philosophers. Their conclusion was that there is more practical value in Confucianism. Why?

B：因为它被广泛运用于中国社会。孔子还是个了不起的教育家,他平等对待学生,教给他们民主、开放的观念。

A：There is also an increasing awareness of Confucianism in other parts of the world, as Confucianism emphasizes "courtesy" when dealing with people or nature, and it is very beneficial for building harmony in any society.

B：有道理。正如一位学者所说,21世纪的生存问题,必须回到25个世纪之前孔子的智慧中去寻求解决的答案。

Exercises

Ⅰ. Interpreting technique practice.

You will hear 10 sentences. Please try to takes notes of each sentence and retell each sentence based on the notes.

1. _____

2. _____

3. _____

4. _____

5. _____

6. _____

7. _____

8. _____

9. _____

10. _____

II. Spot dictation.

Grasping the essence of an old culture like Britain's is always hard. It's even more difficult for foreigners who speak a different language. But Chinese people have a leg up, as the two countries prepare for a "(1)_____" of cultural exchange.

President Xi Jinping's visit to the UK, from Oct. 19 to 23, is the first state visit by a Chinese president since 2005. It's expected to be a (2)_____. Xi led a 150-member business delegation, with billions of pounds of investment planned.

"When people exchange goods, they exchange ideas. (3)_____ _____ go hand in hand," British Chancellor of the Exchequer George Osborne and British Museum director Neil MacGregor wrote in a joint piece on *The Telegraph*. "So as the UK and China broaden and develop their commercial ties, it's natural that the cultural links between the two countries should also grow closer and stronger."

The efforts began with Xi's state visit (4)_____. He was scheduled to travel in a carriage to meet the royal family at the Buckingham Palace. He was set to attend a (5)_____ and visit the Manchester City Football Club.

Xi also headed to the English countryside, to join British Prime Minister David Cameron at his countryside residence Chequers Court for talks and dinner. As British writer Jeremy Paxman once said, "The English mind kept alive the idea that (6)_____ _____ lay in the countryside".

While such experiences are reserved only for world leaders, the U.K. has also designed a (7)_____ for ordinary people in China.

Under the initiatives, some of UK's pre-eminent institutions, including the British Museum, the British Library and the Tate, will share objects and exhibitions with China.

Cultural (8) _____ like *Sherlock Holmes* will be introduced to Chinese audiences, along with plays by Shakespeare and the Royal Opera House.

"The classical repertoire sits very comfortably with technology and (9) _____ _____. It draws on the best of history, with the best of forward thinking," said Nick Marchand, who is the director of arts and creative industries and the first secretary of culture, at the Cultural and Education Section of the British Embassy.

"There's an (10) _____ behind this cultural exchange," wrote the joint piece by Osborne and MacGregor. "Ultimately, however, it's about more than pounds and *renminbi*. It's in our literature, our theater, our paintings and our museums, that we express who we are as a country."

III. Sentence listening and translation.

1. _____
   _____

2. _____
   _____

3. _____
   _____

4. _____
   _____

5. _____
   _____

IV. Paragraph listening and translation.

_____
_____
_____
_____

V. Dialogue interpretation.

A: I always feel spoiled to be a guest in a Chinese household. The host would start preparing for our visit days ahead. Even if there would be a lot of food on the table, the host would still say, "We don't have much, so please bear with us." They keep putting food on my plate despite the fact I may not like certain food. I usually feel very embarrassed. Some hosts even force their children to perform a song or recite a poem for me.

A: 这就是中国人的待客之道,把最好的东西拿出来招待客人。而西方人不会,他们的目的是交流而不是表现待客的热情。

B: Chinese hospitality is meant to show the politeness of the host rather than keeping guests happy. The host might insist on starting a fire so he could make tea for them, despite the fact that the guests might have been clouded by the smoke. At least the host made the impression that he was very hospitable.

A: 这是一百年前的情形,现在有所不同。越来越多的人意识到尊重他人的重要性。待客的方式也在逐渐改变。传统的待客之道也许很快就不复存在了。

VI. Interpreting in groups.

Role-play the following situation with your partners, acting as the Chinese speaker, English speaker and the interpreter respectively. One group will be invited to perform in class.

Characters: 1. Sara
2. Wang Min's mother
3. Wang Min, interpreter

Location: Dining room at home

Task: Sara is an international student who studies Chinese culture at the Confucius Institute in Beijing. As the hostess of Sara's homestay family, Wang Min's mother persuades Sara to celebrate the Spring Festival with them. Wang Min's mother speaks Chinese while Sara is an English-speaker. Wang Min will work as an interpreter.

VII. 3-minute talk on the given topic.

Talk on the following topic in three minutes based on the given reference questions.

Topic: **Being proud of Chinese culture**

Questions for Reference:

1. What are the symbols of Chinese culture in your eyes?
2. Are you proud of Chinese culture? Why?
3. What do you like most about Chinese culture?

VIII. Theme-related expressions.

• 四大发明	the four great inventions of ancient China
• 中国热	Sinomania
•《三国演义》	Romance of the Three Kingdoms
•《西游记》	Journey to the West; Pilgrimage to the West

•《红楼梦》	Dream of Red Chamber; The story of Stone; A Dream of Red Mansions
•《水浒传》	Heroes of the Marshes; Tales of the Water Margin
•《孙子兵法》	The Art of War
•四合院	quadrangle, the traditional Chinese single-story houses with rows of rooms around the four sides of a courtyard
•优秀民间艺术	outstanding folk arts
•文物	cultural relics
•中国结	Chinese knot
•中山装	Chinese tunic suit
•京剧票友	amateur performer of Beijing Opera; Peking Opera fan
•刺绣	embroidery
•文房四宝	the four stationery treasures of the Chinese study—writing brushes, ink sticks, paper and ink stones
•蜡染	batik
•漆画	lacquer painting
•水墨画	ink painting; wash painting
•檀香扇	sandalwood fan
•唐三彩	triocolor-glazed pottery of the Tang Dynasty

Section C Further Exploration

尝试翻译中央电视台春节联欢晚会节目单部分节目内容。

1. 开场曲《欢歌贺新春》，中央电视台48位主持人	1. Opening song *Usher in the Spring with Beautiful Melodies* (48 CCTV hosts and hostesses)
2. 歌曲《十二生肖》	2. Song *Chinese Zodiac*
3. 小品《我要上春晚》	3. Comic skit *I Want to Be in Spring Festival Gala*

Unit 9　Cultural Exchange 文化交流

4. 小品《想跳就跳》	4. Comic skit _____
5. 创意儿童节目《剪花花》	5. Children show *Paper-cutting Flowers*
6. 相声《这事儿不赖我》	6. Cross talk *Do Not Blame Me*
7. 歌曲《我心永恒》	7. Song _____
8. 武术《少年中国》	8. Martial art *China Youth*
9. 杂技《冰与火》	9. Acrobatics *Ice and Fire*
10. 歌曲《一辈子朋友》	10. Song _____
11. 魔术《魔琴》	11. Magic show *Magic Piano*
12. 土耳其风情舞蹈《火》	12. Turkey dance *Fire*
13. 歌曲《净土》	13. Song _____
14. 创意乐舞《指尖与足尖》	14. Piano and ballet performance *On My Fingertips and Toes*
15. 京剧《智取威虎山》片段	15. A segment of Peking Opera from *Taking Over the Weihu Mountain*
16. 相声《东西南北大拜年》	16. Cross talk _____
17. 歌曲《难忘今宵》	17. Song *Unforgettable*

UNIT 10
Health and Medicine
健康医疗

Learning Objectives

1. To learn to convert parts of speech in translation;
2. To learn how to interpret numbers(1);
3. To learn how to translate/interpret passages or dialogues on the topic of health and medicine;
4. To learn useful words and expressions related to health and medicine.

Lead-in

● *Quiz*(**True or False**)

_____ 1. TCM usually stands for traditional Chemical medicine in terms of medicine.

_____ 2. Chinese medicine is sometimes chosen over western medicine because it is more natural, less dangerous and more effective.

_____ 3. When taking Chinese herbal medicine, you should avoid foods like rice and bread.

_____ 4. The three main types of traditional Chinese therapy are acupuncture, cupping and massage.

_____ 5. Chinese medicine has a long recorded history of over 200 years.

_____ 6. Chinese medicine has proved effective in curing any disease that western medicine fails to cure.

_____ 7. There are about 360 acupuncture points all over the body of everyone.

Unit 10　Health and Medicine 健康医疗

● **What are the pictures about? Fill in the blanks with the given English words.**

stethoscope　　acupuncture　　Band-Aid　　massage　　wheelchair
syringe　　　　Chinese herb　　gauze　　　　pill capsule　cough syrup

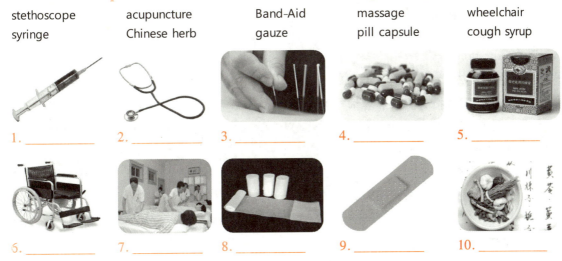

1. _____　2. _____　3. _____　4. _____　5. _____

6. _____　7. _____　8. _____　9. _____　10. _____

Section A　Translation

Translation Technique

词性转换

由于中国和英语国家在历史、文化、风俗习惯等方面的不同,在语言上形成了很大差异。很多时候,需要我们对语言中的词性进行转换,然后再翻译,方可使译文显得通顺、自然。词性转换是指翻译时将某个词从一种词性译成另一种词性。

英译汉时主要有如下词性转换:

1. 英语名词、介词、形容词或副词转换为汉语动词

The <u>cultivation</u> of a hobby is therefore a policy of first importance to a public man. 因此,对于一个从事社会活动的人来讲,培养一种爱好,是至关重要的对策。

The Army marched on bravely <u>against</u> the piercing wind. 军队冒着刺骨的寒风英勇前进。

All were <u>unconscious</u> that this experience was a test of character. 大家都没有认识到这番经验却是一次个性的考验。

She opened the window to let fresh air <u>in</u>. 她把窗子打开,让新鲜空气进来。

2. 英语动词、副词转换为汉语名词、形容词

The inflammation is <u>characterized</u> by red, swelling, fever, and pain. 炎症的<u>特点</u>是红、肿、热、痛。

Our government shows great <u>concern</u> for the Chinese residents abroad. 我国政府十分<u>关心</u>海外华侨。

3. 英语名词转换为汉语形容词、副词

He added: "I understand and respect those views, but I deeply believe in the <u>correctness</u> of my decision." 他还说:"我理解并尊重他们的看法,但我深信我的决定是<u>正确的</u>。"

161

汉译英时主要有如下词性转换：

1. 汉语动词转换为英语名词

他在讲话中特别<u>强调</u>提高产品质量。In his speech he laid special <u>stress</u> on raising the quality of the products.

绝对不许<u>违反</u>这个原则。No <u>violation</u> of this principle can be tolerated.

2. 汉语动词转换为英语形容词或副词

获悉贵国遭受地震，我们极为<u>关切</u>。We are deeply <u>concerned</u> at the news that your country has been struck by an earthquake.

我们决不<u>满足</u>于现有的成就。We are not <u>content</u> with our present achievements.

3. 汉语形容词或副词转换为英语名词

那个家伙<u>笨</u>得出奇。That fellow is a typical <u>fool</u>.

4. 汉语名词转换为英语动词

他的讲演给听众留下了很深的<u>印象</u>。His speech <u>impressed</u> the audience deeply.

Passage Translation 1

Vocabulary

1. 中医药
2. 智慧的结晶
3. 常见病
4. 多发病
5. 疑难病
6. 社区卫生服务机构
7. 乡镇卫生院和村卫生室
8. 临床人才
9. 临床诊疗
10. 中医针灸
11. 人类非物质文化遗产代表作
12. 《黄帝内经》
13. 《本草纲目》
14. 世界记忆遗产名录

Unit 10　Health and Medicine 健康医疗

中医药在中国有着悠久的历史,是中华民族在生产生活实践以及治疗疾病过程中形成和发展的医学科学,是中华民族智慧的结晶,为中华民族繁衍昌盛做出了重要贡献。中医药在治疗常见病、多发病和疑难病等方面独具特色和优势,在治疗传染性疾病方面也有良好效果,并以其费用低、疗效好、副作用小等特点,深受中国公众喜爱,在医疗卫生保健中发挥着不可替代的重要作用。

中国政府一贯积极扶持和促进中医药事业的发展:

建立覆盖城乡的中医医疗服务体系。目前,75.6%的社区卫生服务中心、51.6%的社区卫生服务站、66.5%的乡镇卫生院、57.5%的村卫生室能够提供中医药服务。

形成独具特色的中医药人才培养体系。国家把人才培养作为中医药事业发展的根本,加强优秀中医临床人才培养。

推进中医药现代化。积极利用现代科学技术,促进中医药的理论和技术创新;在中医基础理论、临床诊疗等领域取得重要成果。加速中药产业化和现代化,中药产业规模大幅扩大。

积极开展国际交流合作。目前,已有70多个国家与中国签订了协议,中医药对外医疗、教育、科技合作不断扩大,已传播到世界上160多个国家和地区。"中医针灸"列入人类非物质文化遗产代表作名录,《黄帝内经》《本草纲目》等中医药典籍列入世界记忆遗产名录。

Notes

1. "建立覆盖城乡的中医医疗服务体系。"这句话是典型的汉语无主句,文中有大量这种句子。汉译英处理的时候主要是转成被动语态句或添加逻辑主语。此句中使用被动语态句翻译。全句翻译为:"Networks of TCM medical services have been established to cover both urban and rural areas."

2. "目前,已有70多个国家与中国签订了协议,中医药对外医疗、教育、科技合作不断扩大,已传播到世界上160多个国家和地区。"这句除了是无主句需要处理外,句中的"中医药对外医疗合作"指的是在国外运用中医药的合作。因此,可以译为"cooperation with foreign countries in TCM application"。全句翻译为:"China has signed agreements with over 70 countries, expanding the cooperation with foreign countries in TCM application, education and technology."

3. "'中医针灸'列入人类非物质文化遗产代表作名录,《黄帝内经》《本草纲目》等中医药典籍列入世界记忆遗产名录。"这句翻译难点主要是中医相关术语。这些都是约定俗成的,在平时多积累即可。比如,"针灸"译为"acupuncture",《黄帝内经》和《本草纲目》分别译为"*Inner Canon of the Yellow Emperor*"和"*Compendium of Materia Medica*"。全句翻译为:"'TCM acupuncture' has been recognized as a masterpiece of the intangible heritage of mankind. *Inner Canon of the Yellow Emperor*, *Compendium of Materia Medica* and other classic works have been included in the Memory of the World."

Passage Translation 2

Vocabulary

1. antibiotics
2. infection
3. life expectancy
4. World Health Day
5. drug-resistant pathogens
6. R & D pipeline
7. antimicrobial
8. unabated
9. dose
10. microbe
11. health worker
12. civil society
13. drug resistance

When the first antibiotics were introduced in the 1940s, they were hailed as "wonder drugs", the miracles of modern medicine. Widespread infections that killed millions of people every year can now be cured. The powerful impact of these medicines sparked a revolution in the discovery of new drugs. The human condition took a dramatic turn for the better, with significant jumps in life expectancy.

The message on this World Health Day is loud and clear. The world is on the brink of losing these miracle cures.

The emergence and spread of drug-resistant pathogens has accelerated. More and more essential medicines are failing. The speed with which these drugs are being lost far outpaces the development of replacement drugs. In fact, the R & D pipeline for new antimicrobials has practically run dry.

The implications are equally clear. In the absence of urgent corrective and protective actions, the world is heading towards a post-antibiotic era, in which many common infections will no longer have a cure and, once again, kill unabatedly.

The development of resistance is a natural biological process that will occur, sooner or later, with every drug. The use of any antimicrobial for any infection, in any dose, and over any time period, forces microbes to either adapt or die in a phenomenon known as "selective pressure". The microbes which adapt and survive carry genes for resistance, which can be passed on from one person to another and rapidly spread around the world.

The responsibility for turning this situation around is entirely in our hands. Irrational and inappropriate use of antimicrobials is by far the biggest driver of drug resistance. This includes overuse, when drugs are dispensed too liberally; underuse, especially when economic hardship encourages patients to stop treatment as soon as they feel better; misuse, when drugs are given for the wrong disease, and the massive routine use of antimicrobials in the industrialized production of food.

On this World Health Day, WHO is issuing a policy package to get everyone, on the right track, with the right measures, quickly. Governments can make progress, working with health workers, pharmacists, civil society, patients, and industry. We all can plan and coordinate our response. Drug resistance costs vast amounts of money, and affects vast numbers of lives. The trends are clear and obvious. No action today means no cure tomorrow. We cannot allow the loss of essential medicines to become the next global crisis.

Notes

1. "When the first antibiotics were introduced in the 1940s, they were hailed as 'wonder drugs', the miracles of modern medicine." 这句话中"the miracles of modern medicine"虽是同位语，这儿不一定要译为修饰语，可以译成分句"是现代医学的奇迹"，更符合汉语表达。这句话翻译为："抗生素于20世纪40年代首次现身时,被人们惊呼为'神药',是现代医学的奇迹。"

2. "The emergence and spread of drug-resistant pathogens has accelerated." 这句话中的"emergence and spread"根据汉语表达习惯，翻译时可以由名词转为动词。全句译为："耐药病原体已经加速出现和蔓延。"

3. "The use of any antimicrobial for any infection, in any dose, and over any time period, forces microbes to either adapt or die in a phenomenon known as 'selective pressure'." 句中的"use"可以转译为动词。这句话翻译为："针对某种感染使用某一剂量的某种抗菌剂一段时间,会迫使微生物或是适应,或是死亡;这种现象被称为'选择性压力'。"

4. "The microbes which adapt and survive carry genes for resistance, which can be passed on from one person to another and rapidly spread around the world." 句中的定语从句较多,如果都译为修饰语不利于表达,可以把后面"which can be passed on from one person to another and rapidly spread around the world"译成句子。全句译为："适应并存活下来的微生物携带耐药基因,可以从一个人传给另一个人,并在世界上快速蔓延开来。"

Sentences in Focus

1. 中医药在中国有着悠久的历史,是中华民族在生产生活实践以及治疗疾病过程中形成和发展的医学科学,是中华民族智慧的结晶,为中华民族繁衍昌盛做出了重要贡献。

2. 中医药在治疗常见病、多发病和疑难病等方面独具优势,在治疗传染性疾病方面也有良好效果,并以其费用低、疗效好、副作用小等特点,深受中国公众喜爱,在医疗卫生保健中发挥着不可替代的重要作用。

3. 中国政府一贯积极扶持和促进中医药事业的发展,建立覆盖城乡的中医医疗服务体系。

4. 国家把人才培养作为中医药事业发展的根本,加强优秀中医临床人才培养。

5. "中医针灸"列入人类非物质文化遗产代表作名录,《黄帝内经》《本草纲目》等中医药典籍列入世界记忆遗产名录。

6. The speed with which these drugs are being lost far outpaces the development of replacement drugs.

7. In the absence of urgent corrective and protective actions, the world is heading towards a post-antibiotic era, in which many common infections will no longer have a cure and, once again, kill unabated.

8. The responsibility for turning this situation around is entirely in our hands. Irrational and inappropriate use of antimicrobials is by far the biggest driver of drug resistance.

9. On this World Health Day, WHO is issuing a policy package to get everyone, especially governments and their drug regulatory systems, on the right track, with the right measures, quickly.

10. We cannot allow the loss of essential medicines to become the next global crisis.

Exercises

I. Fill in the blanks with English words according to the given Chinese.

1. Lung cancer is the most _____(常见的疾病) in Guangzhou, with 47 of every 100,000 residents diagnosed.

2. Gender imbalance is another _____(副作用) of the one-child policy, as Chinese parents' preference for sons has led to abortions of female fetuses.

3. China will improve the mechanisms for coordinating _____ _____(城乡发展) in an effort to allow farmers to share the fruits of the country's modernization.

4. Patients can now register after 8 p.m. to attend the _____

_____ (门诊) the next day, eliminating the need to arrive early in the morning to make an appointment.

5. In 2005, the average cost of a prescription at a _____ (社区卫生服务中心) paid by low-income people in Yinchuan was 14.5 yuan.
6. Any _____ (人才培养), without the basis of school education, would not be realistic or sustainable.
7. It is amazing how traditional Chinese medicine can uncover the _____ _____ (病因) without the aid of modern techndogy.
8. China needs _____ (技术创新) to adapt to the new normal of economic growth and realize a transformation and upgrade of the economy.
9. To better guide and standardize clinical treatment of the disease, a _____ _____ (临床诊断) and treatment guideline on AIDS was issued by Chinese Medical Association.
10. Now that traditional Chinese medicine is rapidly entering the mainstream of the practice of medicine in North America, an increasing number of people are interested in finding a _____ (合格的医师).

II. Translate the following medicine terminologies into English or Chinese.

1. aging population _____
2. online registration platform _____
3. drugs that are covered by medical insurance _____
4. community nursing service _____
5. chronic disease _____
6. 中西医结合 _____
7. 公共卫生服务 _____
8. 医疗保健体系 _____
9. 药价改革 _____
10. 专利药 _____

III. Translate the following sentences.

1. We will give full play to the important role of traditional Chinese medicine and folk medicines of ethnic minorities in the prevention and control of disease.

_____

2. Over the past few years, the Chinese social security system has been established and improved through the reform of our health insurance system.

_____

3. Prices of more than 2,700 drugs will soon be determined by the market, rather than the government, as China gets ready to roll out its drug pricing reform plan.

4. China will set up standardized training in 2015 for medical graduates before they become resident doctors, according to the National Health and Family Planning Commission.

5. Not only does *tai chi* help reduce stress and anxiety but it also helps strike the balance between *yin* and *yang*.

6. 中国妇女的人均寿命已从 2000 年的 73.33 岁上升至 2013 年的 77.37 岁。

7. 根据世界卫生组织发布的报告,随着每年新增 1000 多万例癌症病例,癌症已经成为全球最具杀伤力的疾病之一。

8. 让我们携手抗击艾滋病,因为我们有责任为下一代创造一个安全的环境。

9. 尤其在培养合格的专业人才方面,中国与贵国之间的技术合作取得了瞩目的成就。

10. 政府制定了一系列政策来发展中医服务网络,从而更好地服务于农村居民。

IV. Translate the following paragraphs.

1. The origin of traditional Chinese medicine can be traced to Shennongshi, a mythological figure about 5,000 years ago, who sampled hundreds of herbs for use as medicines. The formal history of TCM started about 2,500 years ago with *Inner Canon of the Yellow Emperor*, the first written account of the practice of TCM. TCM views a patient's condition as a reflection of the interaction of five elements of nature: metal, wood, water, fire and earth. Chinese consumers generally perceive TCM as more effective for chronic illnesses, and they view western medicine as being more effective for acute and serious illnesses.

2. 中医有着几千年的历史。它是中国最宝贵的文化遗产之一。有些中医处方拯救了数百万人的生命,有着极高的价值。中国政府将继续保护并向全世界推广中医。我们相信,在医学专家的努力下,中医将在各类疾病的治疗中发挥越来越重要的作用。

Section B Interpretation

Interpretation Technique

口译技能:数字口译(1)

任何话题的口译都可能遇到各种复杂的数字。而数字的口译又必须准确无误,不得有半点疏忽。因此数字口译往往是一大难点。数字口译的压力主要来自两个方面:一是要在较短的时间内有较强的短期记忆能力来准确捕捉数字信息,二是要能自然而快速地进行两种语言间的数字转换。造成汉英数字互译困难的原因有几个方面:一是汉语和英语的数字表达方式和四位以上数字的数位分段法不同。从下图可以看出,汉语四位以上的数字每四位一段,从右往左各段位依次为:个/万/亿/兆。而英语则每三位为一段,从右往左各段位依次为 one, thousand, million, billion, trillion, 这两组段位应该烂熟于胸。

兆/万亿	千亿	百亿	十亿	亿	千万	百万	十万	万	千	百	十	个
tr	h b	ten b	b	h m	ten m	m	h t	ten t	t	h	ten	one

(图中 h 代表 hundred,t 代表 thousand,m 代表 million,b 代表 billion,tr 代表 trillion)

从上图对比中还可以看出,英语中没有与汉语"万""十万""千万""亿"等相对应的词,这就给汉英数字互译带来很大不便。汉译英时遇到以上数字时,译员必须很快推算出与其相对应的英语数位和表达方式。用"ten thousand"表示"万",用"hundred thousand"表示"十万",用"ten million"表示"千万",用"hundred million"表示"亿"等。英译汉时则要做相反的推算和转换。这样,译员在进行语言转换的同时,要不停地进行数位的推导和换算,脑子活动异常紧张,稍不注意便会出错。所以,可适当记忆下面两组英汉数字表达对照表。

万 =10 thousand

十万 =100 thousand

百万 =1 million

千万 =10 million

一亿 =100 million

十亿 =1 billion

百亿 =10 billion

千亿 =100 billion

万亿 =1 trillion

数字口译,还可以使用"点三杠四法"和"缺位补零法"。

1. "点三杠四法"

这种方法是根据英汉两种语言数字分段方法的不同而专门设计的。英文数字是三位一段,汉语数字是四位一段。英文数字以逗点从右至左每三位一点(,),汉语数字以斜杠(/)从右至左每四位一划。在口译时转换过程如下:

(1)汉译英数字口译转换过程

① 听到汉语数字:十五亿三千九百八十七万六千三百二十一

② 在笔记上按照汉语数字的段位依次记下:15/3987/6321

③ 从右至左按英语计数方式三位一点:1,5/39,87/6,321

④ 再按照英语段位读出:one billion five hundred and thirty-nine million eight hundred seventy-six thousand three hundred and twenty-one

(2)英译汉数字口译转换过程

① 听到英文数字:thirty-six million seven hundred and twenty-four thousand six hundred and thirty-one

② 在笔记上按照英语数字的段位依次记下:36,724,631

③ 从右至左按汉语计数方式每四位一划:36,72/4,631

④ 按照汉语段位,读出数字:三千六百七十二万四千六百三十一

2. "缺位补零法"

这种方法是针对数字中有空位的情况设计的。如上例中,假如每一段位上都有数字,那么翻译时直接使用"点三杠四法"即可。但如果某些数位为零,情况就要复杂一些。首先要注意每个段位中的数字是不是三个(英语数字)或四个(汉语数字),如果不足,要及时补零。

(1)汉译英数字口译转换过程

① 听到汉语数字:六亿零五十八万零三十六

② 在笔记上按照汉语数字的段位依次记下:6/58/36

③ 按照汉语数字每个段位有四个数字的特点从右至左在每个段位数字前补零:6/0058/0036

④ 从右至左按英语计数方式三位一点:6/00,58/0,036

⑤ 再按照英语段位读出英文:six hundred million five hundred and eighty thousand and thirty-six

(2)英译汉数字口译转换过程

① 听到英文数字:one hundred billion thirty-six million seven thousand and forty-one

② 在笔记中按照英语数字的段位依次记下:100,36,7,41

③ 按照英语数字每个段位三个数字的特点从右至左在每个段位数字前补零,即:100,036,007,041
④ 从右至左按汉语计数方式每四位一划:100,0/36,00/7,041
⑤ 再按照汉语段位读出:一千亿三千六百万七千零四十一

长数字的口译可以先从练习三位数开始听译,再逐渐进阶到多位数数字的听译。另外,为顺利完成转换,还要对英汉数字的段位划分十分熟练。

Passage Interpretation 1

今年世界无烟日活动的主题是"两性与烟草——关注针对女性的烟草促销行为"。

虽然只有不到十分之一的女性吸烟,但全世界女性烟民人数估计达两亿之多。而且,由于烟草企业花巨资制作针对女性的广告,将吸烟与美和妇女解放挂钩,这一数字还有可能增长。世界卫生组织近期对151个国家的调查显示,有一半国家,男孩和女孩的吸烟人数不相上下。由于青少年在成年后很可能继续吸烟,这一结果越发令人担忧。有证据表明,一些国家女性烟草使用率在上升。各国政府必须采取行动,保护妇女远离烟草广告、促销和赞助活动。

各国政府还要保护女性,远离二手烟。世界卫生组织的数据显示,在每年因二手烟死亡的43万人当中,近三分之二为妇女。在世界各地,每年有超过150万妇女死于烟草使用。其中大多数死亡发生在低收入和中等收入国家。如果不采取协调一致的行动,到2030年,这一数字将可能达到250万。

我们必须遏制全球烟草流行。值此世界无烟日之际,我敦促各国政府设法应对这一公共健康威胁。烟草使用既不时尚也不健康。使用烟草是一种致命的陋习。

Passage Interpretation 2

We all know that exercise is good for our physical health. Might physical exercise boost our health? The research says yes.

Research has established that exercise is good for mood. People are happier after they engage in physical exercise and there is evidence that exercise can help with depression. Critically, studies have demonstrated that people are more likely to perceive their lives as meaningful when they are in a good mood. Thus, by boosting mood, exercise may boost meaning.

Research also suggests that exercise may help people combat anxiety. Similarly, many people exercise to manage stress. Anxiety and stress can compromise health: people are less likely to perceive life as meaningful when they are experiencing anxiety and stress. Thus, by offering relief from stress and anxiety, exercise may promote health.

Finally, research indicates that exercise can improve self-esteem and self-esteem is highly associated with health. When people feel good about themselves, they also feel like their lives are meaningful.

In general, exercise is more likely to be associated with positive self-esteem if people are exercising for health and fitness, not solely to improve body image.

Many exercise enthusiasts will tell you that their daily workouts are a critical part of maintaining their mental health and well-being. Exercise regulates mood and helps people cope with the challenges of life. So exercise. It is good for your health.

Dialogue Interpretation

Patient: Doctor, I have been suffering from "fits" for a few years. I wonder what the matter is with me and hope you'll help me get rid of them soon.

医生：您说的"突然昏倒"是什么意思？

Patient: By "fit" I mean I lose consciousness and fall on the ground suddenly.

医生：什么时候开始的？

Patient: When I was 25 years old.

医生：有多少年了？

Patient: Over three years.

医生：每次犯病持续多长时间？

Patient: About a minute.

医生：每次发作相隔多久？

Patient: Sometimes about a month, and sometimes two months. Could it be related to the environment?

医生：平常在什么情况下容易发作？

Patient: It is difficult to say exactly. Once when I was crossing the street, a swiftly moving car suddenly drove by and I became very nervous. I screamed and blacked out.

医生：您伤着了吗？

Patient: No, the car stopped at once. I came to quickly and then walked home.

医生：还怎样发作过？

Patient: On another occasion, no sooner had I seen a nurse draw blood from a patient than I felt perspiration and weakness followed by loss of consciousness.

医生：在发病的时候还有什么其他的表现吗？

Patient: I was told by witnesses that I got pale and sweated excessively during the attack.

医生：做一个内科和神经科的全面检查吧。这是各项检查单，把所有的检查做完后再来看病。

Patient: Thanks a lot, doctor.

Exercises

I. Interpreting technique practice.

You will hear 5 Chinese numbers and five English numbers. Try to write down the numbers as quickly as possible in the following sentences and interpret them.

1. _____
2. _____
3. _____
4. _____
5. _____
6. _____
7. _____
8. _____
9. _____
10. _____

II. Spot dictation.

The Chinese traditional (1) _____ of acupuncture or piercing the body with a needle is a treatment which focuses on the inside from the outside. It is a therapy that seeks to find acupuncture points as a means of (2) _____ to find the cause of illness and then take the appropriate treatment. Acupuncture is a skill (3) _____ traditional Chinese medical theory, similar to massage and *gua sha*. Acupuncture stimulates points of life (4) _____ in order to keep the *yin-yang* balance and adjust the status of the organs.

"This person is constipated, because of a (5) _____ and too much work. According to her condition, the doctor chooses some acupuncture points to help her rehabilitation."

(6) _____ of new research, modern acupuncture is quickly developing. Today, needles are made of stainless steel rather than gold or silver as they were in the past. Without electricity, doctors used to have to (7) _____ _____ by hand, in order to stimulate the acupuncture points. But now, they can use electrified equipment.

It is estimated that acupuncture has developed for over two and half thousand years and for much of that time, it was used for internal medicine, surgery, gynecology and pediatrics. With the (8) _____ life of the modern world, it serves more to help relieve the pressures of work.

During the Tang Dynasty, Chinese acupuncture (9) _____ Japan, Korea, India and the Arabian peninsula. But now, it is found throughout the world and plays an important role as an (10) _____ to western medicine.

III. Sentence listening and translation.

1. _____

2. _____

3. _____

4. _____

5. _____

IV. Paragraph listening and translation.

_____

V. Dialogue interpretation.

Doctor：早上好！能为你效劳吗？

Patient：Oh, I feel uncomfortable with my stomach and don't have any appetite for food.

Doctor：请伸出舌头……你睡眠好吗？

Patient：No, not very well. I often work extra hours till midnight.

Doctor：你显得很疲劳。内循环(inner circulation)看起来不怎么好。

Patient：It's true. Doctor, could you tell me what I should do to cure my disease?

Doctor：好的。我会用针灸、推拿和中药来治愈你的病。

Patient：Thank you, doctor. My health insurance covers all my medical bills of this year.

Doctor：很好。顺便说一下，别熬夜。

VI. Interpreting in groups.

Role-play the following situation with your partners, acting as the Chinese speaker, English speaker and the interpreter respectively. One group will be invited to perform in class.

participants: 1. Mr. Steve Willis
      2. Doctor
      3. Interpreter

Location: hospital

Task: You are a doctor of Wuxi Hospital of Traditional Chinese Medicine. Mr. Steve Willis is a patient from the United States. Greet him, ask Steve about his physical condition and help him with his illness. You speak Chinese while Steve is an English-speaker.

VII. 3-minute talk on the given topic.

Talk on the following topic in three minutes based on the given reference questions.

Topic: **Healthy lifestyle**

Questions for Reference:
1. Do you exercise? How often do you exercise?
2. Do you think you are in good physical condition? Why?
3. What do you think you should do to improve your physical condition?

VIII. Theme-related expressions.

中医名著	famous TCM work
救死扶伤	healing the sick and saving the dying
相生相克	mutual generation and restriction
新陈代谢	metabolism
艾灸疗法	moxibustion
刮痧疗法	skin scraping therapy with water, liquor or vegetable oil
理疗	physical therapy
切脉	feeling the pulse
偏方	folk prescription
家传秘方	secret prescription handed down from one's ancestors

• 阴阳五行学说	the theory of *yin-yang* and five elements (metal, wood, water, fire and earth)
• 内伤七情（喜、怒、忧、思、悲、恐、惊）	internal causes (joy, anger, worry, thought, grief, fear and surprise)
• 外感六淫（风、寒、暑、湿、燥、火）	external causes (wind, cold, heat, wetness, dryness and fire)
• 中药四性	four properties of medicinal herb
• 中药五味	five tastes of medicinal herb
• 经络	main and collateral channels inside human body; meridian
• 中华医学会	Chinese Medical Association
• 年度体检	annual check-up
• 手术室	operation room
• 输血	blood transfusion
• 急诊室	emergency room
• 药房	pharmacy
• 住院部	in-patient department
• 城镇职工基本医疗保险制度	basic medical insurance system for urban employees

Section C Further Exploration

阅读以下关于中医理论背景下关于症状的描述，根据所给中文在每个空格内填写一个单词使其符合原意。

How to Use Traditional Chinese Medicine Terms
怎样在生活中使用中医的语言

I feel like the circulation of my *qi* and blood is (1) _____ due to long hours of work.	我感觉工作过久导致气血不通。
I'm suffering from (2) _____ in my knees.	我的膝盖有湿气。
Too much air-conditioning in the office and the high temperature made me vulnerable to (3) _____.	办公室空调太冷，外面又太热，导致我受了寒邪。

Unit 10 Health and Medicine 健康医疗

I've eaten too much raw seafood and iced beer, so my body is (4) _____ with humidity.	我吃了太多生冷海鲜和冰啤酒,身体湿气很重。
I feel very dizzy and heavy, and I cannot (5) _____ well. Do you know any food that's good for getting rid of my humidity?	我觉得昏昏沉沉,而且积食不化。你知道吃什么食物可以祛湿吗?
I want to have lamb hot pot because my *yang* has been (6) _____ lately and needs reinforcement.	我想吃羊肉火锅,因为我最近阳虚,需要好好补补。
I'm having an (7) _____, which brought my toothache back again.	我最近上火,牙疼又犯了。
Those easily enraged have linner heat in their (8) _____.	爱生气的人肝火旺。
You looks (9) _____ but your forehead looks dark. Did you drink until 5 o'clock in the morning again?	你看起来面色发白,印堂发黑,是不是又喝酒喝到早上五点钟了?
You have had more white hair recently. You should eat more black sesame to nourish your (10) _____.	你最近白头发变多了,应该多吃黑芝麻补肾。

UNIT 11

Entertainment

影视娱乐

Learning Objectives

1. To know how to translate film titles;
2. To learn how to interpret numbers(2);
3. To learn how to translate / interpret passages and dialogues on the topic of entertainment;
4. To learn useful words and expressions related to film industry.

Lead-in

● **Quiz** (True or False)

_____ 1. Rowan Atkinson is an American actor, comedian, and screenwriter best known for his work on the sitcoms *Mr. Bean*.

_____ 2. British author J. K. Rowling is a British novelist best known as the author of *Harry Potter*, a series of seven fantasy novels.

_____ 3. The Academy Awards or The Oscars is an annual American awards ceremony honoring cinematic achievements in the film industry.

_____ 4. The CCTV Spring Festival Gala has the smallest audience in the world.

_____ 5. Chopsticks Brothers' *Little Apple* wins big at American Music Awards and mixed responses from home.

_____ 6. The film *Ip Man*, starred by Jackie Chan, is based on the story of Yip Kai-man, a Chinese martial artist.

_____ 7. *If You Are the One* is a Chinese dating show hosted by Wang Han and produced by Jiangsu Satellite Television.

Unit 11　Entertainment 影视娱乐

● **What are the titles of these films? Fill in the blanks with English titles.**

The Godfather 　　Avatar　　　　Roman Holiday　　Home Alone
The Lord of the Rings　The Matrix　　Star Wars　　　Transformers
Spider-Man　　　　Titanic　　　　Sleepless in Seattle　Kung Fu Panda

1. _____　　2. _____　　3. _____　　4. _____

5. _____　　6. _____　　7. _____　　8. _____

9. _____　　10. _____　　11. _____　　12. _____

Section A　Translation

Translation Technique

电影片名翻译

1. 音译

在电影片名翻译中，音译的方法使用较少，但又不可或缺。对于片名中涉及的人名、地名，如果为观众所熟知，或具有重要的历史文化意义，则应当音译。音译保留了原片名的韵律节奏，以其浓郁的异域特色吸引广大观众。

如：Titanic《泰坦尼克号》　　Casablanca《卡萨布兰卡》　　Ben Hur《宾赫传》
　　Madam Currie《居里夫人》　《周恩来》Zhou Enlai　　《成吉思汗》Genghis

2. 直译

直译是在片名翻译中，最大限度地保留原片名的内容和形式。当源语与目的语在功能上达到重合时，这是最简单而行之有效的翻译方法。在实际翻译过程中，许多片名中英重合程度惊人，几乎可以达到字对字翻译。

如：Schindler's List　《辛德勒的名单》
　　Four Weddings and a Funeral　《四个婚礼和一个葬礼》

《黄土地》Yellow Earth　　　　《南京大屠杀》Nanjing Massacre

另一些则须根据译语特征，略微改变源语的词序或结构，在总体上仍趋于同源语形式保持一致。

如：Man in Black《黑衣人》　　　　The Silence of the Lambs《沉默的羔羊》
　　《青春之歌》Song of Youth　　　《天云山传奇》Legend of Tianyun Mountain

3. 意译

由于中英两种语言文化的差异，如果片面强调保留片名的形式，就会导致以形害意。为使译语观众能真正领会原片名的内蕴，就需要采用意译法进行翻译。意译强调"得意忘形"，即以改变片名形式为代价，最大限度地保存原片名之内容。在具体操作中，经常运用增译、减译、转换译法等进行翻译，从而起到深入传达原片内容，增强片名感染力的作用。

如：Blood and Sand《碧血黄沙》　　Piano《钢琴别恋》
　　The Three Musketeers《豪情三剑客》

4. 按照电影内容翻译

片名翻译中会出现直译、意译片名都难以恰如其分地体现原片内容，此时就需要抛开原片名的形式和内容，以原片内容为基础，另起炉灶，另立译名。

如：Of Mice and Men《芸芸众生》　　Ghost《人鬼情未了》
　　Forrest Gump《阿甘正传》　　　《纵横四海》Once a Thief

片名另译在很大程度上是一个再创作的过程。通过再创造，语言能够在传达原片信息的同时，沟通观众感情，具有强烈的感染力和审美价值。

Passage Translation 1

Vocabulary

1. 《红高粱》

2. 《英雄》

3. 北京电影学院

4. 西安电影制片厂

5. 主演

6. 《老井》

7. 金鸡奖

8. 百花奖

9. 东京国际电影节

10. 最佳男演员奖

11. 《菊豆》

12. 《大红灯笼高高挂》

13. 《活着》

14. 《秋菊打官司》

15. 《一个都不能少》

16. 《我的父亲母亲》

17. 商业片

18. 惊人的票房

19. 《十面埋伏》

20. 《满城尽带黄金甲》

21. 宣传片

从艺术片《红高粱》到大片时代的《英雄》，再到2008年北京奥运，张艺谋将自己的名字打造成了他的品牌。

1978年，张艺谋才得以进入北京电影学院摄影系学习。他是个天才摄影师，屡屡在国内外获奖。

1987年，张艺谋开始当起了演员，主演西安电影制片厂厂长吴天明导演的影片《老井》，连获国内金鸡奖和百花奖、东京国际电影节"最佳男演员奖"。

但张艺谋的抱负不止于此。张艺谋的导演处女作《红高粱》将一个独特的时代刻画得淋漓尽致。之后，《菊豆》《大红灯笼高高挂》等作品同样以浓烈的色彩让观众印象深刻。后来，他又拍了《活着》《秋菊打官司》《一个都不能少》《我的父亲母亲》等一系列现实主义题材影片。

2002年，拍电影的第15个年头，张艺谋开始挑战商业片，邀请李连杰、梁朝伟等一线明星，投资过亿元，打造了中国第一部功夫商业片——《英雄》。

《英雄》让张艺谋赢得当时惊人的票房，也为他招来恶评如潮。但张艺谋仍在继续创新，很快又拍出了《十面埋伏》，同样招来铺天盖地的恶评。之后的《满城尽带黄金甲》仍然是"大投入、大宣传、高票房、高争议"的商业片，有人质疑他为了商业彻底迷失了方向。

张艺谋是个全才：执导过歌剧、芭蕾舞剧、"印象"系列以及汽车广告，拍过2008年奥运会和2010年世博会的官方宣传片，甚至担任过网络游戏公司艺术总监。无论出现在哪一行，他都会成为焦点。奥运之后，张艺谋成为最具象征性的中国文化名人之一。

Notes

1. "之后，《菊豆》《大红灯笼高高挂》等作品同样以浓烈的色彩让观众印象深刻。"句中的两个片名分别用了两种翻译方法。由于菊豆是人名，所以片名直接用了音译法。后面的片名用的是直译的方法，既容易理解，也能表达出电影中挂红灯笼这个主题场景。全句翻译成："After that, his works such as *Judou* and *Raise the Red Lantern* also made a deep impression on the audience."

2. "张艺谋仍在继续创新，很快又拍出了《十面埋伏》。"句中的片名《十面埋伏》不便直译，这儿采用另译的方法，根据电影内容翻译，抛开片名形式，由于电影讲的是和飞刀门有关的故事，因此，译为 House of Flying Daggers。全句译为："But Zhang Yimou continued his innovation. Soon, he directed House of Flying Daggers."

3. "之后的《满城尽带黄金甲》仍然是'大投入、大宣传、高票房、高争议'的商业片。"句中的"大投入""大宣传"虽然都用了"大"字，但所指不同，英语中的用词是有区别的。"大投入"是指资金投入大，而"大宣传"应该是指宣传范围广，程度深。因此，分别用"heavy"和"large-scale"两个词修饰。全句翻译成："His film Curse of the Golden Flower is also the commercial film following the path of 'heavy investment, large-scale promotion, high office box revenue and great controversy'."

Passage Translation 2

Vocabulary

1. International Jazz Day
2. embrace
3. spontaneity
4. integration
5. civil rights
6. human dignity
7. improvise
8. pay tribute to
9. Goodwill Ambassador
10. Thelonius Monk Institute of Jazz

On 30 April, musicians and music lovers the world over are celebrating International Jazz Day for the third time. Throughout the world, for more than a century, artists have embraced jazz. They are fascinated with its spontaneity and its freedom of expression.

Jazz is much more than music: it is a lifestyle and a tool for dialogue, even social change. The history of jazz tells of the power of music to bring together artists from different cultures and backgrounds, as a driver of cultural integration and mutual respect. Jazz has given rhythm to the struggles of the civil rights movement in the United States, and has done so elsewhere in the world. Through jazz, millions of people have sung and still sing today their desire for freedom, tolerance and human dignity.

UNESCO established International Jazz Day to promote these values. This year, once again, hundreds of events and concerts will be organized or improvised worldwide, by authorities, music schools and concert halls. The main event will take place this year in Japan—in Osaka. With its numerous jazz clubs and its world-renowned annual competition, Osaka is at the heart of the modern jazz movement. By choosing this city to celebrate jazz, UNESCO also wishes to highlight that musical interactions can forge links between cultures beyond borders and oceans.

On behalf of UNESCO, I would like to pay tribute to all our partners, in Japan and all other countries, who are organizing events to celebrate jazz and the values it embodies, along with our Goodwill Ambassador Mr. Herbie Hancock and the Thelonius Monk Institute of Jazz, who have supported us from the start. I invite you to join us in spreading the message of energy, sharing and peace through culture and music.

Notes

1. "On 30 April, musicians and music lovers the world over are celebrating International Jazz Day for the third time." 2011年11月, 联合国教科文组织大会宣布每年的4月30日为"国际爵士乐日(International Jazz Day)", 主要目的是为了提升国际社会对爵士乐的认识: 爵士乐不仅是一种教育工具, 同时也是推广和平、团结以及增强不同民族间对话与合作的一股力量。

2. "Jazz has given rhythm to the struggles of the civil rights movement in the United States, and has done so elsewhere in the world." "rhythm"是节奏的意思, 这儿不能直译, 根据上下文, 爵士乐是在黑人音乐基础上创立起来的, 反映了黑人的悲惨境遇和底层生活状态。因此, 在这儿应该译成"伴随"的意思。全句译为: "是爵士乐的节奏一直伴随着美国和世界其他各地的民权斗争。"

3. "By choosing this city to celebrate jazz, UNESCO also wishes to highlight that musical interactions can forge links between cultures beyond borders and oceans." "UNESCO"是"联合国教科文组织"的缩略语, 全称为"United Nations Educational Scientific and Cultural Organization"。许多常见机构的缩略语有必要经常整理和记忆。全句译为: "联合国教科文组织选择这座城市来庆祝爵士乐日, 也是为了彰显音乐交流能够漂洋过海, 在不同文化之间建立起紧密联系。"

Sentences in Focus

1. 1987年, 张艺谋开始当起了演员, 主演西安电影制片厂厂长吴天明导演的影片《老井》, 连获国内金鸡奖和百花奖、东京国际电影节"最佳男演员奖"。

2. 张艺谋的导演处女作《红高粱》将一个独特的时代刻画得淋漓尽致。

3. 张艺谋开始挑战商业片, 邀请李连杰、梁朝伟等一线明星, 投资过亿元, 打造了中国第一部功夫商业片——《英雄》。

4. 《英雄》让张艺谋赢得当时惊人的票房, 也为他招来恶评如潮。

5. 张艺谋是个全才：执导过歌剧、芭蕾舞剧、"印象"系列以及汽车广告，拍过2008年奥运会和2010年世博会的官方宣传片，甚至担任过网络游戏艺术总监。

6. Throughout the world, for more than a century, artists have embraced jazz. They are fascinated with its spontaneity and its freedom of expression.

7. Jazz is much more than music: it is a lifestyle and a tool for dialogue, even social change.

8. The history of jazz tells of the power of music to bring together artists from different cultures and backgrounds, as a driver of cultural integration and mutual respect.

9. With its numerous jazz clubs and its world-renowned annual competition, Osaka is at the heart of the modern jazz movement.

10. I invite you to join us in spreading the message of energy, sharing and peace through culture and music.

Exercises

I. Fill in the blanks with English words according to the given Chinese.

1. It is reported that the custodian service by Industrial and Commercial Bank of China has won seven _____ (国内外大奖) consecutively since last year.
2. Grayson's youthful _____ (志向、抱负) was to sing opera, but she wasn't able to accomplish that dream until her movie career ended.
3. "The audience, mostly seniors, like to go to theaters, order a cup of tea and enjoy _____ (锡剧)," said Wang Binbin Jr., whose father was a master of the opera.
4. In this session, campers lead every part of the _____ (影片制作) process from pitching a story, writing the script and acting out the roles to the final editing.
5. Actor Paul Walker, the 40-year-old _____ (电影明星) died in a fiery car crash in North Los Angeles.
6. This statistic shows the _____ (票房收入) of the top ten movies worldwide on the weekend of April 3 to 5, 2013.
7. Leonardo DiCaprio enjoys great _____ (受欢迎) in China, which contributed to the success of his new movie.

8. A true _____ (音乐爱好者) won't limit himself to certain types of music because of his skin color or what's popular.

9. Non-verbal _____ (音乐交流) can encourage non-verbal social interaction for those patients who have lost language skills.

10. Music helps _____ (传播讯息) emotions of anger, happiness, sorrow or peacefulness.

II. Translate the following movie titles into English or Chinese.

1. *Sense and Sensibility* _____
2. *Madison County Bridge* _____
3. *Inception* _____
4. *Cleopatra* _____
5. *Sister Act* _____
6. 《真实的谎言》_____
7. 《音乐之声》_____
8. 《卧虎藏龙》_____
9. 《泰囧》_____
10. 《神话》_____

III. Translate the following sentences.

1. Chinese actress Yang Mi is the Goodwill Ambassador of this year's China International Film Festival London.

2. *Wolf of Wall Street* is about a New York stockbroker who refuses to cooperate in a large securities fraud case involving corruption on Wall Street.

3. Ever since Disney announced plans for a live-action version of their hit animated film, *Mulan*, many fans in China and abroad have expressed concerns about it.

4. The science fiction action film *Transformers 4*, by Hollywood director Michael Bay, will start shooting at Wulong county, Chongqing, according to media reports.

5. The Film *If You Are the One* directed by Feng Xiaogang and co-starred by actor

Ge You and actress Hsu Chi was released to the public on Dec. 18.

6. 从事电影拍摄30多年，张艺谋成为一名全球知名的导演。

7. 第五届北京国际电影节吸引了来自全球的930部影片。

8. 《变形金刚》导演迈克尔·贝在拍摄最新一部电影期间遭到攻击而受伤。

9. 成龙在网上公告中否认了关于其退出动作影片的传言。

10. 在这个网站，你可以免费下载情景喜剧，例如《老友记》《成长的烦恼》等。

IV. Translate the following paragraphs.

1. Mr. Dursley was the director of a film called *Grunnings*, which made drills. He was a big, beefy man with hardly any neck, although he did have a very large moustache. Mrs. Dursley was thin and blonde and had nearly twice the usual amount of neck, which came in very useful as the spent so much of her time craning over garden fences, spying on the neighbors. The Dursleys had a small son called Dudley and in their opinion there was no finer boy anywhere.

2. "动感地带"（M-Zone）首届英国电影节是广东省历年来举办过规模最大、质量最高的国际性电影节，所选的9部影片都是2000年后在世界影坛颇有影响的作品，务求让广大年轻电影爱好者欣赏到多元的当代英国电影，促进中英文化的相互交流和发展。

Section B Interpretation

Interpretation Technique

口译技能：数字口译（2）

对于较长和较复杂的基数数字可以用前面一章介绍的方法，但其他数字或带有数字，则需要我们熟悉它们在汉语和英语里的不同表达，这样才能迅速和准确地完成转换。

1. 基数词

（1）英式英语和美式英语在表达整数时的差异。

如：120 在英式英语里可以读成 one hundred and twenty，而在美式英语里读成 one hundred twenty，百位和十位间不用 and。

（2）有时 thousand 可以用 hundred 来表示，如 1,300 可以读成 13 hundred。

（3）年份的表达。如 732 读作 seven hundred (and) thirty-two；1978 读作 nineteen seventy-eight，2006 读作 two thousand and six 或者 twenty o six；AD 98 读作 ninety-eight AD。

（4）电话号码的表达。无重复数字时，从左到右三位一组读。如 123456789 按照 123-456-789 来读。如果有两个数字重复的话，则用 double，如 786623456 读成 78-double six-234-56。

（5）零可以读作数字 zero 或 nought，或是字母 o。

（6）其他。如 $1.23 读作 one (dollar) twenty-three (cents)；-5℃ 读作 minus five degree Celsius；比分 2：1 读作 two-to-one。

2. 分数

（1）简单分数 $\frac{1}{3}$ 读作 one third；

（2）复杂分数如 $\frac{5}{123}$ 读作 five over one hundred and twenty-three 或者 five over one two three；整数带分数则先读整数，再读分数，中间用 and 连接。如 $6\frac{2}{3}$ 读作 six and two thirds。

3. 倍数

倍数的表达在英汉语里有不少固定的表达方式。

（1）两倍在汉语里可以说"两倍""增加了一倍"或"翻了一番"。在英语里可以是：twice as ... as；double；increase 100%。

（2）三倍在汉语里可以说是"增加了 2 倍"或"是……的三倍"。英语里可以是：three times as ... as；triple；increase 200%。

（3）四倍在汉语里可以是"四倍""翻两番"或"增加了三倍"。在英语里可以是：four times as ... as；fourfold；quadruple；increase 300%。

（4）四倍以上的可以用-fold 或 times 来表达。如 10 倍可以说是：10-fold 或 10 times。

4. 一些带有数字的套话和习语

英汉语中都有带有数字的套话或习语。这时就要按照意义视情况而定是否把数字口译出来了。

（1）可以译出数字的情况。如"三三两两"译成"in twos and threes"；"a drop in the ocean"译成"沧海一粟"。

（2）需要用数字，但不是和源语一样的数字。如"乱七八糟"译成"at sixes and sevens"；"Once bitten, twice shy"译成"一朝被蛇咬，十年怕井绳"。

（3）不必译出数字的情况。如"一而再，再而三"译成"again and again"；"second to none"译成"名列前茅"。

建议要熟悉英汉语数字的不同表达，多读，多听译。

Passage Interpretation 1

成龙，是华人社会具有影响力的著名演员和导演，也是国际功夫电影巨星，在世界电影界有很高的声望与影响。

他以主演惊险动作电影为主，其中《警察故事》获得了香港电影金像奖最佳故事片奖。

成龙早在1982年时便开始打入好莱坞市场，但他迈向国际的道路并不顺畅。他首次进军国际的作品票房失利，他只能多年后，再闯好莱坞。真正令成龙打入国际市场的是1994年拍摄的《红番区》，在美国上映时创下高票房纪录。他的第一部好莱坞电影《尖峰时刻》，也获得极高的票房，并登上了《时代》杂志，奠定了他今后在国际影坛的地位。成龙曾经表示，其实好莱坞并不是他的天下，只有回到香港他才如鱼得水。

尽管成龙影片票房不如以往，2007年在北美上映的《尖峰时刻3》仍创下将近1亿4千万美元的票房纪录。《尖峰时刻》系列三部电影在北美累积票房超过5亿美元、全球累积8亿3500万美元。目前为止，没有其他亚洲演员领衔主演的电影能在国际上达到同等成绩。

Passage Interpretation 2

If You Are the One rose to the summit of Chinese television fame. The shows' popularity is easy to explain. There are 180 million single people in China. They and their parents are all worried about whether they can find their Mr. and Miss Right. For Chinese viewers, the twice-weekly, hour-long hit shows have proved riveting, turning traditional matchmaking on its head and celebrating instant celebrity. Although dating programs have aired for almost two decades here, they didn't look like this. In the old shows, people just introduced themselves, and there was no session for mutual selection. But dating programs such as *If You Are the One* for Jiangsu Satellite TV offers confrontation, nerves and suspense.

China's one-child policy has skewed the gender balance over the past three decades because of preference for boys. Parents attach great importance to carrying on the family name, so marriage is a big issue.

Even if women enjoy a greater selection, they face other challenges. As surveys show, men consider women old after 28 and women consider men old after 35. Therefore, matchmakers are rushing to cash in at matchmaking fairs and other events. Many parents are big fans of the dating programs.

"No TV show can fully reflect social reality," says Yin Hong, a Chinese scholar at Beijing's Tsinghua University. He prefers *If You Are the One* because it's more controversial. He claims that China's social environment is changing, as people dare to express their private life and love values in public.

Dialogue Interpretation

K: 你又在看那些花边新闻了?

A: Hollywood gossip. It's all about the history of Hollywood.

K: 听起来蛮有意思, 这方面我也知道一些。

A: The place we call Hollywood today was Rancho La Brea and Rancho Los Feliz. In 1886, Mr. Wilcox bought an area of Rancho La Brea that his wife then christened "Hollywood".

K: 他买那块地是为了给富有的中西部美国人提供一个冬季度假的场所, 而不是为了制作电影。

A: In 1911, the Nestor Company opened Hollywood's first film studio in an old tavern on the corner of Sunset and Gower. That's how it all began.

K: 所以, 由于好莱坞有了新的行业, 这里不再是个小社区。不久之后, 好莱坞大道上几乎所有与三个街角相连的住房都被商业大楼取代了。

A: Right, people needed to work there. Also people need to have fun there. Banks, restaurants, clubs and movie palaces sprang up during the 1920s and 1930s. They also needed grand houses for the stars.

K: 那时候, 明星都住在好莱坞吗? 当然, 现在他们要是住在那里的话肯定会被影迷们蜂拥围观, 所以他们都搬到了比弗利山庄去住。

A: During the 1960s, more and more businesses started to move out of Hollywood, and the nightclubs and bars moved to the west. Hollywood today is a diverse and vital community, striving to preserve the elegant buildings from its past.

K: 但大多数电影公司还在那里发展,是吧?不过我可以猜到当地社区的外观肯定发生了变化。现在他们是怎么保护这些建筑的?

A: In 1985, the Boulevard commercial and entertainment districts along the Hollywood were officially listed in the National Register of Historic Places. This will protect the neighborhood's important buildings so that Hollywood's past can be seen in the future.

K: 太好了!那就是说,当你终于攒够了钱去那里参观的时候,那里的一切还会保留在原地,就跟过去一样。

Exercises

I. Interpreting technique practice.

You will hear 5 Chinese numbers and five English numbers. Try to write down the numbers as soon as possible and interpret them.

1. _____
2. _____
3. _____
4. _____
5. _____
6. _____
7. _____
8. _____
9. _____
10. _____

II. Spot dictation.

January 8 is the birthday of American (1) _____ legend Elvis Presley. He would have turned 80 years old on January 8. But, he died in 1977 at the still young age of 42. Elvis mania is still (2) _____ in America. People go to shows featuring Elvis look-alikes. Hundreds of thousands of people go to Memphis, Tennessee each year to visit his home and (3) _____, Graceland. People also get excited about Elvis memorabilia—(4) _____, objects he touched, any of his writings and other things related to the man called the King of Rock and Roll.

On Friday, someone might get a huge piece of Elvis history. On that day, the company Julien's Auctions will hold a (5) _____ of Elvis Presley's two airplanes. The special sale is called an auction. That is a public sale where objects are sold to the person or people who offer the most money.

The planes have been (6) _____ at Graceland for 30 years. They are currently not airworthy. The Lisa Marie was Presley's first jet. It is also the bigger of the two. It could fly up to (7) _____. Presley bought it in 1975 for $250,000. Then he spent $300,000 more on repairs and making the inside beautiful. It has an area for sleeping, a conference room for meetings, and a bar—a place for making and enjoying alcoholic drinks. The Lisa Marie was (8) _____ Presley's daughter. The plane is rare. There were only 65 of the same kind ever made.

The singer purchased his second jet while waiting for work to be finished on the Lisa Marie. The Hound Dog II could fly 8 to 10 passengers. Julien's Auctions is based on Beverly Hills, California. Officials (9) _____ say they expect the planes to sell for $10 million and $15 million. The company also says the buyer may purchase land near Graceland to keep and show the jets. An agreement between Graceland and the jets' current owners is (10) _____ at the end of April. The identity of the owners has not been released.

III. Sentence listening and translation.

1. _____
2. _____
3. _____
4. _____
5. _____

IV. Paragraph listening and translation.

Ⅴ. Dialogue interpretation.

A: Have you watched the dating show *If You Are the One* produced by Jiangsu Satellite Television?

B: 看过。在这个相亲节目里,24位单身女性向一位男士提问,看他的介绍视频并按下按钮来决定他是否该留下。

A: There must be some lucky guys who will find their true love.

B: 希望如此。你听说过一个名叫马诺,来自北京的模特吗?

A: No. What's up?

B: 她说宁可在宝马车里哭也不愿坐在一个失业小伙的自行车上。她的话引发了广泛的争议。

A: I don't think that she represents most of Chinese young people.

B: 我同意你的看法。

Ⅵ. Interpreting in groups.

Role-play the following situation with your partners, acting as the Chinese speaker, English speaker and the interpreter respectively. One group will be invited to perform in class.

Participants: 1. John
                2. Ms. Li
                3. Interpreter

Task: John, an international student, is conducting a survey on how Chinese people spend their leisure time. He interviews some people, such as Ms. Li, in the street. Ms. Li speaks Chinese while John is an English-speaker.

Ⅶ. 3-minute talk on the given topic.

Talk on the following topic in three minutes based on the given reference questions.

Topic: Is book reading still popular?

Questions for Reference:

1. What kind of books do you usually read?
2. Do you like reading? Why or why not?
3. How do you comment on the phenomenon that people spend less time in reading printed books?

VIII. Theme-related expressions.

惊悚片	thriller
科幻片	science fiction
古装剧	costume drama
恐怖片	horror film
动画片	animated film
动作片	action film
武侠片	swordsmen film
侦探片	detective film
伦理片	ethical film
电影原声	soundtrack
首映式	premiere
演职人员	cast
男女主角	leading actor and actress
男女配角	supporting actors and actresses
制片方	producer
编剧	screenwriter
化妆师	stagehand
特技替身演员	stuntman
字幕	subtitles
票房冠军	top-grossing movie
预告片	film trailer
试映	test screening
视觉效果	visual effects
华表奖	Ornamental Column Awards
金马奖	Golden Horse Film Festival
金球奖	Golden Globes
金草莓奖	Razzie Awards
戛纳国际电影节	Cannes Film Festival
英国电影学院奖	British Academy Awards
柏林国际电影节	Berlin International Film Festival

Section C Further Exploration

将以下获奖名单翻译成中文。

【FILM | 电影类】

Best Motion Picture—Drama | _____
Boyhood _____

Best Actor in a Motion Picture—Drama | _____
Eddie Redmayne—The Theory of Everything _____

Best Actress in a Motion Picture—Drama | _____
Julianne Moore—Still Alice _____

Best Motion Picture—Comedy or Musical | _____
The Grand Budapest Hotel _____

Best Actor in a Motion Picture—Comedy or Musical | _____
Michael Keaton—Birdman _____

Best Actress in a Motion Picture—Comedy or Musical | _____
Amy Adams—Big Eyes _____

Best Director | _____
Richard Linklater—Boyhood _____

Best Supporting Actor in a Motion Picture | _____
J. K. Simmons—Whiplash _____

Best Animated Feature | _____
How to Train Your Dragon 2 _____

Best Foreign Film | _____
Leviathan, Russia _____

Best Original Song—Motion Picture | _____
Glory—Selma _____

UNIT 12
Environmental Protection
环境保护

Learning Objectives

1. To know how to use negation in sentence translation;
2. To learn how to interpret numbers (3);
3. To learn how to translate/interpret passages and dialogues on the topic of environmental protection;
4. To learn useful words and expressions related to environmental protection.

Lead-in

● *Quiz* (True or False)

_____ 1. World Earth Day falls on March 22nd.

_____ 2. Global warming is caused only by natural factors.

_____ 3. When it comes to the environment, the 3 Rs refer to reduce, reuse and recycle.

_____ 4. Electricity is better power than solar energy for the environment.

_____ 5. Flood, drought and population explosion resulted from global warming.

_____ 6. Cities like Beijing and Shanghai have implemented local administrative regulations banning smoking in indoor public venues.

_____ 7. Red tide is likely to break out at the oil-spills-affected sea area.

● What are the possible consequences of environmental pollution? Fill in the blanks with the given English words.

| sandstorm | heat wave | winter storm | flood | smog |
| tornado | wildfire | drought | landslide | red tide |

1. _____ 2. _____ 3. _____ 4. _____ 5. _____

6. _____ 7. _____ 8. _____ 9. _____ 10. _____

Section A Translation

Translation Technique

正面表达与反面表达转换

由于思维方式的不同，英语中有些从正面表达的东西在汉语中习惯从反面来表达，而有些从反面来表达的东西在汉语中则习惯从正面来表达。因此，翻译时常常有必要进行转换。这就是通常所说的"正说反译、反说正译"法。英语正面表达指的是不带否定词"no""not""never"，否定前缀"non-""in-""im-""ir-""dis-"和否定后缀"-less"等的句子。汉语正面表达则是指不带"不""没""非""未""否""无""莫""勿""别"等否定词语的句子。反之，则都是反面表达。

1. **英语正面表达转换为汉语反面表达**

   例如：frost-free refrigerator 无霜冰箱   Freeze! 别动！
   　　　Wet paint! 油漆未干！   mortally ill 不治之症

   The proposal was carried by a very narrow margin. 这项建议差点没通过。

   He went to an outdoor phone booth and dialed Chicago, then New York, then San Francisco. Silence. Silence. Silence. 他到一个户外公用电话亭，先给芝加哥、又给纽约、旧金山打了电话。没有回音。没有回音。没有回音。

   As he sipped his coffee, he opened a still damp morning paper and began reading. 他一面喝咖啡，一面翻开油墨未干的晨报，看了起来。

2. **英语反面表达转换为汉语正面表达**

   例如：You can't be too careful. 你要特别小心。

   The significance of these incidents wasn't lost on us. 这些事件引起了我们的重视。

Such flights couldn't long escape notice. 这类飞行迟早会被人发觉的。

3. 汉语正面表达转换为英语反面表达

例如：有什么问题，尽管与我联系。If you have any questions, don't hesitate to contact me.

在困难的时候，要看到成绩。In times of difficulty, we must not lose sight of our achievements.

处理这件事，越谨慎越好。You cannot be too cautious in handling this matter.

4. 汉语反面表达转换为英语正面表达

例如：我们不会辜负大家的期望。We will live up to your expectations.

他虽然穷，但无论如何也不会说谎。Poor as he is, he is above telling a lie in any case.

你们的供货远远不够。Your supplies are far from enough.

Passage Translation 1

Vocabulary

1. 生态文明
2. 全面建成小康社会
3. 中华民族伟大复兴
4. 战略重要性
5. 现实紧迫性
6. 生态难题
7. 能源危机
8. 淡水危机
9. 气候异常
10. 物种灭绝
11. 资源约束
12. 世界平均水平
13. 发展方式粗放
14. 资源供需矛盾
15. 人均消费量
16. 瓶颈约束
17. 草原退化
18. 水土流失
19. 土地沙化

20. 地质灾害频发

21. 湿地湖泊萎缩

22. 地面沉降

23. 海洋自然岸线减少

24. 温室气体排放

25. 绿色循环低碳发展道路

26. 代际公平

27. 吃祖宗饭，断子孙路

28. 忧患意识

29. 危机意识

生态是自然界的存在状态，文明是人类社会的进步状态，生态文明则是人类文明中反映人类进步与自然存在和谐程度的状态。生态文明建设是关系我国全面建成小康社会、实现社会主义现代化和中华民族伟大复兴全方位全过程的一项神圣事业。我们必须从全局和战略高度，充分认识生态文明建设的战略重要性与现实紧迫性。

坚定推进生态文明建设是缓解资源环境压力，保持我国经济社会持续健康发展的现实需要。当今世界，全球性的生态难题不断增多，能源危机、淡水危机、气候异常、物种灭绝等此起彼伏，在我国也有所反映。由于高投入、高消耗、高污染的传统发展方式没有根本改变，我国在经济快速增长的同时，也付出了很高的代价，人口、资源、环境的矛盾日益突出，对我国发展的制约日益增大。

一是资源约束趋紧。我国人口众多，资源相对不足，淡水、耕地、森林、煤炭、石油、铁矿石、铝土矿等，很多重要资源人均占有量低于世界平均水平。改革开放以来，随着我国工业化、城镇化快速发展，以及发展方式粗放，能源、资源供需矛盾变得十分突出。随着我国工业化、城镇化的进一步发展，未来一段时期内，各类能源、资源的人均消费量还要增加，能源、资源对于经济社会发展的瓶颈约束将更加明显，粮食安全、能源安全、淡水安全面临严重挑战。

二是环境污染严重。我国传统的发展方式导致主要污染物排放量过大，有的超过了环境容量。水、土壤、空气污染加重的趋势尚未得到根本遏制。雾霾天气范围扩大，是大自然向粗放发展方式亮起的红灯。

三是生态系统退化。森林生态系统质量不高，草原退化、水土流失、土地沙化、地质灾害频发、湿地湖泊萎缩、地面沉降、海洋自然岸线减少等问题十分严峻。

四是气候变化问题突出。温室气体排放总量大、增速快。上述情况表明，我国的资源、环境和生态系统已难以承载传统的发展方式，只有大力推进生态文明建设，努力走绿色循环低碳发展道路，才能从根本上缓解资源环境瓶颈制约，为我国经济社会持续健康发展奠定坚实基础。

Unit 12　Environmental Protection 环境保护

> 联合国曾提出这样一句寓意深刻的话来警告世人,"我们不只是继承了父辈的地球,而且是借用了儿孙的地球"。考虑生态的代际公平,既要注重当代人的福祉,也要顾及后代人的利益,不能"吃祖宗饭,断子孙路"。我们一定要增强忧患意识和危机意识,以对国家和人民高度负责、对子孙后代高度负责、对中华民族高度负责的精神,下大决心以壮士断腕的气魄抓紧抓好生态文明建设。

Notes

1. "生态是自然界的存在状态,文明是人类社会的进步状态,生态文明则是人类文明中反映人类进步与自然存在和谐程度的状态。"翻译这三句话关键是要厘清它们之间的逻辑关系,前两句是后一句的原因,翻译时可添加"thus",显化因果逻辑关系。全句译为:"Ecology pertains to the state in which nature exists, whereas civilization refers to a state of human progress. Thus, ecological civilization describes the harmony between human progress and natural existence in human civilization."

2. "由于高投入、高消耗、高污染的传统发展方式没有根本改变,我国在经济快速增长的同时,也付出了很高的代价。"这句在翻译时,前半句话用反译法翻译,"没有根本改变"翻译为"仍需要改变"。全句译为:"Having yet to fundamentally change a traditional growth model characterized by high input, high energy consumption and heavy pollution, China has paid a high price for its rapid economic growth."

3. "雾霾天气范围扩大,是大自然向粗放发展方式亮起的红灯。"这句话翻译时,主要是正确表达"雾霾天气范围扩大"。这儿的"天气范围扩大",指的是在中国受雾霾影响的地方增多了。因此,全句译为:"Smog is affecting larger parts of China which is nature's red-light warning against the model of extensive growth."

4. "考虑生态的代际公平,既要注重当代人的福祉,也要顾及后代人的利益,不能'吃祖宗饭,断子孙路'。"句中,"代际公平"的理解是难点。"代际公平"指当代人和后代人在利用自然资源、满足自身利益、谋求生存与发展上权利均等。因此,"生态的代际公平"翻译成"inter-generational equity in ecological terms"。"不能吃祖宗饭,断子孙路"指的是我们不能过度使用祖先留下的遗产(主要指浪费环境资源而不考虑给后代留下后路),翻译为"neither squander our heritage, nor can we leave future generations with nothing"。因此,全句译为:"In order to ensure inter-generational equity in ecological terms, we need to take into consideration both the well-being of the current generation and the interests of future generations. We can neither squander our heritage, nor can we leave future generations with nothing."

5. "我们一定要增强忧患意识和危机意识,以对国家和人民高度负责、对子孙后代高度负责、对中华民族高度负责的精神,下大决心以壮士断腕的气魄抓紧抓好生态文明建设。"句中的"壮士断腕的气魄"只能意译,在这儿指的是"当机立断,为了长远的利益舍弃眼前的利益的决心",翻译成"bitter resolve"。全句翻译成:"Driven by a strong sense of responsibility for our country, our people, our future generations, and the Chinese nation, we must devote ourselves to the promotion of ecological progress with bitter resolve."

Passage Translation 2

Vocabulary

1. Secretary General
2. consign
3. rising sea level
4. crop failure
5. climate refugee
6. jeopardy
7. magnitude
8. clean energy
9. carbon pollution
10. fuel economy
11. wind energy
12. capture carbon pollution
13. complacency
14. block our progress
15. emitter of greenhouse gas pollution
16. energize our efforts
17. sustainable growth
18. financial and technical assistance
19. low-carbon development
20. pragmatic

I want to thank the Secretary General for organizing this summit, and all the leaders who are participating. That so many of us are here today is a recognition that the threat from climate change is serious. It is urgent, and growing. Our generation's response to this challenge will be judged by history, for if we fail to meet it—boldly, swiftly and together—we risk consigning future generations to an irreversible catastrophe.

No nation, however large or small, wealthy or poor, can escape the impact of climate change. Rising sea levels threaten every coastline. More powerful storms and floods threaten every continent. More frequent droughts and crop failures breed hunger and conflict in places where hunger and conflict already thrive. On shrinking islands, families are already being forced to flee their homes as climate refugees. The security and stability of each nation and all peoples—our prosperity, our health and our safety—are in jeopardy. And the time we have to reverse this tide is running out.

And yet, we can reverse it. John F. Kennedy once observed that "Our problems are man-made, therefore they may be solved by man." It is true that for too many years, mankind has been slow to respond or even recognize the magnitude of the climate threat. It is true of my own country, as well. We recognize that. But this is a new day. It is a new era. And I am proud to say that the United States has done more to promote clean energy and reduce carbon pollution in the last eight months than at any other time in our history.

We are making our government's largest ever investment in renewable energy. We've proposed the very first national policy aimed at both increasing fuel economy and reducing greenhouse gas pollution for all new cars and trucks—a standard that will also save consumers money and our nation oil. We're moving forward with our nation's first offshore wind energy projects. We're investing billions to capture carbon pollution so that we can clean up our coal plants. And just this week, we announced that for the first time ever, we'll begin tracking how much greenhouse gas pollution is being emitted throughout the country.

Because no nation can meet this challenge alone, the United States has also engaged more allies and partners in finding a solution than ever before. We've worked through the World Bank to promote renewable energy projects and technologies in the developing world. And we have put climate at the top of our diplomatic agenda when it comes to our relationships with countries as varied as China and Brazil; India and Mexico; from the continent of Africa to the continent of Europe.

But though many of our nations have taken bold actions and share in this determination, we did not come here to celebrate progress today. We came because there's so much more progress to be made. We came because there's so much more work to be done.

I'm here today to say that difficulty is no excuse for complacency. We must seize the opportunity to make Copenhagen a significant step forward in the global fight against climate change. We also cannot allow the old divisions that have characterized the climate debate for so many years to block our progress. We cannot meet this challenge unless all the largest emitters of greenhouse gas pollution act together. There's no other way. We must also energize our efforts to put other developing nations—especially the poorest and most vulnerable—on a path to sustainable growth. We have a responsibility to provide the financial and technical assistance needed to help these nations adapt to the impacts of climate change and pursue low-carbon development. What we are seeking, after all, is not simply an agreement to limit greenhouse gas emissions. We seek an agreement that will allow all nations to grow and raise living standards without endangering the planet.

But the journey is long and the journey is hard. So let us begin. For if we are flexible and pragmatic, if we can resolve to work tirelessly in common efforts, then we will achieve our common purpose: a world that is safer, cleaner and healthier than the one we found; and a future that is worthy of our children.

Notes

1. "That so many of us are here today is a recognition that the threat from climate change is serious. It is urgent, and it is growing." 句中"recognition"一词汉译时要转换词性,译为动词"认识到"。全句译成:"今天有如此众多的代表到会,这表明人们认识到气候变化构成的威胁有多么严重,认识到威胁迫在眉睫,也认识到威胁正日益增长。"

2. "More frequent droughts and crop failures breed hunger and conflict in places where hunger and conflict already thrive." 句中,"breed"一词指的是"引起"的意思,这儿,由定语从句"where hunger and conflict already thrive"可知,这些地区,饥饿和冲突早就盛行,所以,"breed"一词有"加重"的意思。全句译为:"日趋频繁的干旱和粮荒在饥馑和战乱已然深重的地区进一步加深了灾难。"

3. "We're investing billions to capture carbon pollution so that we can clean up our coal plants." "capture carbon pollution"译为"捕获碳污染"。碳捕获是将大型发电厂、钢铁厂、化工厂等排放源产生的二氧化碳收集起来,并用各种方法储存以避免其排放到大气中的一种技术,是世界发达国家在环保方面的一项新技术。全句译成:"我们投资数十亿美元用于捕获碳污染,以使我们的燃煤工厂变得清洁。"

4. "We also cannot allow the old divisions that have characterized the climate debate for so many years to block our progress." "old division"原意是"原有的分离"。这儿,根据句意,指的是在关于气候变化辩论中的一些分歧之处,译成"意见分歧"。全句译成:"我们也不能听任过去多年来在气候变化问题上反复出现的争论阻挠我们取得进展。"

Sentences in Focus

1. 生态文明建设是关系我国全面建成小康社会、实现社会主义现代化和中华民族伟大复兴全方位全过程的一项神圣事业。

2. 当今世界,全球性的生态难题不断增多,能源危机、淡水危机、气候异常、物种灭绝等此起彼伏。

3. 由于高投入、高消耗、高污染的传统发展方式没有根本改变,我国在经济快速增长的同时,也付出了很高的代价。

4. 我国传统的发展方式导致主要污染物排放量过大,有的超过了环境容量。

5. 森林生态系统质量不高,草原退化、水土流失、土地沙化、地质灾害频发、湿地湖泊萎缩、地面沉降、海洋自然岸线减少等问题十分严峻。

6. Our generation's response to this challenge will be judged by history, for if we fail to meet it—boldly, swiftly and together—we risk consigning future

generations to an irreversible catastrophe.

7. Rising sea levels threaten every coastline. More powerful storms and floods threaten every continent. More frequent droughts and crop failures breed hunger and conflict in places where hunger and conflict already thrive. On shrinking islands, families are already being forced to flee their homes as climate refugees.

8. It is true that for too many years, mankind has been slow to respond or even recognize the magnitude of the climate threat.

9. We are making our government's largest ever investment in renewable energy.

10. For if we are flexible and pragmatic, if we can resolve to work tirelessly in common efforts, then we will achieve our common purpose: a world that is safer, cleaner and healthier than the one we found; and a future that is worthy of our children.

Exercises

I. Fill in the blanks with English words according to the given Chinese.

1. As the country's large population has become a primary factor hampering its economic and social development, whether the population problem can be properly solved _____(直接关系到) the improvement of people's living standard.
2. Global collaboration on _____(气候变化) has entered a new stage as challenges brought by global warming have become increasingly urgent.
3. China's _____(可持续发展) faces greater challenges ranging from a fragile natural ecological environment to resource constraints.
4. "China resolves to tackle its pollution problems and is determined to build an _____(生态文明)," President Xi Jinping said.
5. Man-made climate change will ignite a massive _____(物种灭绝) around the globe, and the earth will be affected.
6. When developing strategies of environmental protection, the central authorities should also _____(考虑到) the interests of both common people and all kinds of businesses.
7. China's _____(粮食保障) is being challenged by a mix of factors, including rising demand, rapid urbanization, scarce natural resources and agricultural labor, and greater risk of food safety and environmental problems.

8. We will devote ourselves to the improvement of the environment with a _____ _____ (责任感) for the next generation.
9. If the carbon dioxide emission of any company exceeds the limits, they will ____ _____ (付出高昂的代价) it.
10. Government officials should view livelihood issues from a _____ _____ (战略高度) and then make long-term comprehensive plans to improve people's lives.

II. Translate the following sentences with the technique of negation.

e.g., Getting a dream job is difficult for many college graduates.
得到一份理想的工作对于许多大学毕业生来说不是容易的事。

1. What we say today will not be long remembered.

2. She is the last wife in the world for a famer.

3. She was never tired of complaining about her new job whenever an opportunity presented itself.

4. A lack of awareness of cultural differences or local customs may cause misunderstanding in communication.

5. Bill is too indecisive to make a good leader.

III. Translate the following sentences.

1. The use of biofuels has already been tested by Boeing and several other airlines around the world have recently trialed similar flights.

2. General Secretary Xi Jinping stresses that "we should protect the environment like we protect our eyes and treat the environment like it is our lives".

3. Several animal species including gorillas in Rwanda and tigers in Bangladesh could risk extinction if the impact of climate change and extreme weather on their habitats is not addressed.

4. More than 134 cities across the world switched off their lights for an hour on Sunday to support action to create a sustainable future for the planet.

5. Residents will have a weekly recycling collection limited to cans, paper and card, plastic bottles and aerosols.

6. 政府将采取切实行动,发展低碳经济。

7. 世界环境日是提高人们环保意识、倡导绿色能源的日子。

8. 中国政府非常重视全球气候变化的问题。

9. 中国将在环保领域加强与各国政府之间的沟通与交流。

10. 在中国,环境污染与食品安全的确已成为严重的问题。

IV. Translate the following paragraphs.

1. This year is crucial for the deepening of reforms, with attention being focused on how the "two sessions" will handle the ongoing development of the country and further improve people's livelihood. "I'm looking forward to a brighter sky in Beijing and other major cities across the nation. Tougher measures should be taken to curb industrial pollution. Now we have no choice but to rely on the wind to blow away pollutants and bring fresh air," one interviewee said.

2. 世界卫生组织表示,据估计,2012年全球约700万人死于油烟与汽车尾气引起的空气污染。无论是室内还是室外,空气污染,都成为当前最大的环境健康问题。它影响着发展中国家和发达国家的每一个人。根据一项最新的调查,2012年全球每8名死者中就有一名死因与污染有关。世界卫生组织将东南亚定为污染最严重的地区,包括印度、印度尼西亚、中国、韩国、日本、菲律宾。

Section B Interpretation

Interpretation Technique

口译技能：数字口译（3）

人们常常通过列举数字来说明某一方面的情况。因此数字虽然十分重要，但也只是说明情况的手段而已。在口译时固然要集中精力记数字，当然也绝不能忽视讲话中所要说明的内容。有时内容比数字甚至要重要得多，因为数字没听清可以说大概，而内容没听清就什么也说不出来了。因此，数字口译练习最终要做到会口译带有信息的数字，光会口译单个的数字或数字表达是不够的。

在听数字信息时要把精力放在三个方面：(1) 描述的是什么内容；(2) 描述的趋势是上升还是下降；(3) 数字本身，注意力重点放在较高数位上。以下是一些与数字有关的表达法。

1. **数字上升、下降的表达法**

增加：increase, rise, grow, go up

增长到：expand to, increase to, go up to, be up to, rise to

增长了：go up by, increase by

爬升：pick up, climb

飙升：surge up, hike sth up, jump up, shoot up, soar, zoom up, skyrocket

下降：decrease, decline, drop, fall, go down, reduce

猛跌：plunge, be slashed, tumble

稍降：be trimmed, dip, slip

超过：outstrip, outpace, surpass, exceed, be more than, be over

2. **与数值搭配的表达法**

达到：reach, amount to, stand at, come to, be up to, arrive at, hit

总计：total, add up to, amount to

占（百分比）：account for, occupy, make up, take

多达：be as much as, be as many as, be up to

大约，约：about, around, some, approximately, roughly, more or less, in the neighborhood of, or so, or thereabouts, in the rough

少于：less than, fewer than, under, below, within

多于：more than, over, above, odd

介于……之间：from A to B, between A and B

现在的发言人越来越喜欢使用各种现代技术和直观的表现手法使演讲更具说服力和感染力,因此口译员也需要掌握读图方法和技巧才能准确地传递出讲演者及其数据蕴含的信息。

3. 与图表相关的表达法

(1) 饼状图相关词汇

扇形 sector;饼状图 pie chart

(2) 柱状图相关词汇

柱状图 bar chart;X 轴 X axis;Y 轴 Y axis;坐标 point

(3) 曲线图相关词汇

曲线图 line chart;实线 solid line;虚线 broken line;点画线 dotted line

(4) 面积图相关词汇

阴影部分 shaded area

4. 图表数据分析表达法

回升,好转的趋势 an upturn	上升,好转的趋势 an upward trend
好转,复苏,回升 pick up, recover	维持升幅 sustain an increase
到达最高点 reach a peak	下降的趋势 downward trend
暴跌,萧条 a slump	持续不断地下降 spiral downward
波动 fluctuate	保持不变,稳定 remain constant/stable
降到最低点 bottom out/level out	

建议在数字口译练习初期可以口译单个数字,但随着熟练程度的提高,应该逐步过渡到听句子里的数字和篇章里的数字,将数字和信息结合起来口译,要能既准确抓住数字,也能够掌握句子或篇章主要意义,这才是数字口译练习的最终目的。

Passage Interpretation 1

主席先生,各位同事,女士们,先生们,

首先,我代表中国政府,对可持续发展高级别政治论坛正式启动表示祝贺。可持续发展的概念由 1992 年联合国环境和发展大会正式提出。

中国政府将可持续发展作为基本国策,强调不能再走"先污染、后治理"的老路,要为子孙后代负责,为国际社会负责。我们正积极落实以人为本、全面、协调、可持续的科学发展观,既发展经济,也保护好环境,维护人民的根本和长远利益。

当前中国的新能源和可再生能源投资已经位居全球第一,森林覆盖率在新世纪的头十年内提高了 3.8%,森林面积增加了 36.51 万平方公里。

2006 至 2010 年期间,通过节能和提高能效累计节约 6.3 亿吨标准煤,相当于减少排放二氧化碳 14.6 亿吨。2011 至 2015 年期间,力争将单位 GDP 能耗降低 16%、单位 GDP 二氧化碳排放降低 17%。

本月公布的大气污染防治行动计划,要求到 2017 年非化石能源消费比重提高到 13%,煤炭占能源消费总量的比重降到 65% 以下。

以中国国情和发展状况,走可持续发展之路面临诸多困难和阵痛,但我们迎难而进,将之作为实现中国梦的必由之路。

Passage Interpretation 2

The International Day of Forests is dedicated to raising awareness of the importance of all types of forests and trees outside forests. Some 1.6 billion people—including more than 2,000 indigenous cultures—depend on forests for food, fuel, shelter and income. Three quarters of freshwater comes from forested catchments. Forests prevent landslides and erosion and mangrove forests reduce loss of life and damage caused by tsunamis.

For these reasons, and more, forests are integral to the post-2015 development agenda. Among their most important functions is their role in building climate-resilient societies. That is why, in this year of action for sustainable development, climate change is the theme for the International Day of Forests.

Sustaining healthy forests and mitigating and adapting to climate change are two sides of the same coin. Forests are the largest storehouses of carbon after oceans. At the same time, deforestation and land-use changes account for 17 per cent of human-generated carbon dioxide emissions.

Forests are on the front lines of climate change. These ecosystems, rich with biodiversity, are increasingly vulnerable to changes in weather, temperature and rainfall patterns. It is essential, therefore, that we work to preserve and sustainably manage our forests.

Despite the ecological, economic and social value of forests, global deforestation continues at an alarming rate. Some 13 million hectares of forest are destroyed annually. This is not sustainable for people or the planet. However, there are some encouraging signs. In the past decade, the rate of global deforestation has decreased by almost 20 per cent, which indicates that solutions exist to reverse this destructive trend.

To build a sustainable, climate-resilient future for all, we must invest in our world's forests. That will take political commitment at the highest levels, smart policies, effective law enforcement, innovative partnerships and funding. On this International Day of Forests, let us commit to reducing deforestation, sustaining healthy forests and creating a climate-resilient future for all.

Dialogue Interpretation

齐教授：首先，我们的网民非常有兴趣了解您一家人在环保、节约能源方面的做法。

Secretary Clinton: Well, first of all, let me thank you for having me be able to speak to the netizens, and I am so pleased that you are focusing on such an important topic as energy efficiency and climate change. In our own lives, we have tried to be much more conscious of what we should do. So, for example, we use compact fluorescent bulbs, installed more insulted windows. We have also recycled. And my husband, of course, with the Clinton Foundation, is running a climate change program with, I think, 40 cities around the world working on higher energy efficiency, and so much else. So, we have tried to do more, but we are constantly asking ourselves what more we can do.

齐教授:太好了,谢谢。您在此次访问中强调了积极合作,您能否对中美如何推进在环保、能源以及气候领域的合作做一下详细的说明?

Secretary Clinton: We wish to create a series of actions and partnerships between our countries, between our businesses, our academic institutions and our citizens. And we hope to work together in the lead-up to Copenhagen at the end of this year, with a new climate treaty. We hope that there will be many opportunities for partnerships between American companies and Chinese companies to produce cleaner energy. And our new Energy Secretary, Dr. Steven Chu, wants to work to help create more intellectual property that would be jointly designed and implemented by Chinese and American researchers. So, we are just at the beginning of this cooperative relationship on clean energy and climate change. But I am very hopeful that it will continue to grow.

齐教授:说得很对。联合国政府间气候变化委员会(IPCC)提出,发达国家要将温室气体排放量削减25%到40%,以避免气候进一步恶化。您认为到2020年美国能达到这个要求吗?

Secretary Clinton: I think that it is technically possible. Our challenge now is to make it politically and personally possible. The science and technology is possible for us to be much more energy efficient. In fact, concentrating on energy efficiency more than renewable energies is a very obvious way of trying to move toward our targets. We just have to convince enough of our fellow citizens to agree with us. You started by asking what my family does. Well, we have tried to change our mental attitude, turning off appliances, turning off lights. My late father grew up with the belief that you didn't waste things like electricity. So, we would turn off the furnace at night. We would turn off all the lights when we left a room. And then, I confess, we got a little bit less aware. And I think most Americans did. We wasted a lot of energy and we wasted a lot of money. We can't do that.

齐教授:我完全同意。感谢您和我们的网友交流,谢谢。

Secretary Clinton: Thank you. It's a pleasure.

Exercises

I. Interpreting technique practice.

You will hear 5 Chinese sentences and 5 English sentences. Try to fill in the blanks by writing down the missing numbers as soon as possible and interpret the following sentences.

1. 全年工业增加值为_____元,比上年增长_____。

2. 全年粮食产量为_____吨,比上年增加_____吨,增产_____。
3. 全年进出口总额达_____美元,比上年增长_____。
4. 全年合同外资金额为_____美元,增长_____;实际使用外资_____美元,增长_____。
5. 全年入境旅游人数_____人次,国际旅游外汇收入_____美元,增长_____%。
6. European unemployment fell by roughly two percent in the _____ quarter of _____.
7. The volume of freight handled by ports throughout the country totaled _____ tons, up _____ percent over the previous year.
8. The total number of privately-owned vehicles was _____ million, up _____ percent.
9. The year _____ saw _____ domestic tourists, up _____ percent. Revenue from domestic tourism totaled _____ billion yuan, up _____ percent.
10. The ASEAN region spans an area of some _____ square kilometers, where _____ official languages are spoken and about _____ religions are followed. Its population was estimated at _____ in _____.

II. Spot dictation.

How to Sort Out Rubbish

Step 1 Check— Check the (1) _____ regarding recycling in your town. Not all communities recycle the same things.

Step 2 Rinse —Rinse glass bottles, (2) _____, and aluminum and tin cans. Labels do not have to (3) _____. Recycle the plastic caps of water and soda bottles, but toss the ones from laundry detergent and food containers.

Step 3 Separate—In general, containers that held food, beverages, (4) _____, or personal care products like shampoo and mouthwash are all (5) _____. Separate plastic, glass, aluminum, tin and aerosol cans.

Step 4 Handle with caution—Contact your local sanitation department for instructions on how to (6) _____ anything that held potentially hazardous material such as motor oil, pesticides, paint, solvents and (7) _____.

Step 5 Bundle paper—Place together all newspapers, magazines, catalogs, junk mail, letters, envelopes and (8) _____. Be sure to keep all paper dry.

Step 6 (9) _____—Remove any tape from cardboard boxes and brown paper bags before flattening them. Check if items like pizza and cereal boxes are recycled in your area. If they are, include them, too.

Step 7 Dispose—Find out when your city (10) _____ recycling, so you know when to leave those bins and boxes by the curb.

Unit 12　Environmental Protection 环境保护

Ⅲ. Sentence listening and translation.

1. _____
2. _____
3. _____
4. _____
5. _____

Ⅳ. Paragraph listening and translation.

_____

Ⅴ. Dialogue interpretation.

A：环境污染导致了许多问题，如全球变暖、海平面上升、沙漠化等。我们该怎样来爱护环境呢？

B：My suggestion is that we should live a low-carbon life. For example, I always walk or ride a bike to workplace instead of driving a car.

A：我很赞同您的观点。幸运的是，越来越多的人意识到了这些问题并采取措施改善环境。

B：Exactly. Have you heard about World Car-Free Day, annually held in some cities and countries?

A：听说过。无锡人也积极参与了这样的活动。

B：Sounds great. In my mind, local governments' efforts also matter. People should be taught to sort out rubbish, use green energy and reduce carbon emission.

A：看来中国要改善环境的话还有很长一段路要走。

VI. Interpreting in groups.

Role-play the following situation with your partners, acting as the Chinese speaker, English speaker and the interpreter respectively. One group will be invited to perform in class.

Participants: 1. Mr. Bill Anderson
　　　　　　　 2. Ms. Wang
　　　　　　　 3. Interpreter

Location: Community service center

Task: Mr. Bill Anderson is an environmentalist who has lived in Wuxi for months. With the upcoming World Car-Free Day, he comes to Ms. Wang, a volunteer living in his neighborhood, for more information about the celebration which will be held in Wuxi next week. Ms. Wang speaks Chinese while Mr. Anderson is an English-speaker.

VII. 3-minute talk on the given topic.

Talk on the following topic in three minutes based on the given reference questions.

Topic: Smoking ban

Questions for Reference:
1. Are you a smoker?
2. What do you think of the people who smoke in public?
3. Does smoking ban in public places work well in China? Why or why not?

VIII. Theme-related expressions.

《生物多样性公约》	Convention on Biological Diversity
生态示范区	eco-demonstration region; environment-friendly region
白色污染	white pollution (by using and littering of non-degradable white plastics)
有机污染物	organic pollutants
城市垃圾无害化处理率	decontamination rate of urban refuse
垃圾填埋场	refuse landfill
森林砍伐率	rate of deforestation
农药残留	pesticide residue

Unit 12 Environmental Protection 环境保护

- 水土保持 — conservation of water and soil
- 生态农业 — environment-friendly agriculture; eco-agriculture
- 造林工程 — afforestation project
- 绿化面积 — afforested areas; greening space
- 森林覆盖率 — forest coverage
- 防风林 — wind breaks
- 防沙林 — sand breaks
- 开发可再生资源 — develop renewable resources
- 环保产品 — environment-friendly products
- 自然保护区 — nature reserve
- 濒危野生动物 — endangered wildlife
- 先天与后天, 遗传与环境 — nature-nurture
- 环境恶化 — environmental degradation
- 城市化失控 — uncontrolled urbanization
- 大气监测系统 — atmospheric monitoring system
- 悬浮颗粒物 — suspended particles
- 清洁能源 — clean energy
- 无铅汽油 — lead-free gasoline
- 电动汽车 — cell-driven vehicles; battery cars
- 世界环境日 — World Environment Day (June 5th each year)
- 联合国环境与发展大会 (环发大会) — United Nations Conference on Environment and Development (UNCED)
- 联合国环境规划署 — United Nations Environment Programs (UNEP)
- 国家环境保护总局 — State Environmental Protection Administration (SEPA)

213

Section C Further Exploration

将以下影片的部分字幕翻译成中文填入空格。

An Inconvenient Truth(选自 纪录片《难以忽视的真相》)

You look at that river	看着河水
gently flowing by.	(1) _____
You notice the leaves rustling with the wind.	听着风中(2) _____
You hear the birds.	鸟儿在鸣唱
You hear the tree frogs.	(3) _____
In the distance, you hear a cow.	远处还有奶牛的哞声
You feel the grass.	(4) _____
The mud gives a little bit on the river bank.	河岸露出了一小块泥土
It's quiet. It's peaceful.	(5) _____
And all of a sudden,	突然间
it's a gear shift inside you.	(6) _____
And it's like taking a deep breath and going,	就像深吸一口气,然后说
"Oh, yeah, I forgot about this."	(7) _____

UNIT 13
Science and Technology
科 学 技 术

Learning Objectives

1. To learn the translation technique of inversion;
2. To learn how to achieve equivalence despite the differences between English and Chinese;
3. To learn how to translate/interpret passages and dialogues on the topic of science and technology;
4. To learn useful words and expressions related to science and technology.

Lead-in

- *Quiz* (**True or False**)

　　　　　　 1. iPhone is the product of Microsoft Corporation.
　　　　　　 2. Nobel Prizes are awarded to the leading scientists in the fields of physics, chemistry, physiology or medicine, literature and economic sciences. Besides, a special prize, the Nobel Peace Prize is awarded to the well-recognized peace lover in this world.
　　　　　　 3. GM food is widely known as the short name for growth modified food.
　　　　　　 4. Today, human cloning is legal in all countries.
　　　　　　 5. The World Wide Web, www, is an information system with the access via the Internet.
　　　　　　 6. The National Scientific and Technological Progress Award is granted to the top scientists who have made significant achievements in science and technology in China.
　　　　　　 7. IT stands for Intelligence Technology.

● They are IT products. Do you know what they are? Fill in the blanks with the given English words.

laptop   UAV/ drone   copier   e-book reader   digital camera
smart phone   selfie sticker   modem   iRobot   3-D printer

1. _____   2. _____   3. _____   4. _____   5. _____

6. _____   7. _____   8. _____   9. _____   10. _____

Section A　Translation

Translation Technique

倒置法

在汉语中,定语修饰语和状语修饰语往往位于被修饰语之前;在英语中,许多修饰语常常位于被修饰语之后,因此翻译时往往要把原文的语序颠倒过来。倒置法通常用于英译汉,即对英语长句按照汉语的习惯表达法进行前后调换,按意群进行倒置,原则是使汉语译句符合现代汉语论理叙事的一般逻辑顺序。有时倒置法也用于汉译英。如:

原文:At this moment, through the wonder of telecommunications, more people are seeing and hearing what we say than on any other occasions in the whole history of the world.

译文:此时此刻,通过通信手段的奇迹,看到和听到我们讲话的人比整个世界历史上任何其他这样的场合都要多。(部分倒置)

原文:I strongly believe that it is in the interest of my countrymen that Britain should remain an active and energetic member of the European Community.

译文:我坚信,英国依然应该是欧共体中的一个积极的、充满活力的成员,这是符合我国人民利益的。(部分倒置)

原文:改革开放以来,中国发生了巨大的变化。

译文:Great changes have taken place in China since the introduction of the reform and opening-up policy. (全部倒置)

Unit 13 Science and Technology 科学技术

Passage Translation 1

Vocabulary

1. 中美互联网论坛
2. 云计算
3. 网络犯罪
4. 隐私保护
5. 在线知识产权保护和标准
6. 互联网法制
7. 新媒体
8. 互联网普及率
9. 宽带网民
10. 应用程序商店
11. 自主知识产权
12. 个性化服务
13. 微博
14. 推特
15. 新兴服务业
16. 物流
17. 下一代互联网
18. 物联网
19. 缩小数字鸿沟
20. 抵制网络色情
21. 网络版权保护

　　大家下午好,由中国互联网协会和美国微软公司联合发起的第四届中美互联网论坛于今天正式拉开帷幕。

　　本届中美互联网论坛的主题是"为了更加有用,更可信赖的互联网"。在为期两天的会议期间,双方代表将围绕云计算、网络犯罪预防和隐私保护的国际合作、在线知识产权保护和标准、互联网法制和新媒体发展等议题进行交流和对话。

　　近两年来中国网民规模急剧扩大,网络基础设施日益完善,互联网普及率不断提高。截至 2010 年 6 月,中国网民规模达到 4.4 亿,互联网普及率攀升到 33%。网民每周上网的时间继续增加,人均每周上网时长达到 19.8 小时,特别值得一提的是中国手机网民的

217

规模达到2.77亿。

　　手机网民快速增长的一个重要驱动力是移动互联网的快速发展。由于3G的普及，基于3G网络的阅读、音乐、互动社区、支付、应用程序商店等各种应用吸引着越来越多的手机上网用户。移动互联网在我国尤其农村地区将进一步普及。当前我国拥有自主知识产权的移动互联网相关产品不断涌现。为用户提供更加便捷和舒适的个性化服务，成为移动互联网产业各方的共识。

　　近年来微博的出现是中国互联网产业的另一个亮点。推特的流行使微博的概念为大众所接受。国内以新浪微博为代表的一批微博服务商迅速发展壮大，开展了中国微博时代。

　　中国的电子商务不断向传统产业渗透、融合，带动相关产业快速发展，并成为基于互联网的新兴服务业。大型企业电子商务应用水平显著提高，并逐渐向网上设计、制造、计划、管理等发展，中小企业电子商务应用在以销售、采购为代表的生产经营各环节中保持高速增长。电子商务服务业的作用也将随着电子商务应用的进一步扩大而显得更加突出，在与电子商务相关的支付、物流、IT、金融领域涌现出越来越多的服务商和服务模式。

　　政府对互联网技术的发展与创新也非常重视，近年来一直积极推进和加快下一代互联网、物联网以及云计算等关键技术的研发和产业化，引领产业快速发展。以云计算为例，当前已有阿里巴巴、腾讯、百度、中国石化等一些大型企业建立自己的云计算平台。

　　尽管近年来中国互联网的发展取得了一定成绩，但仍然有一些方面有待完善，例如缩小数字鸿沟，抵制网络色情，深化网络版权保护和网络安全工作等。双方需要进一步加强相互之间的理解、交流和合作。中国互联网协会非常愿意继续积极推动双方交流。

　　让我们真诚合作携手并进，为营造一个和谐、绿色、更加有用更加可靠的互联网不懈努力，共同创造互联网的美好明天。最后衷心祝愿本届中美互联网论坛圆满成功！谢谢大家！

Notes

1. "手机网民快速增长的一个重要驱动力是移动互联网的快速发展。"这句话可以转换视角翻译，以"互联网的快速发展"为主语，这样"驱动力"可以由名词转动词"drive"。全句译为："The fast development of the mobile Internet network has driven the growth of mobile Internet population."

2. "中国的电子商务不断向传统产业渗透、融合，带动相关产业快速发展，并成为基于互联网的新兴服务业。"句中有很多动词："渗透""融合""带动"和"成为"。翻译时，前两个动词因意思相同，可以减译一个，"成为"译为表结果的分词结构，显化逻辑关系。全句译为："China's e-commerce continues to integrate with traditional industries and promote the development of relevant industries, forming the new service sectors based on the Internet."

3. "中小企业的电子商务应用在以销售、采购为代表的生产经营各环节中保持高速增长。"句中的"应用"有较长的修饰语，即"以销售、采购为代表的生产经营各环节的电子商务"。翻译时主要用"application of ... to ..."短语，将修饰语倒置。全句译为："Small- and medium-size enterprises have witnessed fast growth in the application of e-commerce to production and operation, especially sales and purchasing."

Passage Translation 2

Vocabulary

1. cyber-attack
2. identity theft
3. the hacking of Sony Pictures
4. upper and lower case letters
5. browser history
6. Firefox
7. Chrome
8. wireless network
9. Internet address
10. encryption
11. authenticate
12. phishing
13. e-mail attachment
14. anti-virus software
15. flash drive

An increase in cyber-attacks and identity theft make the Internet seem like a scary place these days. The hacking of Sony Pictures led the news for some time. The U. S. State Department public email system was shut down. Even the White House was a target of cyber-attack. Last week, there were reports of a billion-dollar theft from European banks and secret viruses on millions of computer systems across Russia, China, India, Iran and elsewhere. This raises a question: How can individuals protect or make it more difficult for hackers to access their information?

Here are nine tips that can help you protect against cyber-attacks:

1. Make your password harder to hack. Hard passwords include upper and lower case letters, numbers and special characters. They should be at least eight characters in length. They should also not spell out words easy for hackers to find, like your pet's name or the name of a family member.

2. Change your password regularly. A very common mistake made by users is to create one hard password, but then never change it. Remembering a long list of complicated passwords can be difficult. But no password is unbreakable. Hackers are better able to hack multiple accounts if those accounts all have the same password.

3. Clear your browser history. This goes for all the devices you use in a day, your home

computer, your work computer, or your friend's iPad. Internet browsers like Firefox or Chrome keep track of where you've been and what you've done online. They keep records of every site you visited. Information about what you sent or saved on your computer can be kept for days or weeks. It is very easy for anyone who sees that information to steal a detailed record of your online activities.

4. Do not use free Wi-Fi. An increasing number of public places now offer free wireless access to the Internet. Often, a user does not need a password to connect to these wireless networks. These services might be useful, but they're also an easy way for hackers to access everything on your device. Unless you really need it, it is best not to use it.

5. Use HTTPS. HTTPS is officially known as "hyper-text transfer protocol secure". It is similar to HTTP, which is used to enter Internet addresses. HTTPS adds an extra layer of security and encryption while online. Communications between users and sites that support HTTPS are encrypted. The information is also authenticated. That means that HTTPS can determine whether or not a website is real.

6. Watch what you click. One of the most popular and successful ways hackers infect your computer is through a technique called phishing. Phishing occurs when someone opens an e-mail attachment that looks real. But the attachment is actually a virus that immediately infects the user's computer. If someone sends you a file or a website you did not ask for, it is best not to click on it.

7. Try not to use public computers. For many people, not using a public computer can be difficult. Those without a computer or Internet access at home often use Internet cafes to get online. However, the more different people use a computer, the more likely a virus has infected it.

8. Use anti-virus protection. There are many anti-virus softwares available for users. They can offer many different types of computer protection. Some anti-virus softwares are even free. They are a great way to help users one step ahead of hackers.

9. Be careful while using thumb drive. Thumb drives, also known as flash drives, are small and easy storage devices to use across different computers. They are a popular device that people use to exchange files and documents. They can also spread viruses easily across computers and networks.

Notes

1. "The hacking of Sony Pictures led the news for some time."句中的"led the news"是指该新闻是新闻的头条。全句译为:"索尼影音入侵案一段时间以来一直是头条。"

2. "Hackers are better able to hack multiple accounts if those accounts all have the same password."此句翻译时,要考虑汉语句子重心在后面的表达习惯,用倒置法,将从句置于主句前。全句译成:"如果这些账户密码相同,黑客就更能破解多个账户。"

3. "HTTPS is officially known as 'hyper-text transfer protocol secure'. It is similar

to HTTP, which is used to enter Internet addresses."句中的"HTTPS"是指"hyper-text transfer protocol secure",意为"安全超文本传输协议",为计算机科学术语。全句译为:"HTTPS 的正式名称是'安全超文本传输协议'。它类似于用于输入互联网地址的超文本传输协议。"

4. "But the attachment is actually a virus that immediately infects the user's computer."句中的"virus"和"infect"都是计算机科学术语,分别译为"计算机病毒"和"感染"。全句译为:"但这个附件实际上是一个病毒,它会迅速感染该用户的电脑。"

Sentences in Focus

1. 在为期两天的会议期间,双方代表将围绕云计算、网络犯罪预防和隐私保护的国际合作、在线知识产权保护和标准、互联网法制和新媒体发展等议题进行交流和对话。

2. 近两年来中国网民规模急剧扩大,网络基础设施日益完善,互联网普及率不断提高。截至 2010 年 6 月,中国网民规模达到 4.4 亿,互联网普及率攀升到 33%。

3. 中国的电子商务不断向传统产业渗透、融合,带动相关产业快速发展,并成为基于互联网的新兴服务业。

4. 电子商务服务业的作用也将随着电子商务应用的进一步扩大而显得更加突出,在与电子商务相关的支付、物流、IT、金融领域涌现出越来越多的服务商和服务模式。

5. 政府对互联网技术的发展与创新也非常重视,近年来一直积极推进和加快下一代互联网、物联网以及云计算等关键技术的研发和产业化,引领产业快速发展。

6. An increase in cyber-attacks and identity theft make the Internet seem like a scary place these days.

7. Hard passwords include upper and lower case letters, numbers and special characters. They should be at least eight characters in length.

8. Internet browsers like Firefox or Chrome keep track of where you've been and what you've done online. They keep records of every site you visited. Information about what you sent or saved on your computer can be kept for days or weeks.

9. One of the most popular and successful ways hackers infect your computer is through a technique called phishing. Phishing occurs when someone opens an e-mail attachment that looks real.

10. There are many anti-virus softwares available for users. They can offer many different types of computer protection.

Exercises

I. Fill in the blanks with English words according to the given Chinese.

1. The United Nations released a report that says nearly 3 billion people will _____ _____（可以上网）by the end of 2014.
2. Guangdong Province has made outstanding achievements in protecting _____ _____（知识产权）in China.
3. Governments at all levels should _____（携起手）to tackle the problem of hacker attack.
4. Alibaba may lose its dominance in _____（在线支付）in its home market since China's Central Bank will launch a new platform with other banks.
5. More national technical centers will be set up to enhance _____ _____（技术创新）and development of production.
6. The hotel uses various in-room technologies which brings _____ _____（个性化服务）to guests.
7. "Agriculture has long been regarded as a _____（传统产业）, but is actually a high-tech industry," said the expert.
8. The presidential election is the _____（亮点）of next year's political calendar.
9. Sometimes I _____（网上冲浪）and download e-books to read.
10. _____（隐私保护）is an issue that concerns all the Internet users.

II. Translate the following sentences into Chinese by using the translation technique of inversion.

1. The past decades have witnessed the fundamental change in China since the reform and opening-up in 1978.
   _____
2. We believe that it is right and necessary that people from different cultures should get along well with each other.
   _____
3. We can develop, on the basis of mutual respect and benefits, the friendship between our two countries.
   _____
4. Environmental protection is the common issue that concerns all Chinese people.
   _____

5. Significant achievements have been made in the fields of biotechnology and genetic engineering.

III. Translate the following sentences.

1. China and the United States established an innovation dialogue mechanism to share the views and experience on formulating innovation policies.

2. Since opening its first Network Technology School at Fudan University in September 1998, Cisco has established more than 130 network technology schools in China.

3. The international art and science exhibition, held by Tsinghua University, includes 560 works from 32 universities in 16 countries.

4. China and the United States have achieved laudable progresses in agricultural cooperation, since the signing of the agricultural cooperation protocol between the two countries in 2002.

5. The Chinese-made supercomputer Tianhe-I is not only the fastest supercomputer system running in the world, but also enjoys broad applications.

6. 技术给人们的生活带来了许多新产品,如平板电脑、三维打印机等。

7. 中国将继续加大科技领域的开放度。

8. 科学家们就生物技术、信息技术和新能源展开了热烈的讨论。

9. 科技部部长于4月22日参加了此次科技展的开幕式。

10. 中美将携手加强技术及文化交流。

IV. Translate the following paragraphs.

1. Today, I am thinking much more about Microsoft's future than its past. I believe computing will evolve faster in the next 10 years than ever before. We have already lived in a multi-platform world, and computing will become even more pervasive. We are nearing the point where computers and robots will be able to see, move, and interact naturally, unlocking many new applications and empowering people even more.

2. 随着宽带网络的迅猛发展,人们获取在线数据资源变得容易了。然而,因特网正遭遇越来越多黑客攻击的风险。信息保护已成为网络发展的当务之急。200多位网络安全专家参加了此次论坛,旨在加强政府间合作机制来共同应对这个问题。

Section B Interpretation

Interpretation Technique

口译技能:英汉语差异及转换方法

在记忆信息后,口译的下一步就是把储存在大脑里的信息转换成目标语言。口译转换是口译过程的重要环节。但是,英语和汉语在句法结构等方面存在着较大的差异,如果不熟悉这两种语言之间的转换规则,就会影响口译输出的质量。以下是英汉之间的主要差异及转换方法。

1. 汉语"意合"和英语"形合"

所谓"意合"就是指语言组织主要靠句子内部的逻辑联系,所谓"形合"就是指语言组织主要靠语言本身的语法手段(包括词汇手段和形态手段)。换言之,汉语是"隐性连接",英语是"显性连接"。因此,在进行汉英转换时,一个常见的策略便是要有意识地根据英语"形合"的特点,在语句的衔接与连贯之处添加表示并列、因果、条件等关系的"连接词"。

汉译英时,往往逻辑关系和句间关系都要显性化。

原文: 我们应该牢牢把握中美关系的大局,妥善解决分歧,不断朝着增进了解、扩大共识、发展合作、共创未来的目标前进。

口译: We should take a firm hold of the overall interests of Sino-US relations and settle our differences properly so as to reach the goal of promoting mutual understanding, broadening common ground, developing cooperation and building a future together.

而英译汉时,英语中显性的逻辑关系和句间关系往往要做隐性化处理。

原文: If we persist in our reform, we will be able to turn our ideals into reality.

口译: 坚持变革创新,理想就会变为现实。

2. 汉语"主题突出"和英语"主语突出"

汉语中位于谓语前面的成分是一个主题或话题,但不一定是主语,而且汉语中有很多"无主句",即没有主语的句子;而英语中一个完整的句子(除了祈使句以外)必须有主语。也就是说,汉语是话题凸显的语言,而英语是主语凸显的语言。

因此,我们在汉译英时要先确定主语。

原文: 改革开放胆子要大一些,要敢于试验。

口译: We must be courageous enough to venture on experiments in our reform and opening-up efforts.

这句话中,显然不是"改革开放"可以放大胆子,所以不是主语,这时可以添加逻辑主语"we"。

3. 汉语"多种词类均可充当谓语"和英语"谓语结构以动词为中心"

在汉语中,能充当谓语的绝不仅仅是动词,形容词也是典型的谓语词,甚至名词也可充当谓语;而在英语中,充当谓语的必然是动词。在英语中,"主语+动词"式的句子结构(subject + verb structure)占了绝大部分,是典型的英语句子结构。

在汉英转换时,确定了句子的谓语动词就等于抓住了句子的灵魂。

原文: 我们坚持在和平共处五项原则的基础上,建立发展友好合作关系。

口译: We will establish and develop friendly relations and cooperation with the rest of the world on the basis of the Five Principles of Peaceful Coexistence.

4. 汉语"修饰语+中心词"和英语"中心词+修饰语"

在汉语中,修饰语常出现在中心词前面,但如果修饰语过长,则应另立分句,详细说明。

在英语中,一个典型的语法现象是,"中心词"出现后,其后面的修饰语是开放的,似乎可以无限延长,可以加上多个短语,如介词短语、非谓语动词短语等,还可以加上多个从句,如定语从句、同位语从句、状语从句等。

原文: 中国人将筷子视为一种可以将饭从碗中逐口送入口中的一种最简单和有效的用餐工具。

口译: Chinese people regard chopsticks the simplest possible and the most efficient tool for transporting bite-sized morsels of food from a bowl to the mouth.

5. 汉语"句子重心在后"和英语"句子重心在前"

在复合句中,英语的主句为主要部分,一般放在句首,即"重心在前";而汉语则一般按照逻辑和时间顺序将主要部分放在句尾,即"重心在后"。这也是口译时要注意的英汉转换规律。

原文:航班取消了,我们不得不多待一天。

口译:We had to stay for one more day, for the flight was canceled.

掌握了英汉语的主要差异,我们在口译时才能采用合适的翻译方法进行流利转换。

Passage Interpretation 1

创新是经济结构调整优化的原动力。要把创新摆在国家发展全局的核心位置,促进科技与经济社会发展紧密结合。

加快科技体制改革。强化企业在技术创新中的主体地位,鼓励企业设立研发机构。

新兴产业和新兴业态是竞争高地。要实施高端装备、信息网络、集成电路、新能源、新材料、生物医药、航空发动机、燃气轮机等重大项目,把一批新兴产业培育成主导产业。制订"互联网+"行动计划,推动移动互联网、云计算、大数据、物联网等与现代制造业结合,促进电子商务、工业互联网和互联网金融健康发展,引导互联网企业拓展国际市场。除了已设立的400亿元新兴产业投资基金,国家还需要整合筹措更多资金,为产业创新加油助力。

Passage Interpretation 2

Good morning, ladies and gentlemen. On behalf of Roaming Robots, the largest creative robot entertainment company in Europe, I have the greatest pleasure to introduce to you one of the most exciting robotics events of the year—the Robot Zone at the Royal International Air Tattoo.

The RIAT, short for the Royal International Air Tattoo, is a major annual showcase of UK's aeronautic technologies. It is held at the Royal Air Force, with over 168,000 visitors in 2004!

This year's RIAT is scheduled on July 16th and 17th, at which time the first Robot zone will be inaugurated as showcases for engineering talent in robot design and manufacturing anywhere in the country.

Apart from exhibitions, two major robotics competitions are on our agenda.

One is RIAT Robot Challenge. This activity will take place in the special 120-seat arena, with battles as seen on the popular TV program *Robot Wars*. 51 of the UK's top robots, 25 heavy weights and 26 feather weights will fight throughout the day. Many of the robots participating are winners of various robotics competitions throughout the country that have battled their way into the hearts of robotics fans.

The other is RIAT Youth Robot Competition. Budding roboteers aged 16 and under from around the country are being invited to design and construct a robot and compete on a specially constructed obstacle course to win the inaugural RIAT Youth Robot Competition Trophy.

And, after you have witnessed all the action, you'll have the opportunity to meet the robot makers themselves and see how robot technology is increasingly being applied to our everyday lives.

Unit 13　Science and Technology 科学技术

Dialogue Interpretation 1

记者：被人称作世界上最富有的人感觉如何？

Gates：I'm surprised whenever I hear that! What it really means for me is that I have a lot of resources to give back to my Foundation and hopefully do a lot of good things because of that.

记者：您的公司现在可谓是家喻户晓了，但是有些人说您垄断了整个IT产业。您对此有什么看法？

Gates：Well, Microsoft has had its success by doing low-cost products and constantly improving those products and we've really redefined the IT industry to be something that's about a tool for individuals. So we're proud of what we've done. Meanwhile, we need to keep doing even better to maintain the leadership position we've got.

记者：有些人似乎不喜欢微软成功的方式，您对此有何看法？

Gates：Well, if you look at any survey about the most admired company or the place people want to work the most, Microsoft comes out on top again and again. People are very passionate about software and we like getting their feedback, what they like, what they don't like. And wherever we fall short, we want to just go back and work a little bit harder, do a better job.

记者：好的。您认为微软将继续在市场上保持目前的领先地位吗？

Gates：Well, that all depends on whether we keep making big breakthroughs. People have very high expectations for where we need to go with the software, and now we think we can meet those expectations because we're spending a lot on research and development. We've been able to hire a lot of great people and that's what makes my job a lot of fun.

记者：您认为未来科技的发展方向是什么？

Gates：The advancement of technology is based on making it fit in so that you don't really even notice it. That means having a computer remember what you're interested in and it can help you automatically.

记者：对于软件侵权行为，微软有什么看法？

Gates：Well, I think any author or musician is anxious to have legitimate sales of their products, partly so they're rewarded for their success and partly so they can go on and do new things. In the case of software, we have special prices for education and student-type usage. We always strive to let people know about the software license and we fund the research and development.

记者：最近我读到一篇关于火狐的文章，文章说火狐在各方面的性能都比微软更好，你觉得这个说法公平吗？

Gates：Well, there's competition in every place that we are in. Our commitment is to keep our browser that competes with Firefox to be the best browser—best in security, best in features. In fact, we just announced that we will have a new version of the browser which shows that we are innovating very rapidly there and it is our commitment to have the best.

记者：您会迫于竞争压力而提高浏览器更新换代的速度吗？

Gates：Well, competition is always a fantastic thing. Whether for Google, Apple or Microsoft, some fantastic competitors are always there who keep us on our toes.

Exercises

I. Interpreting technique practice.

1. 明天不下雨，我们就去爬山。

2. 中国历史上产生了许多杰出的哲学家、思想家、政治家、军事家、科学家和文学艺术家。

3. 中国疆域辽阔，人口众多，历史悠久。

4. 过去的一年是重要而非同寻常的一年，是取得显著成就的一年。

5. 我们两国人民的贸易交往可以追溯到很久以前。

6. A right attitude towards the diversity of our cultures will strengthen our trust and confidence.

7. The football player spotted an opening in the human wall, swayed the football a bit to the left, kicked it out from a small angle and scored.

8. The financial crisis is a very complicated issue drawing more and more attention from the international community.

9. The series of *Harry Potter* have been translated into many languages and loved by children across the world.

10. From my experience of working with hi-tech companies in California's Silicon Valley, the biggest problems arise when existing patent protections for business methods are combined with the Internet.

II. Spot dictation.

The American computer company IBM says it has developed a microprocessor—a computer chip—that works much like the (1)_____. IBM calls the chip TrueNorth. It is the size of a postage stamp. The chip has 5.4 billion tiny parts that work like the human brain's neurons and synapses. Neurons and synapses are the cells and electric forces that (2)_____ to and from the brain. TrueNorth has 1 million neurons and 256 million synapses. The human brain has (3)_____

_____ neurons and up to 150 trillion synapses. IBM says it can program the new chip to understand difficult problems and then solve them as humans would.

IBM's brain-inspired architecture (4) _____ a network of neurosynaptic cores. The company says the TrueNorth chip could be used as a brain for search-and-rescue robots. It can also be used for controlling new kinds of wheelchairs or for (5) _____ involving several people and then making a printed record of those conversations. TrueNorth is still being tested. But IBM says it could be available for public use in two to three years.

The chip is just one example of machines becoming more and more like humans. This field of study is called (6) _____, or AI. Some experts believe computers will someday become more intelligent than humans.

Researchers are trying to develop ways for humans and computers to work together more closely. Someday, humans and computers may be joined. The (7) _____ _____ of a human and a computer is called a cyborg.

Jonathan Mugan has written a book about the relationship between humans and computers, called *The Curiosity Cycle*. He told VOA by email that it is time to prepare for a future where computers (8) _____ over our lives. In his words, "Machines are technology. And technology expands as human knowledge expands. (9) ____ _____, human intelligence developed through evolution, which is a much slower process."

Mr. Mugan believes that (10) _____ are good for humans. He says intelligent machines can help humans solve many of our most difficult problems. But he says, "Once computers become broadly smarter than humans, it's hard to predict what will happen."

III. Sentence listening and translation.

1. _____

2. _____

3. _____

4. _____

5. _____

IV. Paragraph listening and translation.

V. Dialogue interpretation.

A: 上海科技馆引入了一个名为"奇怪的东西"的展览,很有意思。
B: Sounds good. What makes it interesting?
A: 展览可让观众与展品进行互动,了解日用材料的一些特点。
B: It must be very instructive for people who have little knowledge about material science.

A: 是啊。既然展览从 7 月 26 号开放到 11 月 9 号,咱们暑假去参观怎么样?
B: It's a good idea. You know, Shanghai is my favorite tourist destination.

VI. Interpreting in groups.

Role-play the following situations with your partner, acting as the Chinese speaker, English speaker and the interpreter respectively. One group will be invited to perform in class.

Participants: 1. Peter
2. Tour guide
3. Interpreter

Location: World Expo, Shanghai

Task: You are a tour guide working with World Expo Shanghai. Peter is an exchange student from the United States, paying a visit to the Expo with his friend. Greet them, introduce briefly the attractions of the Expo and answer their questions. You speak Chinese while Peter is an English speaker. Peter's friend works as the interpreter.

VII. 3-minute talk on the given topic.

Talk on the following topic in three minutes based on the given reference questions.

Topic: To be or not to be a phubber
Questions for Reference:
1. What is phubber?
2. Are you a phubber? Why or why not?
3. What is your advice for phubbers?

Ⅷ. **Theme-related expressions.**

《高技术研究发展计划纲要》	High-Tech R & D Program Outline
《世界版权公约》	Universal Copyright Convention
版税	royalty
猖獗的盗版行为	rampant piracy
发展多种形式的产学研结合	promote the integration of production, teaching and research in a variety of approaches
风险投资基金	venture capital investment fund
改革试点	pilot reform
改造传统产业	renovate conventional industries
高新技术产业开发区	high-tech industrial zone
国家科学技术进步奖	National Award for Science and Technology Progress
基因芯片	genetic chip; biochip (an important component in human gene studies covering gene sequencing, genetic function defining and genetic diagnosing)
技术转让	technology transfer
尖端技术	state-of-the-art technology; cutting-edge technology
抗病转基因小麦	transgenic wheat of disease resistance
科学技术是第一生产力。	Science and technology is the primary productive force.
科研成果商品化	commercialization of research findings
纳米材料	nano materials
企业研发中心	corporate R & D center
侵权行为	infringing act
染色体	chromosome

• 生命科学	life science
• 生物技术	biotechnology
• 生物遥感器	bio-sensor
• 实施科教兴国战略	implement the strategy of rejuvenating China through science and technology
• 推广科研成果	promote the application of research findings
• 星火计划（把先进、适用的技术引向农村的指导性科技计划，1986年经国务院批准）	Spark Program
• 火炬计划（发展中国高新技术产业的指导性计划，于1988年8月经国务院批准）	Torch Program
• 样机	prototypes; mock-up
• 应用型科研机构	application-based research institution
• 优势科技力量	outstanding scientists, engineers and technicians
• 中国科学院	Chinese Academy of Sciences (CAS)
• 专利产品	patented products

Section C Further Exploration

以下是2015中国国际机器人展览会的信息简介，根据所给中文填写英文，每个空格填写一个单词。

展会名称 Exhibition Name	2015中国国际机器人展览会 2015 China International Robot Show (CIROS 2015)
时间 Date	2015年7月8日—11日 July 8-11, 2015
地点 Venue	国家会展中心（上海） National Exhibition and (1) _____ Center

展出面积 Area	28000 平方米 28,000 m²
到场观众 Visitors	50000 人次 50,000
(2) _____ 开放时间 Time	2015 年 7 月 8—10 日 9:00—17:30; 7 月 11 日 9:00—15:00 9:00-17:30, July 8-10, 2015 9:00-15:00, July 11, 2015
展会主旨 (3) _____	以"推动机器人跨越发展,引领制造业深入变革"为主题,引领产业发展,为机器人行业企业和巨大的中国市场打造对接交流平台。 Promoting the leaping development of robotics and leading the (4) _____ transformation of manufacturing industry, CIROS 2015 will take the lead in (5) _____ development to build the communication platform for robot industries and the (6) _____ Chinese market.
展会简介 Introduction	本届展会展出面积共计 28000 平方米,展品范围涵盖工业机器人本体、零部件以及服务机器人技术与产品,是目前中国机器人领域规模最大、行业影响力最强的专业展览会,被誉为中国机器人第一展。 The total exhibition area of CIROS 2015 adds up to 28,000 m². The (7) _____ of CIROS 2015 include industrial robot body and parts, the technology and products of service robots. As the leading robot exhibition in China, CIROS is currently the largest and the most (8) _____ professional exhibition in Chinese robot circle. CIROS 拥有权威的主办机构、优质专业的买家团、全球机器人行业顶级峰会及专业技术论坛,更有海内外机器人协会、科研机构积极参与和专业媒体强势宣传,极大地推动产业发展,促进更多的市场应用。 CIROS 2015 boasts prestigious organizers, high quality and professional buyer group, top-class (9) _____ and specialized technology forum in the global robotics industry. CIROS 2015 will greatly spur the development of industry and market applications, with the active (10) _____ of robotics associations and research institutions at home and abroad as well as the intensive propaganda of professional media.

UNIT 14

Economy

经济活动

Learning Objectives

1. To learn how to translate modifiers;
2. To know the criteria for interpreting;
3. To learn how to translate/interpret passages or dialogues on the topic of business practice;
4. To learn useful words and expressions related to economic world.

Lead-in

● *Quiz* (**True or False**)

_____ 1. Bill Gates is the co-founder and chairman of Apple Inc.

_____ 2. Alibaba Group went public on the New York Stock Exchange in 2014.

_____ 3. Subway is an American fast food restaurant franchise that primarily sells submarine sandwiches and salads.

_____ 4. China Import and Export Fair, also known as the Canton Fair, is held in Guangzhou once a year.

_____ 5. It is Legal Affairs Department that is responsible for recruiting employees for a company.

_____ 6. The abbreviation of "limited company" usually goes like "Co. Ltd."

_____ 7. Business-to-business (B2B) is commerce transactions between businesses, such as between a manufacturer and a wholesaler, or between a wholesaler and a retailer.

● Here are some logos of Fortune 500. Which company does each logo stand for? Fill in the blanks with the given names.

Alibaba Group	Apple Inc.	McDonald's Corporation
Facebook	PepsiCo Inc.	General Electric
Bank of China	Nike, Inc.	Honda Motor Co., Ltd.
Royal Dutch Shell Group	Haier Group	Microsoft Corporation

1. _____

2. _____

3. _____

4. _____

5. _____

6. _____

7. _____

8. _____

9. _____

10. _____

11. _____

12. _____

Section A Translation

Translation Technique

英译汉修饰语的处理

在英语里，修饰语可以放在中心词的前面或后面。充当前置修饰语的有形容词、名词、分词等；充当后置修饰语的有定语从句、形容词短语、分词短语、介词短语等。而汉语修饰语一般会放在中心词的前面，但是也会有一个"度"，不会将所有修饰语全部堆积在中心词的前面。

如果原文修饰语不多（不超过两个）也不长，那么可以把修饰语放在汉语中心词的前面。

如果原文修饰语较多或较长，而且是前置修饰和后置修饰均有，那么译成汉语时就要把简单的修饰语放在中心词前面，较长、结构较复杂的修饰语则转换为分句。

1. 把英语的前置修饰语译成汉语"……的"

原文：The financial crisis is a very complicated issue drawing more and more attention from the international community.

译文：金融危机是非常复杂、越来越为国际社会所关注的问题。

2. 把英语中后置的一重修饰语放在汉语中心词的前面

原文：I am interested in the potential of television as a popular medium which engages audiences in popular drama and I am also interested in the commercial and other pressures which make it difficult to produce high quality work for television.

译文：我很关心电视这一大众媒体吸引观众收看电视剧的潜力，也关心在商业及其他压力下很难制作高质量的电视节目的问题。

3. 把英语中后置的多重修饰语放在汉语中心词后，并用"这""该"等概括词承接

原文：The next part of my speech is what we called the "unsolicited advice", which is rarely valued, seldom remembered, never followed.

译文：我演讲的第二部分是"不请自来的忠告"。这样的忠告甚少受到重视，很少会有人记住，而且绝对没有人会付诸实践。

4. 把英语中有逻辑关系的修饰语（句）转换成相应的汉语关系复句

原文：My visit to China will be an exciting trip, which will enable me to see with my eyes the economic, social and cultural achievements over the past three decades in China.

译文：此次访华之旅将是激动人心的，因为我将亲眼看到中国在过去三十年间所取得的经济、社会和文化上的成就。

Passage Translation 1

Vocabulary

1. 新常态
2. 中高速增长
3. 规模速度型粗放增长
4. 质量效率型集约增长
5. 要素投资驱动
6. 创新驱动
7. 劳动生产率
8. 能耗
9. 服务业
10. 基本国策
11. 投资环境
12. 合法权益
13. 远亲不如近邻
14. 互利合作

15. 互联互通
16. 睦邻友好合作条约
17. 东盟
18. 丝绸之路经济带
19. 21 世纪海上丝绸之路
20. "一带一路"
21. 顺应了地区和全球合作潮流
22. 合作机制或倡议
23. 优势互补
24. 亚洲基础设施投资银行
25. 愿景
26. 丝路基金
27. 基础设施互联互通项目
28. 广阔前景
29. 命运共同体
30. 开创

中国经济发展进入新常态,正从高速增长转为中高速增长,从规模速度型粗放增长转向质量效率型集约增长,从要素投资驱动转向创新驱动。2014 年,中国经济实现了 7.4% 的增长,劳动生产率提高了 7%,能耗下降了 4.8%,国内消费贡献度上升,服务业发展加快,发展质量和效益不断提高。

中国经济发展进入新常态,将继续给包括亚洲国家在内的世界各国提供更多市场、增长、投资、合作机遇。未来 5 年,中国进口商品将超过 10 万亿美元,对外投资将超过 5000 亿美元,出境旅游人数将超过 5 亿人次。中国将坚持对外开放的基本国策,不断完善国内投资环境,保护投资者合法权益,同大家一起,共同驱动亚洲发展的列车,不断驶向更加光明的未来。

远亲不如近邻。这是中国人很早就认识到的一个朴素的生活道理。中国坚持与邻为善、以邻为伴的理念,不断深化同周边国家的互利合作和互联互通,努力使自身发展,更好地惠及周边国家。中国已经同 8 个周边国家签署睦邻友好合作条约,正在商谈签署中国—东盟睦邻友好合作条约,并愿同所有周边国家商签睦邻友好合作条约,为双边关系发展和地区繁荣稳定提供有力保障。

2013 年我访问哈萨克斯坦和印度尼西亚时,分别提出建设丝绸之路经济带和 21 世纪海上丝绸之路合作倡议。"一带一路"合作倡议契合中国、沿线国家和本地区发展需要,符合有关各方共同利益,顺应了地区和全球合作潮流。

"一带一路"建设秉持的是共商、共建、共享原则,不是封闭的,而是开放包容的;不是中国一家的独奏,而是沿线国家的合唱。"一带一路"建设不是要替代现有地区合作机制和倡议,而是要在已有基础上,推动沿线国家实现发展战略相互对接、优势互补。目前,已经有60多个沿线国家和国际组织对参与"一带一路"建设表达了积极态度。"一带一路"建设、亚洲基础设施投资银行都是开放的,我们欢迎沿线国家和亚洲国家积极参与,也张开臂膀欢迎五大洲朋友共襄盛举。

　　"一带一路"建设不是空洞的口号,而是看得见、摸得着的实际举措,将给地区国家带来实实在在的利益。在有关各方共同努力下,"一带一路"建设的愿景与行动文件已经制定,亚洲基础设施投资银行筹建工作迈出实质性步伐,丝路基金已经顺利启动,一批基础设施互联互通项目已在稳步推进。这些早期收获向我们展现了"一带一路"的广阔前景。

　　人类和平与发展的事业是崇高的事业,也是充满挑战的事业。前进的道路不会一帆风顺,期望的成果不会唾手可得。不管征程多么曲折、多么漫长,胜利总是属于那些永不放弃、百折不挠、携手前行的人们。我相信,只要我们大家认准目标、锲而不舍,就一定能携手迈向命运共同体、开创亚洲新未来!

Notes

1. "2014年,中国经济实现了7.4%的增长,劳动生产率提高了7%,能耗下降了4.8%,国内消费贡献度上升,服务业发展加快,发展质量和效益不断提高。"这句话是长句,按照句意,在"国内消费贡献度上升"之前断开,拆分为两句。"中国经济实现了7.4%的增长"为主句,可以将后两个分句理解为经济增长的表现,转为非谓语结构。"国内消费贡献度……不断提高"中的三个分句在意义上是并列的,译成三个并列分句。全句译为:"China's economy grew by 7.4% in 2014, with 7% increase in labor productivity and 4.8% decrease in energy consumption. The share of domestic consumption in GDP rose; the service sector expanded at a faster pace; the quality and efficiency of development continued to improve."

2. "'一带一路'合作倡议契合中国、沿线国家和本地区发展需要,符合有关各方共同利益,顺应了地区和全球合作潮流。"这句话有三个动词"契合""符合"和"顺应",可以将"契合"译成非谓语结构。全句译为:"The 'Belt and Road' initiative, meeting the development needs of China, countries along the routes and the region at large, will serve the common interests of relevant parties and answer the call of our time for regional and global cooperation."

3. "'一带一路'建设秉持的是共商、共建、共享原则,不是封闭的,而是开放包容的;不是中国一家的独奏,而是沿线国家的合唱。"这句话拆分为三句。拆分后都属无主句,要分别添加主语,分别为"China""the programs of development"和"they"。全句译为:"In promoting this initiative, China will follow the principle of wide consultation, joint contribution and shared benefits. The programs of development will be open and inclusive, not exclusive. They will be a real chorus comprising all countries along the routes, not a solo for China itself."

4. "'一带一路'建设不是要替代现有地区合作机制和倡议,而是要在已有基础上,推动沿线国家实现发展战略相互对接、优势互补。"这句话中的四字格"相互对接"和"优势互补"是难点，关键在解释意义，译为："align their development strategies and form supplement"。全句译为："To develop the 'Belt and Road' is not to replace existing mechanisms or initiatives for regional cooperation. Much to the contrary, we will build on the existing basis to help countries align their development strategies and form complementarity."

5. "不管征程多么曲折、多么漫长，胜利总是属于那些永不放弃、百折不挠、携手前行的人们。"句中的"百折不挠"和"永不放弃"同义，不但需要减译一个，而且翻译时重在释义。全句译为："No matter how long and difficult the journey may be, those who work together and never give up will eventually prevail."

Passage Translation 2

Vocabulary

1. fraud
2. business environment
3. corruption
4. rife
5. Enron and Worldcom
6. Sarbannes-Oxley Act
7. reputational damage
8. internal audit
9. perpetrate
10. authorize
11. breach
12. subordinate

The objective of my presentation is to raise the awareness of fraud in the business environment and the potential losses that can and do occur. Generally speaking, fraud is the business equivalent of corruption and many of the symptoms and issues are the same, such as the abuse of a position of trust.

Businesses exist to make a profit. Fraud reduces that profit—sometimes substantially. If a company cannot make a profit, then it will presumably cease trading and the staff will lose their jobs. If a commercial environment exists where fraud is rife, businesses will be reluctant to start operating there.

Fraud can create uncertainty that adversely affects confidence in businesses. The large corporate frauds in the USA—Enron and Worldcom shook stock market confidence and resulted in the Sarbannes-Oxley Act.

The messages I would take from the figures we collected are that dealing with frauds costs a lot of money and that management fear the secondary consequences of share price and reputational damage as much as the cost of the fraud.

Taking into consideration the potential damage a fraud can do to an organization and to a manager's career if a fraud is discovered in an area he is responsible for, I strongly suspect that many frauds are unconsciously or willfully ignored.

The interesting fact is that most frauds are discovered by accident, not by internal audit who you would expect to find the most. I would suggest that the reason for this is that auditors are well trained, highly disciplined professionals. They have minds that are trained to think according to their discipline. The fraudster will always present what the auditor expects to see. Otherwise, he wouldn't be a good fraudster!

Most frauds are perpetrated by staff within a business. This is maybe for the simple and obvious reason that a member of staff has access to the process, and they have the knowledge. Managers not only have access and knowledge, they have the ability to authorize larger amounts or influence decisions. The fraud includes a breach of trust by the manager.

When a manager abuses his position of trust, then fear makes it hard for a subordinate to report their suspicions, and loyalty makes it difficult for fellow managers to suspect a colleague whom they may have known and worked with for many years. Therefore, suspicions of frauds go unreported or dismissed.

Notes

1. "The objective of my presentation is to raise the awareness of fraud in the business environment and the potential losses that can and do occur." 句中"that can and do occur"是后置修饰语，汉译时要前置，此处在语境中意为"潜在的或已发生的"。全句译为："我发言的目的是提高各位对商业环境中的诈骗以及诈骗所引发的潜在的或实际损失的认识。"

2. "The large corporate frauds in the USA—Enron and Worldcom shook stock market confidence and resulted in the Sarbannes-Oxley Act." 句中的安然公司(Enron Corporation)原是世界上最大的综合性天然气和电力公司之一，世通公司(WorldCom)是一家美国的通讯公司。2001至2002年间，两家公司相继爆发财务丑闻，参议院议员Paul S. Sarbanes等提出沙宾法案(Sarbanes-Oxley Act, SOA)，原名为《2002年上市公司会计改革和投资者保护法案》。"Enron and Worldcom"为同位语，解释为"The large corporate frauds"。全句译为："美国几宗大的商业诈骗案，如安然丑闻和世通公司事件动摇了股市的信心，引发了沙宾法案的制定。"

3. "The messages I would take from the figures we collected are that dealing with frauds costs a lot of money and that management fear the secondary consequences of share price and reputational damage as much as the cost of the fraud." 句中的"the secondary consequences"是指诈骗对股价和公司声誉造成的影响。全句译为："从我们收集

到的数据中,我得出的结论是,应对诈骗耗资巨大,而且公司管理层不但担心诈骗造成损失,而且担心诈骗对股价和公司声誉造成不良影响。"

4. "Taking into consideration the potential damage a fraud can do to an organization and to a manager's career if a fraud is discovered in an area he is responsible for, I strongly suspect that many frauds are unconsciously or willfully ignored." 此句需要按照汉语表达习惯,倒置部分语序。由于"Taking into consideration"后的内容过长过复杂,可以先翻译,然后再翻译"Taking into consideration",使句子表达更流畅。全句译为:"诈骗对公司的潜在破坏严重,同时,如果一个经理被发现在其负责的领域出现诈骗,他的职业生涯也会被破坏。考虑到这些情况,我强烈怀疑许多诈骗都被有意无意地瞒报了。"

Sentences in Focus

1. 中国经济发展进入新常态,正从高速增长转为中高速增长,从规模速度型粗放增长转向质量效率型集约增长,从要素投资驱动转向创新驱动。

2. 2014年,中国经济实现了7.4%的增长,劳动生产率提高了7%,能耗下降了4.8%,国内消费贡献度上升,服务业发展加快,发展质量和效益不断提高。

3. 中国经济发展进入新常态,将继续给包括亚洲国家在内的世界各国提供更多市场、增长、投资、合作机遇。

4. 未来5年,中国进口商品将超过10万亿美元,对外投资将超过5000亿美元,出境旅游人数将超过5亿人次。

5. 在有关各方共同努力下,"一带一路"建设的愿景与行动文件已经制定,亚洲基础设施投资银行筹建工作迈出实质性步伐,丝路基金已经顺利启动,一批基础设施互联互通项目已在稳步推进。

6. The objective of my presentation is to raise the awareness of fraud in the business environment and the potential losses that can and do occur.

7. Generally speaking, fraud is the business equivalent of corruption and many of the symptoms and issues are the same, such as the abuse of a position of trust.

8. If a company cannot make a profit, then it will presumably cease trading and the staff will lose their jobs. If a commercial environment exists where fraud is rife, businesses will be reluctant to start operating there.

9. The messages I would take from the figures we collected are that dealing with frauds costs a lot of money and that management fear the secondary consequences of share price and reputational damage as much as the cost of the fraud.

10. When a manager abuses his position of trust, then fear makes it hard for a subordinate to report their suspicions, and loyalty makes it difficult for fellow managers to suspect a colleague whom they may have known and worked with for many years.

Exercises

I. Fill in the blanks with English words according to the given Chinese.

1. The Chinese economy, in the last ten years, has essentially been _____ _____ (投资驱动).
2. The country may choose other means, such as boosting _____ _____ (国内消费) and increasing imports, to achieve a trade balance.
3. The number of _____ (出境游) from the Chinese mainland is expected to reach 94.3 million this year.
4. It is the _____ (基本国策) of China to adhere to the principle of "One Country, Two Systems".
5. The core issue is to protect farmers' _____ (合法权益) and their property rights over their land.
6. The _____ (繁荣稳定) of Hong Kong Special Administrative Region benefits Hong Kong itself and the world as well.
7. The 21st Century _____ (海上丝绸之路) is a cooperation initiative proposed by Chinese President Xi Jinping during his visit to Indonesia last October.
8. There are far more _____ (共同利益) than disputes between China and the United States.
9. The cooperation between China and Kazakhstan enjoys _____ _____ (广阔前景) and will certainly bring benefits to the two peoples.
10. _____ (命运共同体) is the key to building new Asian regional order.

II. Translate the following into English or Chinese with the translation technique learned in this section.

1. global integration of economy _____
2. high-tech park _____
3. "naked official" whose family live abroad _____

4. sense of belonging to the community _____

5. under-developed country _____

6. 稳定的社会与政治环境 _____

7. 东西方文化差异 _____

8. 蓝领工人 _____

9. 社会主义市场经济 _____

10. 各界人士 _____

Ⅲ. Translate the following sentences.

1. Foreign investment in Shanghai and its surrounding areas has quadrupled in recent years.

2. Nearly half of all China's e-commerce sales, totaling $505.7 billion, are made with mobile devices.

3. Premier Li Keqiang stresses that the government will provide a good environment for the development of private banks.

4. Amazon will establish its new cross-border e-commerce platform in Shanghai Free Trade Zone.

5. More than 1,000 Chinese and overseas companies in the auto industry, including manufacturers, suppliers and dealers, are involved in anti-monopoly investigations.

6. 服务业的发展有助于推动国内消费。

7. 中国经济新常态将给世界各国带来更多的贸易机会。

8. 亚欧国家表示支持丝绸之路经济带的建设。

9. 我发言的目的是提高各位对网络安全的认识。

10. 上海自贸区将为更多中小企业的发展创造良好的环境。

IV. Translate the following paragraphs.

1. Teamwork is essential in almost any work environment. Questioning your ability to work in a team is therefore one of an interviewer's favorites. They'll be looking for evidence of the following core abilities:
The ability to communicate effectively with others;
The ability to recognize and understand the viewpoints of others;
The ability to appreciate the contribution you are expected to make.

2. 2014年,中国经济实现了7.4%的增长。创新将取代投资成为中国经济主要的驱动力。此外,丝绸之路经济带的建设将给中国及亚洲发展中国家创造广阔的前景。我们相信,中国经济的发展会给世界各国带来更多的好处而不是威胁。

Section B Interpretation

Interpretation Technique

口译技能：口译中的表达

完成英汉语之间的转换后,口译的下一阶段就是口头表达了。口译工作者和笔译工作者不同,需要在人前、在交流现场工作,因此,良好的口头表达能力对译员十分重要。良好的表达能增加交流双方以及听众对译员的信任感,也有助于沟通的顺利进行。

良好的口头表达能力包括反应迅速,表达简练、流畅,音量、语速适中。

译员应该做到在说话者话音落后的 2—5 秒之内就开口翻译,间歇太长必然影响交流。如果现场听众较多,间歇超过 5 秒钟,会场的气氛就会受到破坏;交流双方或说话者以及听众会表现出不耐烦、不信任,这些反过来又会影响译员的情绪和自信心,形成恶性循环,不利于接下来的口译。

译员应该口齿清晰,表达流畅。要注意培养良好的语言习惯,说话干脆利落,简洁明了,停顿得当,条理清楚。尤其是有的发言者可能表达能力不强,说话犹豫、重复、啰唆。但人们一般感兴趣的是他们讲话的内容,对他们的讲话技巧并不苛求。译员却不同,他是专职的语言工作者,说话人的犹豫、重复、啰唆都应该经过译员的加工变得清楚、简练、流畅。一般说来,口译时译文的长度不应超过原文长度的四分之三,译员在口译过程中可以压缩说话人的客套话,省略说话人无意重复的话和口头禅。中文表达大约是每分钟 150—180 字,英文则是每分钟 120—150 单词,译员讲话的速度往往要比说话人略快。

译员还应该语音正确,语调自然。要注意把握语调的分寸。语调过于呆板、平淡会使听者感到厌倦、昏昏欲睡;而语调过于丰富、高昂会给人哗众取宠的印象。一般说来,译员讲话保持比说话人稍微平淡一些的语调为宜。

译员应该根据需要,随时调节自己的音量和语速。译员口译时应该与不同方位的听众都有眼神交流。这不仅是出于礼貌,也有助于随时观察听者的反应,以便及时调整音量和语速。在听者需要做记录的情况下,口译需要重复或将重点简单归纳。

做口译时少用或不用手势,即兴发言时难免有口误甚至被人纠正错误,这时应表现出良好素养,不做鬼脸,不皱眉头,虚心接受批评,立即改正。

建立自信、充分准备和适应变化是消除紧张心理的主要途径。译员表达能力的高低和他是否怯场关系密切。译员和运动员一样,有的平时水平很高,但临场发挥不好。要培养自己在众人面前讲话不怯场,可以练习在课堂上站在台前口译,或在课堂上练习做简短发言。总之,良好的表达能力是必须培养而且是可以培养的,平日的课堂讨论、角色扮演和小会发言等都是练习的好机会,不应错过。

Passage Interpretation 1

上海地处长江三角洲前缘,位于我国南北海岸线的中部,地理位置优越。上海的面积从 1949 年的 636 平方公里增至现在的 6340.5 平方公里,人口从 1949 年的 520 万人,增至现在的 2479 万人。上海正向着现代化国际大都市的目标迈进。

工业总产值占全国的 1/12,港口货物吞吐量占全国的 1/10,口岸进出口商品额占全国的 1/4,财政收入占全国的 1/8,上海为全国现代化建设做出了重大的贡献。

上海作为一个国际化的大都市,交通十分发达。上海有各种铁路线近百条,两个国际机场,通往世界 100 多个城市的国际航线,以及 14 条海上国际航线。这里有中国最大的港口,与世界上 200 多个国家和地区的 1100 多个港口建立航运关系。便利的交通,促进了上海与世界各国的交往。

上海也是一个金融发达的城市。中国人民银行、中国银行、中国工商银行、中国建设银行、中国农业银行、交通银行等设立的分行,以及众多的证券交易网点遍布大街小巷。更值得一提的是,已有诸多的外国银行在上海设立了分行和办事机构。

上海还有良好的投资环境和优惠的投资政策。为了吸引外国投资,凡投资额大的项目,除一般外资待遇之外,还有特别优惠。

欢迎大家来上海投资!谢谢!

Passage Interpretation 2

The UK has a strong equity culture and our companies traditionally use the capital markets rather than relying on banks to raise money for growth. This process was designed for fairly large companies who could afford to devote the time and attention to flotation that a listing on a public equity market demands. But for smaller companies the options for raising capital were more limited.

At the London Stock Exchange, we saw that many smaller but dynamic entrepreneurial companies needed access to funds to grow and develop. The banks were not always the best way of providing the capital they needed at a sufficiently low cost. Many smaller firms felt prohibited from seeking a Main Market listing. Indeed many were essentially too small for a Main Market listing, so we identified the need for a market that could provide smaller companies, across all industry sectors, with appropriate and pragmatic regulations tailored to suit them. And in 1995, we launched Alternative Investment Market especially for smaller firms.

And since 1995, AIM has gone from strength to strength, admitting almost 1,500 companies, including over 122 international companies. Last year alone AIM attracted 162 new companies and now has 917 companies on the market. Last year saw a doubling of money raised on AIM, a doubling in shares  traded and a four-fold increase in their value. AIM is becoming more global too. AIM's growing international profile, with 85 overseas companies, makes it an important resource for smaller and medium-sized companies all over the world. And international companies have good reasons for considering AIM as a capital-raising tool.

Dialogue Interpretation

记者:今晚我们的客人是星巴克咖啡公司的董事长,霍华德·舒尔茨先生。他用自己对咖啡的热情创造了价值数十亿的全球生意,在全世界1万多个地方经营咖啡店。欢迎您的到来,舒尔茨先生。

Schultz: That's my pleasure, thank you.

记者:星巴克是如何进入您的生活的?或者更确切地说,在20世纪80年代初期,您是如何开始在星巴克工作的?您可以说说吗?

Schultz: Sure. Well, the story is that I actually joined Starbucks as an employee. In the fall of 1982 and when I joined the company, we had three stores, getting ready to open up our 4th. What attracted me to the company at that point was the entrepreneurial opportunity and I was really drawn to the quality of the coffee. I honestly never dreamed at the time that I would one day own the company or be in a position where we would have, as you said, 10,000 stores around the world.

记者：你们的生意涉及很多不同文化氛围的销售市场，比如法国、中国、约旦和世界上许多其他国家。你们怎样处理这些文化差异呢？会在开店之前做很多市场调查吗？会在当地招聘经营管理团队吗？你们的战略是怎样的呢？

Schultz: I've never been a believer in market research personally. So we haven't done a lot of that over the years. But we have fantastic local partners. We co-author the strategy with them and leave the execution to them.

记者：是的。这些年来您的公司一直保持高速的发展，您也正在进入不同的市场，将产品进行差异化组合，甚至涉及了音乐领域，一个如此成功的公司如何超越自我呢？

Schultz: Well, I appreciate the compliment of being so successful. We try to create long-term value for our shareholders while integrating a social conscience in everything we do. But I would also say that we have taken a very long view of the opportunity despite the fact that we've grown this significantly and these are still the very early stages for growth and development of the company. We want to emerge as one of the most recognized and respected brands in the world and we have a long way to go to ultimately accomplish that.

记者：我知道您很想开拓中国的市场，并去了那里很多次。中国有什么特殊之处？

Schultz: I just returned from a two-week trip to Asia and a week in China and I must say I was stunned and overwhelmed with the growth and development and the significance of the cultural change in China, in terms of the people and what's happening there. We have approximately 170 stores in mainland China and 70 in Hong Kong, China and 150 or so in Taiwan, China and believe that ultimately China will be the second largest market in the world for Starbucks after the U.S.

Exercises

I. Spot dictation.

More than 40 countries and districts, including Russia and China's Taiwan, have agreed to be founding members of China's proposed Asian Infrastructure Investment Bank. However, two of the world's (1) _____, the United States and Japan, have held off at this time.

China proposed the bank last October as a way to finance roads, bridges, ports and other needed (2) _____ in Asia. The time limit for joining as a founding member was March 31.

In only a few months, the number of countries seeking membership nearly doubled. They came from Africa, Europe, South America, Asia and the Pacific. Some (3) _____ added themselves to the list. They include Britain, Germany, France and Italy. Other important economies include South Korea, Australia and Russia.

247

China's Taiwan also (4) _____ become a founding member. But it is not clear how China will react. Relations (5) _____ _____ since the election of Taiwan regional leader Ma Ying-jeou in 2008. The two sides also are working on details of a trade agreement.

The U. S. and Japan have said they are (6) _____ the governance of the Asian Infrastructure Investment Bank, or AIIB. The United States has urged countries to consider details about the bank's governance and standards—its (7) _____ _____ policy—before joining AIIB. Critics say the AIIB threatens the work of the existing development banks such as the World Bank, the International Monetary Fund and the Asian Development Bank.

Yet, the Asian Development Bank itself noted in a (8) _____ _____ that the need for infrastructure projects in Asia is great. The institution, led by the U. S. and Japan, estimated last May that the Asia Pacific area needed $800 billion each year in infrastructure development.

Experts are watching to see how China will take its leadership role in the new bank. The AIIB is (9) _____ start with $100 billion in capital, mostly from China. Some experts point to the high interest in membership. Shi Yinhong is a political scientist at Renmin University of China in Beijing. He says China's leading part in the bank comes with (10) _____.

In other words, while China has gained from the effort to develop the AIIB, it will also have to satisfy other bank members and multi-national institutions. Officials at the World Bank, International Monetary Fund and Asian Development Bank say they are looking for ways to cooperate with the AIIB.

II. Sentence listening and translation.

1. _____
   _____
2. _____
   _____
3. _____
   _____
4. _____
   _____
5. _____
   _____

III. Paragraph listening and translation.

_____
_____

Ⅳ. Dialogue interpretation.

W: 你好,容我自我介绍一下。我叫王林。
S: Pleased to meet you. I'm Bill Smith. I haven't seen you around before.
W: 对。我刚来通用电气工作,在销售部。
S: What do you do there?
W: 我是搞市场调研的。你呢?
S: Well, I've been with GE for years. I'm Mr. Vincent's personal assistant. He is the After-Sales Service Director.
W: 我还不认识他。他来参加这次聚会了吗?
S: Yes, that's him. Let me introduce you.

Ⅴ. Interpreting in groups.

Role-play the following situation with your partners, acting as the Chinese speakers, English speaker and the interpreter respectively. One group will be invited to perform in class.

Participants: 1. Mr. John Vincent
2. Wang Yu
3. Interpreter

Location: Personnel Department

Task: Mr. John Vincent comes from the headquarters of General Motors in the U. S. It is the first day he works with the team of the Personnel Department in GM (Shanghai). Wang Yu, the personnel manager, greets Mr. Vincent and introduces him to the team.

Ⅵ. 3-minute talk on the given topic.

Talk on the following topic in three minutes based on the given reference questions.

Topic: **Self-employment**

Questions for Reference:

1. Do you know any leading entrepreneurs who have made great success by starting their own business? Share some stories of success with the class.
2. What is your dream job?
3. Do you plan to start your own business after graduation? Why or why not?
4. What is your career plan?

VII. Theme-related expressions.

保税区	bonded zone
产业结构升级	upgrading of an industrial structure
城乡居民收入	income of urban and rural residents
持续快速健康发展	sustained, rapid and sound development
传销	pyramid sale; multi-level marketing
村办企业	village-run enterprise
电视广告	TV commercial
独资公司	exclusively-funded venture
非公有制经济	non-public sectors of the economy
首付	down-payment
业主	home owner
房屋空置率	housing vacancy rate
按揭	mortgage
房地产开发商	real estate developer
高新技术产业	high and new technology industry
股份制	joint-stock system
固定资产投资	investment in the fixed assets
国有企业	state-owned enterprise (SOE)
混合所有制经济	a mixed sector of the economy
计划经济体制	planned economy system
经济杠杆作用	economic leverage
经济特区	special economic zone (SEZ)
扩大内需	expand domestic demand
粮食主产区	main grain producing areas
泡沫经济	bubble economy
市政工程	municipal works; public works
试点工程,试点项目	pilot project

Unit 14　Economy 经济活动

• 消费税	consumption tax
• 个人所得税	personal income tax
• 财产税	property tax
• 关税	tariff
• 逃税,漏税	tax evasion
• 外向型经济	outward-looking economy
• 外资企业	overseas-funded enterprises; foreign-funded company
• 稳定物价	stabilize prices
• 外汇汇率	foreign exchange rate
• 西部大开发	the large-scale development of China's western region
• 需求疲软	weak demand
• 质检	QC（quality check）
• 国家重点工程	national key projects
• "南水北调"	South-to-North Water Diversion
• "西气东输"	West-East Natural Gas Transmission Project

Section C　Further Exploration

将文中的句子翻译成中文填入空格。

The Wal-Mart Culture

Wal-Mart Stores, Inc. was founded on the principles developed by Sam Walton. These principles carried out every day by hard-working and friendly associates have created a unique corporate culture that is key to Wal-Mart's competitive edge. The basic beliefs guiding Wal-Mart Stores, Inc. are:

Three Basic Beliefs

1. Respect for the Individual

Every associate's opinion is respected. Managers are considered "servant leaders" who help new associates realize their potential through training, praise and constructive feedback. An "open door" management philosophy encourages associates to raise questions and concerns in an open atmosphere.

2. Service to the Customer

"The customer is the boss." Everything possible is done to make shopping at Wal-Mart a friendly, pleasant experience. The "Ten-Foot Attitude" means that associates are to greet each person they see. The "Satisfaction Guaranteed" refund and exchange policy allows customers to be fully confident of Wal-Mart's merchandise and quality.

3. Strive for Excellence

Wal-Mart associates share an exceptional commitment to customer satisfaction. At the start of each day, store associates gather for the Wal-Mart cheer, review sales from the previous day, and discuss their daily goals. "The Sundown Rule" requires a continual sense of urgency, with questions asked in the morning answered before the end of the day.

沃尔玛公司文化

沃尔玛公司是在山姆·沃尔顿所倡导的原则上建立起来的。执行这些原则的正是那些辛勤工作且友好待客的员工们,这已然创造了沃尔玛独特的企业文化,是(1)_____。引领沃尔玛百货有限公司的基本信仰是:

三项基本信仰

1. 尊重个人

尊重每位员工提出的意见。经理们被看作"公仆型领导",通过(2)_____。运用"开放式"的管理哲学,在开放的气氛中鼓励员工多提问题、多关心公司。

2. 服务顾客

"顾客就是老板。"沃尔玛公司尽其所能使顾客感到在沃尔玛购物是一种亲切、愉快的经历。"三米微笑原则"是指(3)_____;"保证满意"的退换货政策使(4)_____。

3. 追求卓越

沃尔玛公司员工们特别承诺,要做到令顾客满意。每天营业前,员工们会聚集在一起高呼沃尔玛口号,总结前一天的销售情况,讨论当天的目标。此外,"日落原则"要求员工们(5)_____。

UNIT 15
Laws and Regulations
法 律 法 规

Learning Objectives

1. To learn the basic techniques for the translation of laws and regulations;
2. To learn coping tactics in interpretation;
3. To learn how to translate/interpret passages or dialogues on the topic of laws and regulations;
4. To learn useful words and expressions related to Chinese laws and regulations.

Lead-in

- *Quiz* (**True or False**)

    _____ 1. Chengdu adopts 72-hour visa-free transit policy which allows transit passengers with passport of 51 countries to stay for up to 72 hours without a visa on direct transit.

    _____ 2. Boarding pass, a document, tells you which seat you are going to take on the airplane.

    _____ 3. Visa is a document indispensable for your international flight, which is separate from your passport.

    _____ 4. Passengers are expected to submit their customs declaration form when they are at check-in counters of the airport.

    _____ 5. There is only one international airport in Shanghai, i. e. Shanghai Pudong International Airport.

    _____ 6. If you pick up an overseas visitor at the airport, you should wait for your guest at the arrival gate.

    _____ 7. Free baggage allowance is the maximum number, size, and weight of baggage that each customer is allowed with no additional charge.

● What does each public sign symbolize? Fill in the blanks with Chinese translation.

1. _____   2. _____   3. _____   4. _____   5. _____

6. _____   7. _____   8. _____   9. _____   10. _____

Section A　Translation

Translation Technique

法律法规翻译基本技巧

1. 法律英语用词正式而庄重,任何情况下都不能使用口语、俚语和方言

比如,不用"before"而用"prior",不用"but"而用"provided that",不用"after"而用"sequent",不用"tell"而用"advise",不用"begin"或"start"而用"commence",不用"use"而用"employ",不用"according to"而用"in accordance with",不用"show"而用"demonstrate",等等。

2. 正确使用古体词能使法律语言庄重严肃并具备神圣性、权威性和严密性,因此,英译时使用一些当代法律英语中常用的副词,主要体现在大量使用以"here""there"和"where"与介词合成的词

今后 hereafter =after this time

特此 hereby =by means/reason of this

此中,于此 herein =in this

在下文 hereinafter =later in this contract

此后,后来 thereafter =afterwards

因此,由此,在那方面 thereby =by that means

在那里,在那点上 therein =from that

以下,在下文 thereinafter =later in the same contract

由是,凭那个 whereby =by what; by which

在哪里,在哪点上 wherein =in what; in which

3. 法律英语要使用特定的法律术语、行话和套话

例如,"termination(终止)"不能用"finish"代替,"invoke(援引)"不能用"quote"代

替,"peremptory(最高)"不能用"supreme"代替,"a material breach(重大违约)"不能用"a serious breach"代替。

4. 为使国际条约表意准确和规范严谨,条约制定者在行文中大量使用词语并列结构,用"and"或"or"把两个或多个短语并列起来

这种并列结构有更强的包容性,同时也更加具有弹性。例如:"under or in accordance with","signed and delivered","in whole or in part","within EU or elsewhere","revocation, suspension or imposition","by the government or by any government, public or local authority … or by any person other than the person claiming relief"等。

5. 法律条文中使用最多的三个情态动词是"shall""may"和"must"

(1)"shall"在法律英语中的词义不同于普通英语中的词义。它在法律英语中主要表示"指示性""施为性"含义和行使权利的"义务"和"责任",主要可以被译成"须""应"和"应当"等。如:

原文: 委员长、副委员长连续任职<u>不得</u>超过两届。

译文: The Chairman and Vice-Chairman of the Standing Committee <u>shall</u> serve <u>no more than</u> two consecutive terms.

原文: The rights and freedoms enjoyed by Hong Kong residents <u>shall not</u> be restricted unless as prescribed by law. Such restrictions <u>shall not</u> contravene the provisions of the preceding paragraph of this Article.

译文: 香港居民享有的权利和自由,除依法规定外不得限制,此种限制不得与本条第一款规定抵触。

(2)在法律文件中,可汉译为"不得"的情态动词当然并非是只有跟"shall"有关的否定句,与"may"相关的否定句也同样可译成"不得"。如:

原文: 中央人民政府所属各部门、各省、自治区、直辖市均<u>不得</u>干预香港特别行政区根据本法自行管理的事务。

译文: <u>No</u> departments of the Central People's Government and no province, autonomous region, or municipality directly under the Central Government <u>may</u> interfere in the affairs which the Hong Kong Special Administrative Region administers on its own in accordance with this Law.

(3)"may"在法律英语中主要有两种解释。一是表示"给予许可"或者"给予某人做某事的授权"(be allowed to or have permission to),这一含义多用于法律法规中。二是表示"也许"或者"可能性"(be in some degree likely to),这一含义多用于法律合同中。如:

原文: 民事法律行为<u>可以</u>采取书面形式、口头形式或者其他形式。

译文: A civil juristic act <u>may</u> be in written, oral or other form.

原文: 承租人<u>可以</u>要求减少租金或者不支付租金。

译文: The lessee <u>may</u> request a reduction of rent or not to pay the rent.

(4)在具权威性法律文献的翻译实践中,以"must"对应"必须"的惯例似乎早已确立。如:

原文: 中华人民共和国公民<u>必须</u>遵守宪法和法律,保守国家机密,爱护公共财产,遵守劳动纪律,遵守公共秩序,尊重社会公德。

译文: Citizens of the People's Republic of China <u>must</u> abide by the Constitution and the

Law, keep state secrets, protect public property, observe labour discipline and public order, respect social ethics.

但在法律篇章中几乎没有该词直接的否定形式(即 must not),尽管该词的否定形式在普通篇章中并不少见。

6. 法律英语大量使用被动语态

被动结构的最大功能就是隐藏和弱化动作的行为者,在法律语境下就是隐藏和弱化法律主体,从而模糊了对法律行为主体的认定。被动结构可以使法律语言显得更加客观公正。如:

原文:中国人民解放军气象工作的管理办法,由中央军事委员会制定。

译文:Administrative measures governing the meteorological work in the Chinese People's Liberation Army shall be formulated by the Central Military Commission.

7. 名词化结构的运用

名词化结构是将形容词或动词等非名词词类转化成名词使用的一种语言表述方法,除了使语言表述更加紧凑外,还可以帮助立法者使法律条文的表述更加准确,另一方面也使法律条文更具有包容性。如:

原文:禁止抢采掠青、毁坏母树。

译文:Plundering of unripe seeds and doing damage to mother trees are prohibited.

8. 为了使条款明确清晰,排除一切可能产生的歧义和误解,严格界定条约各方的义务和权利,条约的句式中常常使用大量结构复杂、重叠的状语来修饰条款中的动词

多个状语同时修饰一个动词,或者一个状语包含另一个状语的现象也很常见。在翻译中不可一概而论,针对不同的状语要采取不同的翻译技巧。例如,翻译下面句子时可以把长状语转换成并列句来处理。

原文:The Security Council shall encourage the development of pacific settlement of local disputes through such regional arrangements or by such regional agencies either on the initiative of the states concerned or by reference from the Security Council.

译文:安全理事会对于依区域办法或由区域机关而求地方争端之和平解决,不论其系由关系国主动提出,或由安全理事会提交,应鼓励其发展。

9. 法律条文需要周密严谨的叙述,语句也就相应变得复杂冗长,长句多使用复合句,有很多的从句和修饰语,结构上相互重叠,前后编插,往往一个句子就是一个段落

具体翻译一般可用顺序法、逆序法和分译法三种。如:

原文:Subject to the provision of Article 12, the General Assembly may recommend measures for the peaceful adjustment of any situation, regardless of origin, which it deems likely to impair the general welfare or friendly relations among nations.

译文:联合国会在不违背第十二条规定的前提下,对于其认为足以妨害国际公共福利或友好关系的任何情况,不论其起源如何,都应建议和平调解方法。

> Passage Translation 1

Vocabulary

1. 章程

2. 法定代表人

3. 奖罚

4. 决算

5. 任免

6. 清算

7. 终止和期满

8. 代理人

9. 会议记录

10. 裁决

11. 董事会领导下的总经理负责制

12.《中华人民共和国工会法》

13.《中国工会章程》

14.《中华人民共和国个人所得税法》

15. 外籍员工

16. 正当收入

17. 汇往国外

18. "三金"

19.《中华人民共和国外资企业法》

20.《中国国家外汇管理》

外资公司章程（节选）

第一章 董事会

第1.1条 本公司设立董事会。董事会决定公司的一切重大问题。本公司注册成立之日即为董事会成立之日。

第1.2条 董事会由10人组成，设董事长一名，副董事长一名。董事长是公司的法定代表人。董事长不能履行职责时，应授权副董事长或其他董事代表本公司。

第1.3条 董事会的职权：

1. 制定和修改本公司章程；
2. 决定本公司的发展规划及经营方案；
3. 制定员工的劳动工资、福利和奖罚等制度；
4. 审查经营状况、财务预算和决算；
5. 决定利润分配和亏损的弥补办法；

6. 任免本公司总经理、副总经理、总工程师、会计师和其他高级管理人员及确定其职权、待遇；
7. 负责本公司终止和期满时的清算工作；
8. 讨论决定本公司的其他重大问题。

第1.4条 董事会会议应每年召开二次。如经二位以上董事提议，可由董事长召开临时会议。

第1.5条　董事会会议由董事长召集并主持,如董事长不能出席时,应授权副董事长代理并主持董事会会议。

第1.6条　董事因故不能出席董事会议时,可以书面委托代理人出席董事会,如届时委托代理人也未出席,则视为弃权。

第1.7条　董事会会议应有三分之二以上董事出席方能举行。

第1.8条　每次董事会会议内容均应详细记录,并由出席会议的全体董事签字。会议记录用中文书写,由本公司存档备查。

第1.9条　董事会对本公司重大问题的裁决应采取全体董事一致同意通过为原则。

第二章　管理机构

第2.1条　本公司实行董事会领导下的总经理负责制,设总经理1人,副总经理1人;总经理、副总经理由董事会聘任。

第2.2条　总经理直接对董事会负责,执行董事会各项决议;组织和领导本公司的全面生产。副总经理协助总经理开展工作。

第2.3条　总经理的职责:

1. 贯彻执行董事会的决议;
2. 组织和领导本公司日常的经营管理;
3. 在董事会授权范围内,对外代表企业处理企业业务,对内任免下属管理人员;
4. 负责董事会授权的其他事宜。

第三章　劳动管理

本公司雇用中国员工应遵守中国有关法律和珠海市劳动管理的有关规定并依法签订合同,并在合同中订明雇用、解雇、报酬、辞职、工资、福利、劳动保护、劳动保险、劳动纪律等事项。

第四章　工会组织

本公司的职工有权按照《中华人民共和国工会法》和《中国工会章程》的规定建立基层工会组织开展工会活动,以维护职工合法权益。

第五章　税务、财务、外汇管理

第5.1条　本公司按照中国的有关法律和有关规定缴纳各种税金。

第5.2条　本公司职工须按照《中华人民共和国个人所得税法》缴纳个人所得税。外籍员工收入和其他正当收入,依法纳税后,可以汇往国外。

第5.3条　本公司缴纳所得税后的利润扣除"三金"后按《中华人民共和国外资企业法》的规定,可汇往外国。

第5.4条　本公司的会计制度,按照中华人民共和国有关财会管理制度办理和执行。

第5.5条　本公司的会计年度为公历年制,即公历一月一日起至十二月三十一日止。

第5.6条　本公司外汇汇出事宜,依照《中国国家外汇管理》的规定办理。

Notes

1. "董事会会议应每年召开二次。如经二位以上董事提议,可由董事长召开临时会议。"句中的"应"意为"应该",译为"shall"。全句译为:"Board meeting shall be held twice a year, and a temporary board meeting shall be held as proposed by two or more than two directors."

2. "董事因故不能出席董事会议时,可以书面委托代理人出席董事会,如届时委托代理人也未出席,则视为弃权。"这句话翻译要使用被动语态,才能使条文更加客观公正。另外,"视为弃权"为常用法律术语,译为"is deemed as waiver"。"代理人"是指法律代理人,译为"attorney"而不是"agent"。句中的"可以"用情态动词"may"。全句译为:"An attorney may be entrusted in written form to attend the board meeting should the director fail to attend for some reason, and it is deemed as waiver should the attorney entrusted fail to attend."

3. "本公司的职工有权按照《中华人民共和国工会法》和《中国工会章程》的规定建立基层工会组织开展工会活动,以维护职工合法权益。"这句话中,"《中华人民共和国工会法》和《中国工会章程》的规定"中的"规定"可以译为"articles",意思为"条例"。法律根据内容需要可以分为编、章、节、款。"编"一般译为"part","章"为"chapter","节"为"section","款"为"article"。全句译为:"The staff and workers of this company shall have the right to set up a trade union to secure their legal rights and carry on its activities in accordance with the stipulations of the Trade Union Law of the People's Republic of China and the Articles of Association of Chinese Trade Union."

4. "外籍员工收入和其他正当收入,依法纳税后,可以汇往国外。"句中的"可以"表示"给予许可"或者"给予某人做某事的授权",所以译为"may"。全句译为:"The salaries and legal income of the overseas staff may be remitted abroad after being taxed."

5. "本公司缴纳所得税后的利润扣除'三金'后按照《中华人民共和国外资企业法》的规定,可汇往外国。"句中的"三金"指的是按照《中华人民共和国中外合资经营企业法》提取储备基金、企业发展基金、职工奖励及福利基金,翻译时要增译解释,译为"compulsory accumulated fund, voluntary accumulated fund and fund for public interest"。全句译为:"The profits after being taxed and deduced of compulsory accumulated fund, voluntary accumulated fund and fund for public interest may be remitted abroad in accordance with the stipulations of Foreign Investment Laws of the People's Republic of China."

Passage Translation 2

Vocabulary

1. country of origin

2. be preventive from dampness, rust, erosion and shock

3. Do not stack upside down.

4. stencil

5. shipping marks

6. irrevocable Letter of Credit

7. negotiation

8. collection

9. commercial invoice

10. weight memo

11. courier

12. dead freight

13. demurrage charges

14. Letter of Quality Guarantee

15. China Commodity Inspection Bureau

16. hereinafter

17. be borne by

18. force majeure

19. aforesaid

20. thereafter

21. jurisdiction

22. thereof

23. China International Economic and Trade Arbitration Commission (CIETAC)

24. arbitral award

25. INCOTERMS

26. the International Chamber of Commerce

Purchase Contract

Contract No.: _____
Date: _____
Signed at: _____
The Buyer: _____
Address: _____
Tel: _____ Fax: _____
E-mail: _____
The Seller: _____
Address: _____
Tel: _____ Fax: _____
E-mail: _____

The Seller and the Buyer agree to conclude this Contract subject to the terms and conditions stated below:

1. Name, Specifications and Quality of Commodity: _____
2. Quantity: _____% more or less allowed

3. Unit Price: _____
4. Total Amount: _____
5. Terms of Delivery (FOB/CFR/CIF) _____
6. Country of Origin and Manufacturers: _____
7. Packing: _____

The packing of the goods shall be preventive from dampness, rust, moisture, erosion and shock, and shall be suitable for ocean transportation/multiple transportation. The Seller shall be liable for any damage and loss of the goods attributable to the inadequate or improper packing. The measurement, gross weight, net weight and the cautions such as "Do not stack upside down", "Keep away from moisture", "Handle with care" shall be stenciled on the surface of each package with fadeless pigment.

8. Shipping Marks: _____
9. Time of Shipment: _____
10. Port of Loading: _____
11. Port of Destination: _____
12. Insurance:

Insurance shall be covered by the _____ for 110% of the invoice value against _____ Risks and _____ Additional Risks.

13. Terms of Payment:

Letter of Credit: The Buyer shall, _____ days prior to the time of shipment/after this Contract comes into effect, open an irrevocable Letter of Credit in favor of the Seller. The Letter of Credit shall expire _____ days after the completion of loading of the shipment as stipulated.

14. Documents Required:

The Seller shall present the following documents required to the bank for negotiation/collection:

(1) Signed commercial invoice in _____ copies indicating Contract No., L/C No. (Terms of L/C) and shipping marks;
(2) Packing list/weight memo in _____ copies issued by _____;
(3) Certificate of Quality in _____ copies issued by _____;
(4) Certificate of Quantity in _____ copies issued by _____;
(5) Insurance policy/certificate in _____ copies (Terms of CIF);
(6) Certificate of Origin in _____ copies issued by _____;
(7) Shipping advice

The Seller shall, within _____ hours after shipment effected, send by courier each copy of the above-mentioned documents.

15. Terms of Shipment:

The Seller shall, 30 days before the shipment date specified in the Contract, advise the Buyer by _____ of the Contract No., name of commodity, quantity, amount, packages, gross weight, measurement, and the date of shipment in order that the Buyer can charter a vessel/book shipping space. In the event of the Seller's failure to effect loading when the vessel arrives duly at the loading port, all expenses including dead freight and/or demurrage charges thus incurred shall be for the Seller's account.

16. Shipping Advice:

The Seller shall, immediately upon the completion of the loading of the goods, advise the Buyer of the Contract No., names of commodity, loading quantity, invoice values, gross weight, name of vessel and shipment date by _____ within _____ hours.

17. Quality Guarantee:

The Seller shall guarantee that the commodity must be in conformity with the quality, specifications and quantity specified in this Contract and Letter of Quality Guarantee. The guarantee period shall be _____ months after the arrival of the goods at the port of destination, and during the period the Seller shall be responsible for the damage due to the defects in designing and manufacturing of the manufacturer.

18. Inspection:

The manufacturers shall, before delivery, make a precise and comprehensive inspection of the goods with regard to its quality, specifications, performance and quantity/weight, and issue inspection certificates certifying the technical data and conclusion of the inspection. After arrival of the goods at the port of destination, the Buyer shall apply to China Commodity Inspection Bureau (hereinafter referred to as CCIB) for a further inspection as to the specifications and quantity/weight of the goods. If damages of the goods are found, or the specifications and/or quantity are not in conformity with the stipulations in this Contract, except when the responsibilities lies with Insurance Company or Shipping Company, the Buyer shall, within _____ days after arrival of the goods at the port of destination, claim against the Seller, or reject the goods according to the inspection certificate issued by CCIB. In case of damage of the goods incurred due to the design or manufacture defects and/or in case the quality and performance are not in conformity with the Contract, the Buyer shall, during the guarantee period, request CCIB to make an inspection.

19. Claim:

The Buyer shall make a claim against the Seller (including replacement of the goods) by the inspection certificate and all the expenses incurred therefrom shall be borne by the Seller. The claims mentioned above shall be regarded as being accepted if the Seller fails to reply within _____ days after the Seller received the Buyer's claim.

20. Late Delivery and Penalty:

Should the Seller fail to make delivery on time as stipulated in the Contract, with the exception of force majeure causes specified in Clause 21 of this Contract, the Buyer shall agree to postpone the delivery on the condition that the Seller agree to pay a penalty which shall be deducted by the paying bank from the payment under negotiation. The rate of penalty is charged at _____ % for every _____ days, odd days less than _____ days should be counted as _____ days. But the penalty, however, shall not exceed _____ % of the total value of the goods involved in the delayed delivery. In case the Seller fails to make delivery _____ days later than the time of shipment stipulated in the Contract, the Buyer shall have the right to cancel the Contract and the Seller, in spite of the cancellation, shall nevertheless pay the aforesaid penalty to the Buyer without delay.

The Buyer shall have the right to lodge a claim against the Seller for the losses sustained if any.

21. Force Majeure:

The Seller shall not be responsible for the delay of shipment or non-delivery of the goods due to force majeure, which might occur during the process of manufacturing or in the course of loading or transit. The Seller shall advise the Buyer immediately of the occurrence mentioned above and within _____ days thereafter the Seller shall send a notice by courier to the Buyer for their acceptance of a certificate of the accident issued by the local chamber of commerce under whose jurisdiction the accident occurs as evidence thereof. Under such circumstances the Seller, however, is still under the obligation to take all necessary measures to hasten the delivery of the goods. In case the accident lasts for more than _____ days the Buyer shall have the right to cancel the Contract.

22. Arbitration:

Any dispute arising from or in connection with the Contract shall be settled through friendly negotiation. In case no settlement is reached, the dispute shall be submitted to China International Economic and Trade Arbitration Commission (CIETAC), Shenzhen Commission, for arbitration in accordance with its rules in effect at the time of applying for arbitration. The arbitral award is final and binding upon both parties.

23. Notices:

All notices shall be written in _____ and sent to both parties by fax/courier. If any changes of the addresses occur, one party shall inform the other party of the change of address within _____ days after the change.

24. The terms FOB, CFR, CIF in the Contract are based on *INCOTERMS 2000 of the International Chamber of Commerce.*

25. This Contract is executed in two counterparts each in Chinese and English, each of which shall be equally binding. This Contract is in _____ copies, effective since being signed/sealed by both parties.

Representative of the Buyer
(Authorized signature): _____
Representative of the Seller
(Authorized signature): _____

Notes

1. "The measurement, gross weight, net weight and the cautions such as 'Do not stack upside down', 'Keep away from moisture', 'Handle with care' shall be stenciled on the surface of each package with fadeless pigment."虽然合同条款中多使用被动语态,但由于英汉语表达差异,汉译时常将被动语态句译为主动语态。全句译为:"卖方应在每个包装箱上用不褪色的颜料标明尺寸、毛重、净重及'此端向上''防潮''小心轻放'等标记。"

2. "In case of damage of the goods incurred due to the design or manufacture defects and/or in case the quality and performance are not in conformity with the Contract, the Buyer shall, during the guarantee period, request CCIB to make an inspection."句中的"due to the design or manufacture defects and/or in case the quality and performance are not in conformity with the Contract"使用"and"或"or"词语并列结构,使条款更具包容性,表意准确、规范、严谨,翻译时只须直译即可。全句译为:"在保证期内,如货物由于设计或制造上的缺陷而发生损坏或品质和性能与合同规定不符时,买方将委托中国商检局进行检验。"

3. "The Buyer shall make a claim against the Seller (including replacement of the goods) by the inspection certificate and all the expenses incurred therefrom shall be borne by the Seller."句中的"therefrom"译为"自那以后",是古英语词汇,使合同语言显得庄重严肃并具备神圣性、权威性和严密性,汉译时只须根据句意译出意思即可。合同中还有一些这类词"aforesaid""thereafter""hereinafter""thereof"等。全句译为:"买方凭其委托的检验机构出具的检验证明书向卖方提出索赔(包括换货),由此引起的全部费用应由卖方负担。"

4. "Should the Seller fail to make delivery on time as stipulated in the Contract, with the exception of force majeure causes specified in Clause 21 of this Contract, the Buyer shall agree to postpone the delivery on the condition that the Seller agrees to pay a penalty which shall be deducted by the paying bank from the payment under negotiation."这是句典型的合同条款长句,通过使用介词短语、状语从句和定语从句等,使条款语句严谨。译成汉语时如果采用一个汉语句子对原文进行翻译,容易导致句义混乱,这种情况下,可以使用分译法把长句中的从句或短语化为句子分开来翻译。全句译为:"除合同第21条不可抗力原因外,如卖方不能按合同规定的时间交货,买方应同意在卖方支付罚款的条件下延期交货。罚款可由议付银行在议付货款时扣除。"

5. "The Buyer shall have the right to lodge a claim against the Seller for the losses sustained if any.""if any"在这儿意为"若有的话",是一种补充说明,使法律条文更为严谨。全句译为:"买方有权对因此遭受的其他损失向卖方提出索赔。"

Sentences in Focus

1. 董事会由10人组成,设董事长一名,副董事长一名。董事长是公司的法定代表人。

董事长不能履行职责时,应授权副董事长或其他董事代表本公司。

2. 总经理直接对董事会负责,执行董事会各项决议;组织和领导本公司的全面生产。副总经理协助总经理开展工作。

3. 本公司雇用中国员工应遵守中国有关法津和珠海市劳动管理的有关规定并依法签订合同,并在合同中订明雇用、解雇、报酬、辞职、工资、福利、劳动保护、劳动保险、劳动纪津等事项。

4. 本公司的职工有权按照《中华人民共和国工会法》和《中国工会章程》的规定建立基层工会组织开展工会活动,以维护职工合法权益。

5. 本公司职工须按照《中华人民共和国个人所得税法》缴纳个人所得税。外籍员工收入和其他正当收入,依法纳税后,可以汇注国外。

6. The Buyer shall, _____ days prior to the time of shipment /after this Contract comes into effect, open an irrevocable Letter of Credit in favor of the Seller.

7. In the event of the Seller's failure to effect loading when the vessel arrives duly at the loading port, all expenses including dead freight and/or demurrage charges thus incurred shall be for the Seller's account.

8. The manufacturers shall, before delivery, make a precise and comprehensive inspection of the goods with regard to its quality, specifications, performance and quantity/weight, and issue inspection certificates certifying the technical data and conclusion of the inspection.

9. The Seller shall not be responsible for the delay of shipment or non-delivery of the goods due to force majeure, which might occur during the process of manufacturing or in the course of loading or transit.

10. This Contract is executed in two counterparts each in Chinese and English, each of which shall be equally binding.

Exercises

I. Fill in the blanks with English words according to the given Chinese.

1. Think tanks play an important role in helping the government to _____ (制定政策).

2. The government will no longer _____ (批准) or fund science and technology projects directly.
3. China called on Malaysia to _____ (履行义务) to compensate families of Flight MH370 passengers.
4. The _____ (发展蓝图) for the Beijing-Tianjin-Hebei region will be released soon.
5. The municipal government is to _____ (采取措施), including restricting traffic according to license plate numbers, during the APEC Economic Leaders' Meeting in November.
6. China, _____ (在……的领导下) the CPC Central Committee, has made a series of social and economic achievements during the past 10 years.
7. I'm _____ (负责) purchasing building materials and I hear that you know the boss of a building material company.
8. Hopefully the new _____ (管理条例) will lay a basis for the formation of sound internal control and risk management schemes in domestic banks.
9. China urged Sri Lanka to provide a sound legal environment to _____ (保障) further Chinese investment.
10. The buyers shall open Letter of Credit _____ (依照) the terms of this contract.

II. Translate the following names of laws and regulations into English or Chinese.

1. Food Safety Law of the People's Republic of China
   _____

2. Interim Regulations of the People's Republic of China on Business Tax
   _____

3. Regulations of Foreign Investment in Commercial Fields
   _____

4. The Basic Law of the Hong Kong Special Administrative Region of the People's Republic of China
   _____

5. Regulation on Realty Management
   _____

6. 《中华人民共和国婚姻法》
   _____

7. 《中华人民共和国义务教育法》
   _____

8. 《中华人民共和国劳动合同法》
   _____

9. 《中华人民共和国消费者权益保护法》
   _____

10. 《中华人民共和国公务员法》
    _____

III. Translate the following sentences.

1. The people's congress system is the fundamental political system of the People's Republic of China (PRC), and the system of government of the country.
   _____
   _____

2. The Standing Committee of National People's Congress is composed of the chairman, vice chairmen, the secretary-general and members.
   _____
   _____

3. Premier Li Keqiang has called for reduction in the fee of cellphone data plan.
   _____
   _____

4. China has designated June of each year "National Ecological Civilization Month" as it plans a campaign to encourage its public to lead green lifestyles.
   _____
   _____

5. China has further relaxed its more than three-decade-old family planning policy and adopted the universal two-child policy to actively address the country's aging trend.
   _____
   _____

6. 中国禁烟令禁止人们在公共场所吸烟。
   _____

7. 北京、上海和广州采取了72小时免签证政策以吸引更多的海外游客。(72-hour visa-free policy)
   _____
   _____

8. 许多地方政府颁布了优惠政策以鼓励大学毕业生参军。(join the military)
   _____
   _____

9. 3月19日，北京取消了针对小学生的期中考试。(abolish)

10. 农民工没有像持有城市户口的人那样享受到同样的好处。(migrant workers)

IV. Translate the following paragraphs.

1. East China's Anhui became the third province to relax the decades-old one-child policy, allowing couples to have a second baby if either parent is an only child. About one week earlier, the neighboring province, Zhejiang, took the lead in the country to relax the strict family planning rules. Jiangxi Province followed suit on Jan. 18. Following the rapid economic growth in the past decade, China's population advantage has shrunk. China has become an aging society with too few young working people supporting parents and grandparents. For years, experts from many walks of life have been calling for the relaxation of the policy.

2. 中国是全球人口最多的国家。为了解决人口问题，自20世纪70年代以来，中国政府就实行了独生子女政策。然而，在经历了过去十年经济的快速发展之后，许多人看到了这项政策的弊端，那就是年轻劳动力过少，不足以支撑起不断老龄化的社会。因此，呼吁放开计划生育政策的时候到了。

Section B Interpretation

Interpretation Technique

口译技能：临场应变技巧

口译前一定要做好充分的准备，包括语言准备、心理准备和相关主题的准备。然而无论准备多么充分，在口译现场都难免遇到一些突发情况。这时一定要沉着冷静，根据具体情况采取具体的处理措施。一般说来，口译现场常见的问题主要有以下6种。

1. 没听清、听漏了或者没听懂

由于口译现场环境、讲话人语速、语音等因素，或者由于译者译前准备有疏漏，在现场一时疲惫分神等原因，就会出现这种情况。首先要分清这部分内容是否重要、是否影响对其他部分的理解，如果是次要内容，并不影响大局，可以省略不译或采取模糊处理的办法。如果是关乎全文的关键性内容，就必须认真对待。

如果情况允许，最好立刻询问讲话人，或者请教现场的相关专家，不能硬着头皮往下译，造成误解，影响会谈和交流。如果是正式场合或者是大会发言，只能先用比较中性或模糊的话过渡，然后集中注意力，伺机调整补救。

2. 错译

最优秀的译员在现场口译中也难免出错。一旦认识自己译错了，不要惊慌，也不要说"对不起，我译错了"，或者"I'm sorry, I made a mistake"。这样不仅会让听众产生理解混乱，还会损害译员和译文的可信度。这时不妨重译，并且对正确的译文采取重音重复的办法，就像平时说话要强调某事一样。或者以解释的语气和方式，用"I mean …"或"就是说""确切地说"引出正确的译文。

3. 不会译

不会译是由两种原因造成的，一是没听懂，此时可以按本文的第一种情况进行处理。二是听懂了，却一时找不到恰当的表达，此时可先直译，再按自己的理解进行解释。虽然译文难免生涩，原文韵味丧失殆尽，但不会造成误解，也不会影响交流的进程。

口译中遇到习语、典故、诗词、幽默表达或专有名词时，如果没有充分的准备或事前不了解讲话内容，一时就很难在目的语中找到对应的表达。此时要力争译出原文的大意，传达讲话人的主旨，使交流顺利地进行下去，哪怕译文欠妥也无伤大雅。译专有名词时，如果拿不准，还可以在译文后重复原文，听众中的专业人士会立刻明白原文意思。

4. 讲话人说错

口译中也可能遇到讲话人说错的情况，如果是有违事实、史实或常识的错误，或者是讲话人口误，译员意识到了这个错误，并且能改正，应该在译文中予以纠正。如果译员怀疑讲话人说错，却又不能肯定，在方便的情况下，应向讲话人确认。

5. 讲话人逻辑混乱

口译常常译的是即席讲话或发言，而人们在即席口头表达中，由于思维和语言水平的限制，经常会出现不必要的重复、拖沓、语言含糊，或者断句、层次不清、逻辑关系混乱等现象，这给口译造成了很大困难。译员要善于对原文进行梳理，分清逻辑层次，迅速抓出主次，对于啰唆重复的部分，应删繁就简、同义合并；对于逻辑不清的部分，要尽量理出层次和头绪，并在译文中体现出来;对于断句或语意不完整的部分,应首先进行句法转换,并加以补充,力求完整。

6. 讲话人语言不得体

由于英汉两种语言的文化背景迥异,思维和表达方式上差异很大,双语交流时难免有文化的冲突。汉语中的一个问候译成英语可能就变成无理的冒犯,而英语的一句赞扬译成中文也许会令人难堪。译员应掌握两种文化背景知识,提高敏感度,在讲话人言语不得体的时候,要灵活处理,可略去不译、淡化或者变通,避免误解,使交流能顺利进行。

Passage Interpretation 1

"一国两制"是一个完整的概念。"一国"是指在中华人民共和国内,香港特别行政区是国家不可分离的部分,是直辖于中央人民政府的地方行政区域。中华人民共和国是单一制国家,中央政府对包括香港特别行政区在内的所有地方行政区域拥有全面管治权。

"两制"是指在"一国"之内,国家主体实行社会主义制度,香港等某些区域实行资本主义制度。"一国"是实行"两制"的前提和基础,"两制"从属和派生于"一国"。"一国"之内的"两制"并非等量齐观,国家的主体必须实行社会主义制度,这是不会改变的。在这个前提下,从实际出发,充分照顾香港等某些区域的现实情况,允许其保持资本主义制度长期不变。

"一国两制"在香港特别行政区的实践,取得了举世公认的成功。实践充分证明,"一国两制"不仅是解决历史遗留的香港问题的最佳方案,也是香港回归后保持长期繁荣稳定的最佳制度安排。坚定不移地推进"一国两制"事业,是包括香港同胞在内的全体中华儿女的共同愿望,符合国家和民族根本利益,符合香港的整体和长远利益,也符合外来投资者的利益。

Passage Interpretation 2

Last week China put some flesh on the bones of its plans to reform its *hukou* (household-registration) system, which determines where people can settle based on a series of exacting requirements akin to many countries' visa rules.

Under the *hukou* system, which dates back to the 1950s, migrants have limited access to health care, education and other social benefits outside their hometowns. This forces many migrant workers to leave their children behind when they move to cities to find work so that their children can attend school. Transferring a *hukou* can be extremely challenging.

The system has succeeded in preventing the emergence of shantytowns around China's cities (though many migrants still live in rotten conditions). But it comes at the cost of breaking up families and forcing migrants from the countryside to live an under-privileged life in urban areas.

To address this injustice, China's government has promised changes. But its plans are cautious, with restrictions to be lifted first in small towns. More strict requirements will remain on those who want to live in larger cities, which are generally more attractive to migrants.

The State Council set out guidelines last week, emphasizing that cities have plenty of leeway to set their own residency requirements. Even so, the very largest cities, defined as those above 5 million in population, are still advised to strictly control the scale of the population, using a points-based system to give priority to high-calibre talents.

Unit 15　Laws and Regulations　法律法规

But reform could still run into trouble. A survey by the Sichuan Province Bureau of Statistics, found that 90% of migrant workers don't even want an urban *hukou*. For many migrant workers, the benefits of better health care and being able to bring their children with them don't outweigh the perks of rural residency, which include a guaranteed (though generally very small) allocation of agricultural land, the survey found.

Dialogue Interpretation

Anna: Sir, I'd like to report a robbery. I got robbed on the street just now.
警察: 请坐。请问您的全名、国籍及在华身份?
Anna: My name is Anna Robinson. I'm an American student.
警察: 抢劫案具体是什么时候发生的?
Anna: About 25 minutes ago. I was window shopping with my friend on Beijing Road, when this guy grabbed my bag and ran away. We chased him and shouted "stop", but he was too fast. And there were too many people. He just disappeared in the crowd.
警察: 您还记得那人的模样吗?
Anna: It was too dark. I didn't see him clearly. But he is tall and big, about 185 cm tall.
警察: 他穿什么样的衣服?
Anna: I couldn't remember exactly what kind of clothes he was wearing, but I think he was in a black jacket.
警察: 好的,能描述一下您的提包吗?
Anna: It is a black handbag, with two round handles. There is also a pink ribbon on one side of the bag.
警察: 包里有什么?
Anna: A purse, a cell phone, some cosmetics, and my passport.
警察: 钱包里有多少钱?
Anna: Some two hundred *yuan* and around 100 U.S. dollars.
警察: 好的,我已经将您所提供的信息都记录下来了。您还有其他要补充的吗?
Sarah: No.
警察: 现在请您看一下这份记录有没有错误,如果没有请在这里签名。
Anna: OK.
警察: 非常感谢。我们会尽快派人调查。如果有任何进展会及时联系您。还有什么需要帮忙吗?
Anna: Since my passport has been lost, how can I get the new one here in China?
警察: 您应向派出所挂失,写出丢失经过,由派出所出具证明,到出入境管理处领取相关文件,然后去本国驻华使领馆申领新护照,再到出入境管理处办理签证。
Anna: I see. Thank you!

Exercises

I. Spot dictation.

Today's the first (1) _____ of the opening of the Shanghai Free Trade Zone and the State Council has marked the event by (2) _____ the elimination of some restrictions that will affect 27 industries.

Overseas investors will have more options in the Shanghai Free Trade Zone now that the State Council has opened (3) _____ in the trade zone to foreign capital ahead of the one-year milestone. Chinese-foreign joint ventures will be allowed to participate in the (4) _____ of a variety of commodities, including sugar and vegetable oil. (5) _____ also will be able to establish wholly owned wholesale salt ventures. That's a big change because the salt sector has been a (6) _____ industry since China's early dynasties.

"The salt sale has been controlled by the government in China, which is because of national (7) _____," Chen Bo, Deputy Director of FTZ Research Center, Shanghai University of Finance & Economics said.

The opening of the salt sector has (8) _____ lots of attention but Chen says there's greater meaning to the decision. "We don't have any problem in salt (9) _____. But the administrative control cannot match the (10) _____ economic situation," Chen said. "Now it's the time for us to consider giving the market a bigger say on such industries."

Some more industries will also open to sole foreign investment, including (11) _____, yachts, luxury liners, and high-speed rail technology. Those sectors (12) _____ require overseas companies to have a local partner.

"Domestically, we are cautious about the opening up of such sectors," Chen said. "But at the same time, we also need to open them to foreign investment (13) _____ exchange markets with overseas countries. China now has already gained strong ability to compete and possess advanced industries. Some industrial protections are already (14) _____."

There are efforts to remove the protections. The State Council's statement on Monday said that foreign companies in some industries in the (15) _____ could invest 51 percent or more in joint ventures with Chinese firms, up from the previous 49 percent.

II. Sentence listening and translation.

1. _____

2. _____

3. _____

4. _____

5. _____

Ⅲ. Paragraph listening and translation.

_____
_____
_____
_____

Ⅳ. Dialogue interpretation.

A: Poverty is a major issue in the world and should be solved as soon as possible.

B: 没错。在中国,有些儿童因为贫困而不得不辍学,帮助父母干农活。

A: Has Chinese government issued any laws or regulations to help those dropouts?

B: 有的。九年制义务教育就要求每个孩子都完成九年正规教育。此外,希望工程的启动就是为了让这些辍学的孩子重返学校。

A: It is a great challenge for the government, isn't it?

B: 是的。但是有了许多志愿者们的无私奉献,希望工程在过去的十年里取得了巨大的成就。

A: I'd like to donate some money to the children in poor areas. Mr. Wang, do you know about any official charity organization in China?

B: 知道。我建议你浏览中国青少年发展基金会官方网站再捐款。

A: Thank you.

Ⅴ. Interpreting in groups.

Role-play the following situation with your partners, acting as the Chinese speaker, English speaker and the interpreter respectively. One group will be invited to perform in class.

Participants: 1. Henry Brown
　　　　　　　　2. Cashier
　　　　　　　　3. Wang Lin, interpreter

Location: Ticket office of a bus station

Task: You are Henry Brown who is going to work in Wuxi for half a year. You want to buy a bus passenger card at the ticket office of a bus station. Wang Lin, a student of Jiangnan University, comes up to help you when you find it hard to communicate with the Chinese-speaking cashier. Wang Lin works as an interpreter for both sides.

VI. 3-minute talk on the given topic.

Talk on the following topic in three minutes based on the given reference questions.

Topic: Birth control

Questions for Reference:
1. Are you the only child in your family?
2. What do you think about the birth control policy in China?
3. Are you willing to have two babies as you are allowed to in the future? Why?

VII. Theme-related expressions.

和平共处五项原则	The Five Principles of Peaceful Coexistence
"引进来"和"走出去"政策	"Bring in" and "Going out" policy
依法治国	rule (run) the country by law
反腐倡廉	combat corruption and build a clean government
民主集中制	democratic centralism
被告	defendant
辩护词	defense; pleadings
辩护律师	defense lawyer
调解	mediation
法律援助	legal aid
民事诉讼	civil litigation
人民法院	People's Court
审判长	presiding judge
原告	plaintiff
法案,草案	draft
政府议案	government bill
生效	to come into force
立法	legislation
撤销	revocation
豁免,豁免权	immunity

• 宪法	constitutional law
• 行政法	administrative law
• 商法	commercial law; mercantile law
•《民事诉讼法》	Civil Procedure Law
•《刑事诉讼法》	Criminal Procedure Law
•《兵役法》	Conscript Law
• 遗产税	inheritance tax

Section C Further Exploration

翻译以下签证申请表,并假设以留学为目的填写该申请表。

VISA APPLICATION FORM

Recent photograph to be attached here

Visa Fee Received: ....

Date: ....

Visa No.: .... (For official use only please do not write in this space)

Please read carefully. ALL questions MUST be answered in block letters

1. Family Name: ....
2. Other names: ....
3. Former Name(s): ....
4. Father's Name: .... Mother's Name: ....
5. Address/Telephone:
    a. Permanent Address: ....
    b. Present Address: ....
    c. Telephone No(s): Home: .... Work: ....
    d. E-mail: ....
6. Nationality: ....
7. Date and Place of Birth: ....
             Day/Month/Year   Place
8. Marital Status: (check/tick one): ☐ Married ☐ Single ☐ Divorced
9. Spouse's Name: .... Age of Spouse: ....
10. Other family members accompanying applicant: (complete appropriate line/s)

| | Name | Date of Birth | Place of Birth |

    a. Spouse: ....

    b. Child: ....

    c. Child: ....

11. Passport No. : .... Issued at: .... On: ....

    Type: (check/tick one) ☐ Diplomatic ☐ Official ☐ Ordinary

12. Type of Visa required (check/tick one)

    a. ☐ Transit   ☐ Single Entry   ☐ Multiple Entry

    b. Category: ☐ Business   ☐ Tourist   ☐ Student

13. Proposed Date of Arrival: ....

                                Day/Month/Year

    Duration of Stay: ....

14. Reason for Journey: ....

    Applicant(s) Signature: ....Date: ....